Islamic Law

Theory & Interpretation

Islamic Law
Theory & Interpretation

Michael Mumīsa

Foreword by
Dr. Shaikh Zaki M. A. Badawi.
Professor of Islamic Law and
Dean of London Postgraduate Muslim College,
Chairman of the Muslim Law (*Shari'ah*) Council of Great Britain,
Vice-chairman of World Congress of Faiths.

amana publications

First Edition
(1423AH / 2002AC)

© Copyright 1423AH / 2002AC
amana publications
10710 Tucker Street
Beltsville, Maryland 20705-2223 USA
Tel: (301) 595-5777 / Fax: (301) 595-5888
E-mail:amana@igprinting.com
Website: www.amana-publications.com

Library of Congress Cataloging-in-Publication Data

Mumisa, Michael.
Islamic law : theory and interpretation / Michael Mumisa.
    p. cm.
Includes bibliographical references.
ISBN 1-59008-010-6
1. Islamic law-Philosophy. 2. Islamic law-Interpretation and construction. I. Title.
LAW
340.5'9'01--dc21

2002010370

Printed in the United States of America by
International Graphics
10710 Tucker Street
Beltsville, Maryland 20705-2223 USA
Tel: (301) 595-5999 Fax: (301) 595-5888
E-mail: ig@igprinting.com
Website: igprinting.com

Dedications to:

Shaikh Ali Dawud (1901-1986)
Prof. Abdur Rahman Ibrahim Doi (1933-1999)
Shaikh S. Abdullah Khan
And to my beloved Mother.

May Allah's Mercy be upon them.

Table of Contents

Acknowledgments

All praises be to the Almighty Allah. There are many people who, though they may not have been directly involved, have made it possible for me to complete this book. Among those who contributed to my academic formation, I would like to express my gratitude to my first teacher the late Shaikh Ali Daud, may Allah have mercy upon him, who introduced me to the field of Islamic studies while I was just a young boy, but could not live long to see the fruits of his work. My acknowledgement also goes to Shaikh Muhammad Amin Hamandishe, Shaikh Shabir and Musa Menk, Shaikh Umar Phiri, Shaikh Ibrahim Sumani (*Tarkib Tawsifi*) and all those who taught me while at the Iqra College in Harare, Zimbabwe

I wish, further, to express my appreciation to all my lecturers at the Darul Uloom al-Islamiyah College at Newcastle (South Africa). There, I learnt the canonical texts of *hadith* and studied Arabic and Islamic sciences for over six years with Shaikh Muhammad Cassim Sema, Shaikh Abdul Kader Hoosen, Shaikh Fairuz al-Din Adam, Mufti Fayyaz, and many others. Not forgetting all my previous Professors at the Rand Afrikaans University as well as those who are assisting me now at the University of Birmingham in the United Kingdom, and I would like to single out Professor Sigvard von Sicard, Dr David Thomas, and Dr. Jabal Muhammad Buaben who has proved to be both teacher and brother. I also would like to mention here my friends, Hasan Muhammad, Jariullah, Zahir Mahmood, my two cousins Tayyib Makwemba and Muhammad Milazi, who, although not aware of it, were a great inspiration to my work.

I have benefited greatly from the comments and criticisms of others. Shaikhah Zainab Awazi of the University of Cape Town read the manuscript and made valuable remarks.

I must also mention here my wife Shaikhah Khadijah Fatimah at the Jami'ah al-Hudaa College-Nottingham for her patience, encouragement, and understanding.

As far as the publication of this book is concerned, it gives me great pleasure to record my sincere gratitude to Amana Publications for agreeing to publish it and without its support this book would not have materialized.

March 11, 2002

Michael Mumīsa
Birmingham, UK

Foreword

The need for new development in Islamic law is universally recognized. Nevertheless, attempts by Muslim scholars at reform have so far been timid providing only piecemeal solutions to the challenges of fast changing social, economic and political conditions.

The old procedure of eclecticism (*talfiq*) is helpful only in a limited number of cases. The modern jurists (*fuqaha*) are shackled by the ancient rules of principles of jurisprudence. These rules form the road map for the scholars; if they follow its guidance they will end exactly where their predecessors have ended.

No project at *Shari'ah* development is possible without redrawing this map. '*Ijtihad*,' that is the intellectual effort to formulate Islamic legal solutions to current problems, will only trim at the edges without creating a dynamic methodology to help transform the whole discipline and the Muslim community with it. There are at the moment two methodological approaches to the Islamic intellectual discourse: One is the traditional approach that rejects any attempt at re-thinking Islamic thought and advocates a fixed and rigid understanding of the classical texts. The second way is that of Muslim apologists who propose re-interpretation based on the same old methodological tools and theories of *Usul al-fiqh*. This second way amounts to a recycling of ideas and solutions and fails to provide meaningful solutions to the contemporary challenges facing Muslims in a globalised postmodern world.

Michael Mumīsa has recognized this fact and called for a new set of rules to be derived, as they must, from the *Qur'an* and the Prophetic *Sunna*. This means therefore that the Islamic legal theory itself (*usul al-fiqh*) needs to be re-interpreted taking into consideration the new challenges faced by the present generation. This is based on the recognition that these theories and principles of law in Islam are themselves contextual and therefore reflect the historical, cultural, social and political conditions under which they were formulated and drawn. In order for any religion or system to function within a society, it has to take a form that is common and relevant to its context. This was the case with Islam and the historical beginning of the *Shari'ah*. Michael Mumīsa challenges the attempt to universalize the historical context of the *Qur'an* or the conditions under which Islamic thought developed.

He writes with the authority of a scholar who is steeped in the traditional system of education and modern Western Studies.

The reader of this work will find a lot of useful information and deep insight into the *Shari'ah*.

Dr. Shaikh Zaki M. A. Badawi
Professor of Islamic Law and Dean of London Postgraduate Muslim College,
Chairman of the Muslim Law (*Shari'ah*) Council of Great Britain,
Vice-chairman of World Congress of Faiths.

Chapter One

Definition, Rationale and Methodology of *Usul al-Fiqh*

If you differ in anything among yourselves, refer it to Allah and His Messenger, if you believe in Allah and the Last Day; this is best, and most suitable for final determination. (*Qur'an* 4: 59)

The Twentieth century has been a period of profound changes particularly in Islamic studies and theological studies in general. Globalization and technological advancements have resulted in faster means of communication between nations of the world. This rapid development has been instrumental in boosting the exchange of ideas between the East and the West. The first and second world wars caused the academia the world over to realize that rationalism alone does not and cannot provide the solutions to life's problems and it is, perhaps, no accident that naziism and fascism emerged in a nation where reason was the dominant source of knowledge. During the same period existentialism (Heidegger, Bultmann, Sartre) emerged as a prominent and influential philosophical school. All of these twentieth-century phenomena have influenced how one approaches scriptures and the way one comprehends and interprets them. Theology and religious studies have become more intellectual, thought provoking, and important for and in everyday life. Even the most secularized nations such as the United States have taken a greater interest in theology and their emphasis has been upon making Christianity more practical. The influence of pragmatism (an American philosophical school of thought starting from C. S. Peirce, William James and John Dewey) has been so clearly reflected in American theology that American Christian Colleges have not only emphasized biblical studies, church history, and systematic theology as academic disciplines, but they also have introduced new fields of study such as education, counselling and practical theology. The Muslims have not been immune to these developments, and accordingly there has been a realization among Muslim theorists that the *Qur'an* and *Sunnah*

1

(*imitatio Muhammadi*) are finite sources of law and cannot suffice the needs of infinite events. The Islamic world has also been rapidly expanding to encompass diverse races, cultures and environments of various kinds. Consequently, jurisprudential problems have been arising for which there is no clear precedent or reference in the *Qur'an* or *Sunnah*. This has caused a great need among the Muslims, particularly the youth, women, and other concerned Muslim scholars for the re-reading of the sources of Islamic law and for trying to understand the message of the *Qur'an* and *Sunnah* in a way that is meaningful of the contemporary world. This in fact is the problem the Muslim has been facing since the completion of the Islamic message with the *Qur'an* and the normative practice of the Messenger of Allah [*Sunnah*] fourteen centuries ago, and will continue to face as he moves forward in the new century: how to make the Qur'anic and Prophetic text existentially meaningful to him, here and now.

Muslims have historically referred matters of everyday life, worship and reflection to Allah and His Messenger, as they were commanded in the *Qur'an* (4: 59). Traditionally, this act of reference developed in the form of legal discourse with recourse to the established principles of Islam, called *usul al-fiqh* [or *usul al-ahkam al-shari'ah*] in Arabic; but for many reasons the dynamism and vitality of the traditional *usul al-fiqh* has not been sustained into the contemporary era. The result is an *usul al-fiqh* where the final form is remembered but the purpose, function, and essence is either forgotten or overlooked. We now have something of a *fiqh*, a transmitted body of legal decisions, which pertained to another time and place, but we seem not to have retained the original vitality and spirit of the *fiqh*. We seem to have ignored the origins, the sources, and the immediacy – the "*usul*" part of *fiqh*. In other words, we have forgotten how to refer our questions directly to the sources [*usul*] of Islamic Law; that is, to the Qur'anic text and Prophetic tradition [*Sunnah*]. This book is an effort and a call to revive and broaden the discipline of *usul al-fiqh* in order to bring about a methodology which will truly enable us to refer all our matters to Allah and His Messenger. We see the very methodology of *usul al-fiqh* to be radical, constructive, and emancipatory: we want to restore these characteristics of *usul al-fiqh* as practiced by the jurisconsults [*fuqaha*]. We realize that the credibility of Islam as a universal way of life and its

2

contribution to the transformation of this world will be measured first of all by the Muslims' readiness to participate in the wider human endeavors on the fundamental questions of humankind, past and present.

Our approach in this book of referring matters directly to the sources of Islam rejects the modernist approach, that thinly-disguised plan to compromise Islam so as to make it fit with modern society. Instead, we want to make Islam more relevant and more applicable to contemporary society of today. Recognizing that the contemporary world is dominated by a discourse and a civilization that are inimical to Islam, this book concedes that it is the modern (or post modern) world whose terminology must be engaged in order to avoid being subsumed in its world view and sophisticated discourse. In fact, in order to ensure that our contemporary discourse is Islamic, we must understand and meet the challenges of this dominant discourse. This is so because the dominance of the modern Western idiom is such that the scholar of Islam [the *alim*] must now conduct not merely a traditional discourse, but also a discourse cognizant of modernity. To fail to do so would invite the unseen or unacknowledged penetration of ideas quite probably alien to Islam. This book, therefore, attempts to contribute to a truly Islamic *usul al-fiqh* for the contemporary age, where the traditional scope and breadth of Islam may be recovered and restored, and this work will thereby incorporate the contemporary disciplines of the social sciences, recognizing of course, that these disciplines were formed and shaped by forces applicable only to what has by now become the dominant portion of the European or Western experience.

The fact that post-modernism has entirely collapsed or imploded the disciplines confirms this recognition. Nevertheless because the Muslim thinker is very often exposed to these disciplines, and thereby exposed and possibly co-opted by their associated worldviews and assumptions, it becomes imperative to address contemporary issues which are associated with the Western disciplines. Islamic scholarship can no longer ignore the host of other world-views, religious or secular, with which it competes for the attention of contemporary human beings. To wish for Islamic disciplines which have no connection to the West is to forget that because of colonialism or imperialism, the Muslim thinker is all too often caught up in images and concepts of *homo economicus* or power politics or national security or development, all paradigms quite alien to classical and medieval Muslim scholarship.

To address the recasting of *usul al-fiqh* with (but not within) the context of the Western disciplines then finds two audiences. One is the modernist or "progressive" element which sees no need for such an exercise and advocates an unconditional subjection to a particular collection of intellectual, cultural, philosophical and ontological elements formulated in renaissance humanism and later Western thought, especially following the 18th century or the "age of enlightenment". The other is the "conservative" or traditionalist element which mistrusts any attempt at addressing problems which arise in the context of occidental philosophy and considers this development a serious departure from orthodoxy and orthopraxy. To the proponents of traditionalism there is no other alternative but a strict and rigid adherence to the interpretations of Muslim classicists. The interpretations done by the classical jurisconsults are seen as the final and only true meaning of the Qur'anic and Prophetic texts. *Fiqh* itself, the *fatawa* texts (books on legal rulings by classical Muslim Jurists) and the various schools of *fiqh* have become the *asl* – primary aim and object of the traditionalist and not the original *asl* – the *Qur'an* and *Sunnah*. For him there is no need for a re-reading of the *Qur'an* and *Sunnah*, in fact, in most of the Colleges of *Shari'ah* Laws more time is devoted to a study of the commentaries done on the commentaries of the Jurists. Little time is spent on referring back to the *usul* (sources) of Islamic Law and discovering what the *Qur'an* and *Sunnah* have to say to the reader here and now. The importance of maintaining the link with the Islamic legacy [*turath*] is often given as reason for this methodology and approach in the studies of *fiqh*. The primary Muslim concern cannot be mere survival of an old tradition [*turath*], but the actualization of a challenging message for our generation.

There exists no doubt that this kind of appeal to authority has its origin in Greek Philosophy, and medieval Muslim scholarship, being influenced by Greek thought and culture, naturally took over this assumption since it fitted in too well the social and political conditions of the time. According to Windelband, it first appeared in the sense of a confirmation on and strengthening of an author's own views, but not as a decisive and conclusive argument. The *jurare in verba magistri*, he maintains, was usual enough among the subordinate members of the school, but the heads of schools, and in general the men who engaged in independent research, maintained an attitude towards the teachings of the former time that was much more of criticism than of unconditional subjection; and though in the schools, chiefly the academic and Peripatetic, the inclination to preserve and maintain the teaching of the founder as an unassailable treasure was fostered by the custom of commenting upon his works. Yet in all the conflict with regard to the criteria of truth, the principle had never been brought forward that something must be believed just because some great man said it. The admiration of Socrates, in which all the followers were in unison, did not itself lead to his being regarded as the valid authority for definite philosophical doctrines.[1] The belief in authority in the later period grew out of the need felt for salvation and help. Another psychological root of this belief was the enhanced importance of personality. This shows itself in the great men of the past, as found in Philo and in all lines of Platonism, and not less in the unconditional trust of the disciples in their masters, which, especially in later Neo-Platonism, degenerated to an exaggerated veneration of the heads of schools.[2]

Ibn Khaldun, in his *Prologomena*, describes the genesis of this phenomenon in Muslim Thought:

> When it was feared that independent judgement and interpretation of the texts (*ijtihad*) would be attributed to those who were not befitting and to those whose opinion was not to be relied upon, they stated that it was something that people were now incapable of. Instead they turned them to blind-following and warned from accepting from more than one Imam since that, they argued, would be to make a game of it. So nothing remained except for the schools of *fiqh* [*madhhabs*] to be passed on and for each blind follower to stick to his own school of *fiqh* [*madhhab*], after its principles had been settled and its ascription affirmed by narration, such that there is no means of attaining *fiqh* today except through their way and any claiming new interpretation and independent judgement *ijtihad* today has his claim rejected and is not followed, and the people of Islam today blindly follow these four Imams.[3]

I am not arguing here that these fatawa books belong to the museum and are a novelty as suggested by other scholars [4], rather, I feel that there must be a realization among Muslim scholars that no interpretation takes place in a social, political, psychological, cultural or existential vacuum.

The *fatawa* books are a result of interpretations, which obviously affected the self-understanding of their societies. They were largely influenced by the social, cultural, political and historical conditions in which they were written. Times, places and conditions which are far different from ours. Moreover, a large part of this literature was produced by interpreters who were not only interpreting the Qur'anic and Prophetic injunctions but were also interpreting the interpretations! Obviously, these scholars were interested in not only what the *Qur'an* and *Sunnah* had to say, but equally or at times even more so in what the interpreter had to say. For the *fuqaha* and writers of these texts, their interpretations of the *Qur'an* and *Sunnah* were an attempt at finding answers for people of their times and not for tomorrow's people and future problems. The re-interpretation of the *Qur'an* and *Sunnah*, therefore, is a challenge which every Muslim society and generation must face since no act of interpretation of Islamic law or any legal system can anticipate solutions for concrete cases which might arise in the future of a society, in perpetual change.

This book attempts to make the Muslim realize that he or she has been left with the world in one hand, and the *Qur'an* and *Sunnah* in the other, and we attempt to address the methodological problems he or she encounters in approaching them. The message of Islam is not merely about rituals, neither is it only about life above the heavens and life below the earth; preparing ones life in the hereafter and saving oneself from the punishment of the grave, and this message will be true and as much applicable tomorrow as it is today. In other words, the effort to make Islam real for our lives in contemporary societies is nothing more than the perennial effort to refer all matters to Allah and His Messenger, which has been traditionally expressed in the discourse of *usul al-fiqh*. The importance of maintaining the link with the Islamic legacy, of modifying and moulding rather than toppling and destroying, cannot be overestimated.

The call for a re-reading of *fiqh* or a re-interpretation of the Islamic texts is not without its problems. It will not necessarily provide the true meaning of what Allah's or His Messenger's intention is in a given text, as required by traditional scholarship. This is mostly because each one understands the text according to his or her *a priori* position. The experience of re-reading texts shows us that we never read a text "objectively". It is always we who read and that means that it is through the application of our very particular perspectives that we allow a text to speak to us. The idea that one can approach the *Qur'an* and *Sunnah* without presuppositions is romantic. There is always the danger of ideological behavior and ideological readings of the *Qur'an* and *Sunnah*, the unwillingness of having one's perspective challenged at all. Among Muslim scholars there are some who, due to personal, social or political reasons, will defend their particular "reading" at all cost and remain hostile to all calls for a change of attitude, perspective or world-view.[5] There is a great need for every Muslim reader of the *Qur'an* and *Sunnah* to become as aware as possible of his or her presuppositions which may be challenged, corrected and possibly transformed during the process of interpretation.

Like any other intellectual discourse, *usul al-fiqh* is temporal – it has a past, a present, and a future. Classical and contemporary writers on *usul al-fiqh* have produced two genres of *usul* literature: apologetic literature produced by Muslim scholars, and *deconstructionist* literature produced by western as well as liberal Muslim scholars. What these two approaches have in common, however, is that they have always given the historical development of the science of *usul al-fiqh* but they have not presented a number of contemporary hermeneutical options. Moreover classical books were written in a context and culture much different from that of the contemporary century. The contemporary century is a period in which the various cultures, societies, and nations are in various stages of development ranging from the most primitive to highly developed and technologically advanced. Obviously, globalization and post-modernity should affect how we interpret usul. This book, we hope, will not be another exercise in Muslim historical romanticism and apologetics, but hopefully it will reflect upon the possibility for a future *usul al-fiqh*. Obviously any *usul* discourse of the future will build upon the past, be understood in the present, and will consist of projections into the future, from here and this very moment.

Conceptual Definitions

Usul is the plural of *asl* which literally mean "root", "origin", "source" or "foundation" [*ma yubna alayhi ghayruhu*].[6] The plural *usul* means "principles", or "fundamentals" and the science of source methodology in Islamic jurisprudence [*usul al-fiqh*] has been defined as the aggregate, considered *per se*, of legal proofs and evidence [*adillatuha al-tafsiliyyah*] that, when studied properly, will lead either to certain knowledge of a *Shari'ah* ruling [*hukum shar'i*] or to at least a reasonable assumption concerning the same; the manner by which such proofs are adduced, and the status of the adducer.[7] *Usul al-fiqh* is a science in which reason and revelation come together, where considered opinion is accompanied by revealed law. Yet *usul* does not rely purely on reason in a way that would be unacceptable to revealed law, nor is it based simply on the kind of blind following or authority [*taqlid*] that would not be supported by revelation or reason.[8]

The traditional sphere of *usul al-fiqh* included all aspects of human activity, be they religious or mundane. The framework within which all matters were referred to Allah and His Messenger was the *usul al-fiqh.* But when the political power shifted out of the hands of Islamic leaders, the community was unable to make Islamic Law the overriding and primary source of jurisdiction, and thus the legal discourse of Islam suffered. The ascendancy of Western common law beclouded the Islamic legal system. The situation now is that the Muslim finds it very difficult in contemporary society to refer matters to Allah and His Messenger, for a number of reasons, foremost of which are reasons which come under the rubric of colonialism and its effects. The attempts to refer matters to the sources of Islam may be generally considered efforts to make Islam the dominant source of social values, individual values, legal authority, and education. The development of the science of *usul al-fiqh,* from a purely human perspective, may be described as a prime Muslim contribution to human civilization.

Evidence of the difficulty of making Islamic law relevant to Muslims in any but the most private, devotional aspects of their lives lies in the almost total atrophying of what are now called the social and political sciences in the *ummah.* By illuminating the connection between these social and human sciences and political power, it becomes clear that the flourishing of these sciences in the West has nothing to do with Muslim decadence or deviance, but with Muslim subjection to alien or corrupt rule. The onslaught of nation-state-propelled secularism and modernism has meant that religion for a few centuries at least has been relegated to a personal and private realm. Perhaps the fact that most of the world's religions have not been well preserved may account for the ease with which religion as a way of life is displaced by secularism or modernism

8

as a complete and exclusive way of life, through a mechanism of capitalism. In contrast, the Muslim believes that Islam has been preserved in its final form of the *Qur'an* and *Sunnah* in pristine purity. We can therefore say that Islam is a complete way of life, a way which is generated through the perfectly preserved tradition. The concept of "way of life" is expressed in Arabic by "*din*". Because Islam embraces one's total existence, the word religion is perhaps not an appropriate description. Neither, then, is the term jurisprudence to describe the external dimension of Islam as "*din*" or a universal way of life.

The famous story of Mu'adh bin Jabal (d.18 A.H.), although its authenticity has been disputed,[9] bears repeating. When the Prophet sent him to Yemen and appointed him as judge, he asked him how he planned to administer justice. He replied that he would depend first on the *Qur'an* and if the *Qur'an* did not give him the direct solution to the particular issue, he would turn to the *Sunnah* of the Prophet. Then the Prophet asked what he would do if the issue were not found there either. Mu'adh bin Jabal replied that if the suitable answer was not found in either the *Qur'an* or *Sunnah*, then he would rely on his individual judgement. For this response, he drew the blessings and appreciation of the Prophet. Mu'adh bin Jabal's perceptive nature and understanding of the essence of Islamic *fiqh* earned him praise from other Companions. Umar said at Jabiah, "Let him who desires to seek knowledge of *fiqh* go to Mu'adh bin Jabal." The importance of understanding *fiqh* and using *fiqh* to establish justice is clearly demonstrated by the Prophet himself, who prayed for the famous scholar and jurist Abdullah bin Abbas (d. 68 A.H.) with the words: "O Allah, grant him deeper understanding in the religious sciences."[10]

The Arabic term "*fiqh*" is loosely translated as Islamic jurisprudence, but this term does not do it justice. It is very important to understand, right at the outset, the difference between the translation of the term "*fiqh*" and its definition. The classical writers of *fiqh* began their works with a section on worship [*ibadat*] and then proceeded to the discussion of personal law [*ahwal al-shakhsiyyah*], transactions [*mu'amalat*], evidence and witnesses [*murafa'at*], crimes and punishments [*janayat*], and international law [*siyar*]. This hierarchy of *fiqh* reflects the ideal that the Muslim's life is really nothing but worship [*ibadat*]. The Muslim who truly recognizes and accepts Islam through the *Qur'an* and *Sunnah* lives in a state of worship. His every action is *ibadah* and according to the Prophetic tradition even if he does not see Allah he always remains mindful that Allah sees him. The state of worship is characterized by a sense of gratitude and joyful thankfulness. Unlike the ascetic who mortifies the flesh to defeat carnal nature, the Muslim lives in the world without any sense of duality and conflict. Recognizing the reality that he has been left with the world in his hands and that the world is but a resting-place before the final and eternal abode, the Muslim seeks to follow divine guidance in order to make his or her life in this world and in the hereafter one of harmony and success. The effort to achieve a life of harmony and success takes place within the framework of *fiqh*, and we may therefore define *fiqh* as the interpretation and application of divine guidance in a world of transient conflict. Imam Abu Hanifah, described *fiqh* as "the knowledge of what is for a man's self and what is against a man's self."

Sadr al-Shari'ah points out that the science of *fiqh*, in so far as it is concerned with actions, deals with the consequences of actions, in the sense of which actions are spiritually profitable and which are injurious. In other words, the object of *fiqh* is the knowledge of spiritual rewards and punishment. He further suggests that the definition of *fiqh* is based on the following Qur'anic verse:

> For every soul there will be on the day of judgement) whatever it has earned and against it whatever it has earned. (2: 286)

There are also aspects of *fiqh* which do not immediately suggest their pertinence to the above definition. Imam Abu Hanifah (d. 150 A.H.) expands his definition to include acts which are spiritually indifferent, such as contracts of sale, leases, and the like. About these, he comments that *fiqh* also means the knowledge of what is permissible and what one is under obligation to do. This is why the science of *fiqh* covers both worship [*ibadah*] as well as transactions [*mu'amalat*] and other aspects of human activity.

The Arabic language is generally based on three letter roots, and the root *fa-qa-ha*, from which *fiqh* is derived, is found twenty times in the *Qur'an*. The Qur'anic phrase *tafaqquh* [*fa-qa-ha*] *fi al-din* (9: 122) encompasses guidance in all aspects of the Muslim's life, whether religious, social, political, economic, legal, domestic or international, since Islam as a universal way of life cannot be parceled off into or restricted to religious and secular realms.

In order to restore to *fiqh* its rightful role as the source of knowledge conducive to human felicity and social justice, we must break out of the bonds placed on us by secular or colonial powers, whether we accepted these bonds passively or attempted to resist. We also need to liberate ourselves from authority and blind following [*taqlid*]. Breaking out of these bonds will mean recognizing once again the ontological kinship of knowledge, law, and the divine. We must recognize once again that the *faqih* (jurist), the *qadi* (judge), and the *alim* (theologian) are ideally one and the same person. That is, the person well versed in the Islamic law [*fiqh*] should be the judge who helps people reach just decisions [the *qadi*]; this person must also be someone knowledgeable [the *alim*, plural *ulama'*]. This ideal person was not terribly rare in many traditional societies through the ages, because the Islamic systems of education tended to produce people who were educated in the essence of Islam, but not necessarily sophisticated in a particular speciality. It has been narrated on the authority of Thawban that the Messenger of Allah, upon whom be peace, said:

> A group of people from my *ummah* will always remain victorious (against their opponents) fighting for truth and justice. He who deserts them shall not be able to do them any harm. They will remain in this position until Allah's Command in executed.[11]

While commending on the above tradition, Imam Nawawi wrote:

> Regarding this group of people, Bukhari said, "they are the scholars [*ahl al-'ilm*] and Ahmad bin Hanbali said, "if they cannot be the *ahl al-hadith* (Traditionists or scholars of *hadith*) then I do not know who they are."[12]

Certainly, there are periods when the Islamic systems of education produced scholars full of pride and venality and subservience to power, but these periods always had their great *alim* and reviver who stood up to denounce the wrongs and re-establish the good. It is therefore unfair to see Islamic civilization sliding into a decadence from which it is only now awakening. And it is simplistic to see the kind of clear speaking and honesty in the face of tyrants to be something related to resistance to the historical phenomenon of colonialism, instead as something essential and fundamental to Islam itself. For it is the duty of Muslims who are able to change wrongs with their hands, or to speak out against injustice and oppression with their tongues, or at least to reject in their hearts what wrongs they see. This is a duty not bound by any time or space, but is instead a perennial, universal aspect of Islam. The Muslim who believes in Allah will have to believe that Allah is the God of liberation and justice.

With this in mind, we can understand why the terms *al-faqih, al-qadi,* and *al-alim* were used interchangeably by the Companions and their Successors to refer to one and the same thing. It is quite clear from the evidence of the early Muslims that the *faqih* was the respected person entrusted by the community to ensure justice prevailed. If the Muslims were to fulfill their duty to Allah and obey the command to refer all their matters of dispute to Him and His Messengers, they were going to need people with particular piety and a special sense of the essence of Islam to help them understand and apply the divine guidance of the *Qur'an* and the *Sunnah*. The Companions put forward by the Prophet were called *fuqaha*, people able to apply *fiqh*. The year 94 A.H. was called in the annals of history as the year of the jurists [*sanat al-fuqaha*] because several of the celebrated jurists of Madinah, such as Sa'id bin al-Musayyab and Abu Bakr bin Abd al-Rahman, died in that year.

The famous early scholar of Islam, Hasan al-Basri, described the qualifications of a *faqih* in these terms: "the real *faqih* was a person who despised the worldly temptations, was interested in the hereafter, possessed a deeper and more comprehensive knowledge of religion and religious law, was regular in his prayers, was pious in his dealings, refrained from disparaging Muslims, and was the well-wisher of the *ummah*"

The great jurisprudent, Imam Malik (d. 179 A.H.) frequently used the term "jurist of the greatest jurists [*faqih al-fuqaha*]" in his masterpiece describing the well-trodden path of Islamic practice (titled *al-Muwatta'* in Arabic) when describing Sa'id bin Musayyab of Madinah. Imam Abu Hanifah (d. 150 A.H.) compiled his work under the title "*al-fiqh al-akbar*" (The Grandest *fiqh*). This evidence points to the thesis that the concept of *fiqh* is not a later development or the result of an evolving legal discourse. Instead, it is essential to Islam and received its formation in the early days of the Islamic *ummah*. *Fiqh*, the science of Islamic jurisprudence, developed in the time of the Prophet, deriving both its *raison d'etre* and substantive form from the prime source of Islam, the *Qur'an* and the *Sunnah*.

Gai Eaton describes the term *"fiqh"* perceptively in these terms: "Christians are puzzled when told that jurisprudence, not theology, is the principle religious science in Islam and that the *alim*, the religious scholar, is primarily a jurist who tells people what to do rather than to believe". He comments further, "for the Muslim there is no problem in knowing what to believe; his concern is with what to do under all circumstances in order to conform to the Word of God and to walk without stumbling on the road which leads to Paradise. The word *fiqh*, usually translated as 'jurisprudence', comes from the verb *faqiha*, which means neither more nor less than 'he understood'. *Fiqh*, then, has to do with understanding the divine commands and their ramifications in the fabric of daily life. For the occidental, jurisprudence is a dull and sterile topic of little interest (unless one becomes involved with the police), which is hardly surprising since secular law is a web of man-made complexities; a solicitor's office is not a place where the Christian is likely to seek his soul's salvation."[13]

Orientalist scholars, such as H. A. R. Gibb, tend to transpose European experiences onto the history of Islam. Thus, if the priests and popes were anti-rationalists and firmly opposed to human reason, then the same case must have prevailed for the scholars of Islam, the *ulama'*. If the Catholic Church, in their estimation, stifled human thought, restricted human endeavor, and allowed for concessions and favors, then the same must hold true of Islam. Thus Gibb assumes that the evolution of a school of Islamic jurisprudence can only be explained as starting from the prior conviction of the imperfection of human reason and its inability to apprehend the nature of the good or indeed or any reality whatsoever. Western scholars of Islam take the emergence of the schools and the proliferation of sayings of the blessed Prophet [*ahadith*, singular, *hadith*] in the second century *hijrah* as proof of the incredibility of the Islamic legal philosophy.

It is quite clear, however, that the concept of *fiqh* is intimately tied onto the notion of justice, liberation, application of divine guidance, and the idea of Islam as a universal way of life. That this concept developed and became firmly established while the Prophet was still alive is obvious. Concerning the proliferation of sayings, a far simpler and more persuasive case can be made that the rapid expansion of the Islamic world and the active pursuit and collection of Islamic traces and sayings laid the way for the systematic and exhaustive gathering of widely dispersed information, not the *ex nihilo* creation of sayings.

Western scholars are accustomed to conceive of jurisprudence as a development from rudimentary forms of laws to a logically construed system of legal discourse. We should therefore not be startled and perplexed by the orientalist view that *fiqh* is an after-thought which evolved as a result of the formalization of law as its justification.

As we shall see later, the development of the schools of *fiqh* did not arise from needs of the later community; instead, the development of the schools has its roots in the needs of all communities seeking to refer matters to Allah and His Messenger, from the first community of believers surrounding the Prophet to the present day. Concepts such as mutual consultation [*shura*], analogical deduction [*qiyas*], independent judgement [*ijtihad*], choosing the most apt injunction [*istihsan*], and judgement stemming from public interest [*masalih al-mursalah*] were not spontaneously created by the schools in the second and third centuries of the Islamic era. Instead, they have their very basis in the early Muslim community as it worked out its affairs with the guidance of the Messenger of Allah.

At one level *fiqh* is not exactly the same as the revealed *Shari'ah*, the divine guidance, because while based on the *Qur'an* and *Sunnah*, some injunctions have been reached on the basis of personal opinion, analogy or legal argument. This is why an entire science of *usul al-fiqh* developed which had as its sole goal the determination of which legal arguments and which kinds of extrapolation were in fact Islamically legal. This science seeks to examine the principles or roots of *fiqh* to see how these principles inform legal discourse, the process of referring all matters to Allah and His Messenger.

Usul al-fiqh is concerned with the essence of law, how laws are derived, how laws may change with exigencies, and how to determine the priority of seemingly conflicting instructions. The term *usul al-fiqh* can be derived from the following Qur'anic verse:

14

"The example of a good word is like that of a tree whose roots are firm in the earth but its branches have spread up to the sky." (14: 24)

In this verse, the operative words seem to be "roots" and "branches" (in Arabic *usul* and *furu'*), hence the science of roots and the science of branches or subsidiaries (in Arabic *ilm al-usul* and *ilm al-furu'*).

Specifically, the majority extant schools of *fiqh* agree on the following sources [*masadir*] of law.

1. The *Qur'an*.
2. The *Sunnah* of the Prophet.
3. *Ijma'* (consensus).
4. *Qiyas* (analogical deduction) or *aql* (reason).

The last source of law depends on a concept of divine motive or the intent of the law. That is, in order to perform analogical deduction [*qiyas*], the community must have in mind what a particular law was meant to achieve: only then can this motive or intent [*illah*] be shifted to cover another, related situation.

With the concept of *maqasid al-shari'ah* (intent and motive of Islamic Law), it becomes possible to apply divine guidance to changing times and changing conditions in society, so that the *data revelata* remain dynamic and creative, always applicable and always invigorating society. This concept of legal intent also developed sub-concepts of legal preference and the idea of the law or message being for the benefit of society. The two Arabic terms are *istihsan* (from the roots *hasana*, meaning "best") and *masalih al-mursalah* (from the roots *salaha* meaning "benefit") Thus, the scholar could weigh two injunctions and decide which one was most applicable. He could also decide which law was of most benefit to society, understanding the entire divine message to be directed to the benefit of society.

The creative tension of *usul al-fiqh* is that Muslims have always believed that the divine revelation preserved in the *Qur'an* and *Sunnah* is perfect and complete, and that no further revelation is possible, or even conceivable. They therefore understand on one hand that their law is immutable. On the other hand, they have always believed that Islam is applicable to all places and times, and therefore must admit of some flexibility. This creative and dynamic tension between immutability and flexibility is an instance of essential unity in diverse forms, where the essential unity of Islam is clear in all Muslim communities through time, though the forms of these communities differ.

This book has been divided into six chapters: the first chapter discusses the rationale, definition and methodology of *usul al-fiqh*. Chapter two examines the use of the *Qur'an* as the prime source of referring matters to Allah, where the *Sunnah* is the source of referring matters to His Messenger. The context of occasions of revelation is examined in order to generate insights into the way Islam works in society. Then, the way Islam is made real for the early community by the Messenger of Allah is investigated with the aim of understanding how *usul al-fiqh* later developed as the method of referring matters to Allah and His Messenger. The position of *Sunnah* as a source of law in Islam is examined, and reference is made to the development of the concept of *Sunnah* as evidenced by the usage of this concept from the period of *jahiliyyah* through the second century. An examination of *Sunnah ahl al-madinah,* and *Sunnah al-nabawiyyah* is carried out. Also discussed in this chapter are the conventional as well as contemporary theories of Qur'anic Hermeneutics. A detailed discussion on the *tafsir* genre, the various schools of Qur'anic Hermeneutics in the first half of the first century of the *hijrah* (Islamic Calendar), as well as the differences between *tafsir* and *ta'wil* also presented in this chapter.

Chapter three provides the definition as well as the historical development of the doctrine of *ijma'*. Inter alia, this chapter also discusses in detail the types of *ijma'* and the democratization of the *ijma'* process. The chapter also tries to explain how globalization and post-modernity can affect *ijma'* in modern times. The abrogation of *ijma'* by a new *ijma'* has been discussed as well. The chapter also covers the definition and historical development of *ijtihad* and *qiyas* from the Prophetic period to the period of Abu Bakr, Umar, Uthman, and Ali.

Chapter four is divided into three parts. The first part deals with the definition and development of the doctrine of *masalih al-mursalah* as per Islamic Law, the classification of *masalih* (Interests) into *Mu'tabara, mulghiya,* and *mursalah.* Examples are given to show how the doctrine of *masalih* accommodates social change. Part two addresses other juristic devices such as *istihsan* (juristic preference), *istidlal* and *istihbab* (legal presumption) and *sadd dari'ah* (deterrent laws). The last part examines customary laws and practices [*urf* and *adat*] and how they influence the Islamic legal system.

Chapter five examines the *taqlid* regime, its definition, historical development, and the position of the schools of Sunni jurisprudence regarding the subject. The methodology of the four *Imams* in the study of *fiqh* has also been detailed in the chapter.

The last chapter examines problems and possibilities for a future *usul al-fiqh* and the process of legal reasoning under social change, the use of the social sciences in doing *fiqh*, and the importance of distinguishing between *bid'ah* and *masalih al-mursalah* in the re-interpretation of *fiqh*.

Notes

1. Windelband, W, *A History of Philosophy: The Formation & Development of its Problems and Concepts*, London: Macmillan & CO., 1914, pp.219-220.

2. Ibid, p. 223.

3. Ibn Khaldun, A, *al-Muqaddimah*, Beirut: Dar al-Fikr, 1988, vol.1, p. 448.

4. See Wali Allah al-Dehlawi, S, *Hujjat Allah al-Balighah*, Lahore: Matba' al-Salafiyyah, [s.a.], vol.1, p.153.

5. The author recalls, while working as a research fellow at an Islamic research centre in South Africa, when he was requested to look for proof from the *Qur'an* and *Sunnah* which would corroborate the position that listening to a lady's voice was unlawful in Islamic Law! This would then be used before an Independent Broadcasting Authority and allow the Muslim organization to retain its Radio License which was in danger of being revoked if women presenters were not allowed on the Muslim Radio station in line with the new South African constitution. Even though the *Qur'an* and *Sunnah* do not contain such proof, one approaching them with such an attitude risked the danger of imposing his perspective uncritically and violently on the text.

6. See Abu Zuhra, Imam Muhammad, *Usul al-fiqh*, Cairo: Dar al-fikr al-arabi, [s.a.], pp. 5-6; & Al-'Alwani, Taha Jabir, *Usul al-fiqh*, Virginia: IIIT, 1990, p.1.

7. Ibid

8. Ibid

9. This story of Mu'adh was reported by Tirmidhi in *Abwab al-ahkam,* by Nasai in the chapter on Qudat, Ibn Majah in *Manasik,* and Abu Dawud in his introduction to the *Sunan,* as well as by others. However, according to some *hadith* scholars this tradition is not authentic. After reporting this tradition and mentioning his sources, Imam Tirmidhi writes: "We do not know this tradition except from this source and I personally say its chain (*isnad*) is not complete." One of the reporters Al-Harith bin Amr is *majhul.* Imam Bukhari also questioned Al-Harith reliability: "he is not reliable and he is not known except by this tradition (the tradition of Mu'adh)." See *Tarikh al-kabir* and also *al-Awsat* in the chapter of those who died during the period between 100 A.H. and 110 A.H. Al-Uqayli, Ibn al-Jarud, and Abu al-Arab mentioned Al-Harith bin Amr among the weak reporters. Ibn Hiban, however, mentioned him among the reliable narrators but his verdict regarding Al-Harith was not accepted because Ibn Hiban, like Al-Hakim, was classified among the lenient (*mutasahil*) scholars of *jarh wa ta'dil* whose verdicts will only be accepted when collaborated by Al-Dhahabi or other moderate *mu'tadil* scholars of *hadith.* According to Al-Dhahabi and other moderate as well as *mutashaddidin* (strict) scholars, Al-Harith is not reliable. The other scholar who is regarded as having made a mistake while studying the *hadith* of Mu'adh is Imam al-Haramayn Abu al-Ma'ali al-Juwayni who claimed that the story was mentioned in Bukhari's *Sahih.* As we have already discussed Bukhari is among those scholars who do not accept the authenticity of this story. There are even some *hadith* scholars who have claimed that the tradition is *mutawatir* (has a Celebrated chain) and Mubarakpuri has provided detailed answers to this claim in his commentary on Tirmidhi, the *Tuhfat al-ahwadhi,* vol. 4, pp.556-559. Perhaps the reason why some scholars have afforded *tawatur* status to this tradition is because almost all *usul al-fiqh* books which discuss *ijtihad* use this tradition as basis for the whole discussion on *ijtihad.* However, according to *hadith* scholars traditions mentioned in *fiqh* or *tassawuf* (sufism) books will not be accepted unless collaborated by *hadith* scholars. While commenting on a *hadith* reported in *Nihaya* the commentary of *Hidaya,* the Indian *hadith* scholar Mullah Ali al-Qari, wrote: "it is unfounded and the fact that the writer of *Nihayah* or other commentators of *Hidayah* have mentioned this tradition does not mean that it is founded and authentic since they were not *hadith* scholars and they failed to establish a source for this tradition from any of the known *hadith*

scholars." See *Risalat al-mawdu'at*, p.85. However, according to the *hadith* scholar al-Shawkani (*Irshad al-fuhul*, p.227), this tradition is not entirely without claim and may be classified as *hasan* and qualifies as substantiating evidence since it has been reported from other sources.

10. *Sahih al-Bukhari: Kitab al-manaqib* (Chapter of Virtues).

11. In Ibn Qutaybah's version of the tradition we do not find the words "they will remain in this position." See *Sahih Muslim: kitab al-imarat & iman*; also Bukhari: *I'tisam, manaqib & tawhid;* Abu Dawud's *Sunan: kitab al-jihad, fitan*; Bin Majah`s *Muqaddimah*; Tirmidhi`s *kitab al-fitan*.

12. *Sahih Muslim*, Karachi: Qadimi kutub khana, 1952, vol. 2, pp.143-144.

13. See, *Islam and the Destiny of Man*, Cambridge: Islamic Texts Society, 1985, pp.166-167.

Chapter Two

The Primary Sources of Islamic Law: The *Qur'an* and *Sunnah*

A s opposed to modernity whose philosophical foundation is based on René Descartes's *"Cogito, ergo sum"* (I think, therefore I am): the thesis that as long as any discourse is rational or *wissenschaftlich*, it is justified and true, and post-modernity which is anti-foundational and refuses to posit any one premise as the privileged and unassailable foundation for established claims to truth, the Muslim admits that it is impossible to determine good and bad within a strictly rational framework. On the one hand this suggests that there is no good or bad save what Allah has designated as good or bad The perfect example of this is the *qiblah* (direction to face while in prayer), which Allah changed from the direction of Jerusalem to that of Makkah, making the persistent use of the old *qiblah* faulty, while the previously faulty direction (Makkah) became the correct orientation.

On the other hand, with the use of reason guided by, and, originating in the contemplation of the divine sources of guidance, it is possible to understand what is good and what is evil. The tendency to have some internal conflict is recognized in the verse which suggests that the *Qur'an* stands as the unshakable foundation to maintain or bring back to truth our human faculties of reason: "Perchance you dislike a thing which is good for you and you love a thing which is bad for you." (2: 216) To the Muslim therefore the *Qur'an* is the supreme foundation and source of knowledge and truth. The precepts of the *Qur'an* are the normative guidelines for humankind. Specifically, the *ummah* (Muslim nation) is to be the catalyst in the world for justice, and in fact the *Qur'an* may be read as the source for a society to base itself on good deeds, termed in Arabic *ma'rufat* (from *amr bi al ma'ruf*, "encourage the doing of good"), with its antithesis of bad deeds, *munkarat* (from *nahy an al-munkar*, "purge bad deeds"). Thus, the *Qur'an* calls for the raising of righteous [*sulaha*] and pious [*atqiya*] people who will participate in the struggle against injustices and will also enjoin others to do the same.

Unfortunately, in recent years, the *Qur'an*, the decisive authority of Islam, has not been able to play an elucidative role in a Muslim's life. There has been a discontinuity from the original sources of Islamic Law. Instead, spurious and suspicious traditions have become seemingly more acceptable to many modern Muslims and have begun to dominate their lives. Thus, theology and law have developed outside of the *Qur'an*. As a result of this discontinuity or lack of relation and attention, thorough study of the Qur'anic text has given way to perfunctory reading and study. Furthermore, these readings have not considered the practical aspects of life and special social influences. They have mainly been theoretical rather than concrete, disregarding *ummatic* considerations. Hence, the result has been nothing more than an abstract knowledge which fails to answer many of the human problems in the society of today. Regarding our social life, the structure of society, responsibility and duty, these studies have not offered any clear and special proposition. In this way the *Qur'an* has become a means of demagogy in the hands of some corrupt and biased Muslim scholars and rulers. Its unfortunate that the same *Qur'an* which came to liberate Bilal and the oppressed women at the dawn of Islam is being used today by many to oppress the weak and create disharmony among the *ummah*.

Those of us committed to a revitalized, self-assertive and liberating Islam are worried and concerned that the Islamic discourse has become theoretical and far removed from the practical concerns of Jurisprudence. We see a great need to go back to the sources of Islamic Law, but then again this has been the call of all Muslim movements from the fundamentalist, sufi, feminist, and even the modernist movements. Therefore, before referring back to Allah and His Prophet, we need to agree on how we are to interpret and understand them since each and every one of us understands the text according to his or her *a priori* position defined by political, theological, social or economical factors. Central to this process, we believe, is the assessment of Qur'anic Hermeneutics.

Ilm al-tafsir

Every Muslim believes that the *Qur'an* was not revealed all at once and as a complete text, and that the legal instructions were revealed in the context of particular affairs over a period of twenty-three years. This was mainly because the *Qur'an* came to answer and solve the problems of a constantly changing society. Furthermore, this system of progressive revelation confirms the proposition that law and society must co-relate and the operative canonical laws are subject to change to meet the needs of the constantly changing society. The very concept of *naskh*, which has been understood to mean "abrogation", is nothing more than substitution of one law with another to accommodate social change. The law is suspended and may be re-implemented in similar circumstances to those in which it was passed or again be suspended in similar situations to those it was suspended.[1] As the early Muslim community was developing, the Qur'anic revelation also kept changing along with the changing conditions.

Whenever a situation or question would arise for which divine guidance was needed, Allah would reveal a verse or a *surah* (chapter) to provide the solution. These situations were then recorded and were later known as the *asbab al-nuzul* (reasons for revelation). In the same way, whenever the Companions had a problem regarding the meaning or reading of a particular verse they would always refer back to the Prophet who would provide the correct interpretation of the reading. For this reason there existed little differences of opinion among the Companions regarding the meaning of the Qur'anic verses. These interpretations from the Prophet were recorded together along with the text of the *Qur'an* in such a way that it later became difficult for one with rudimentary knowledge of the *Qur'an* to distinguish between the Qur'anic text and the interpretation. Each Companion had his or her own copy [*mushaf*] of the *Qur'an* with explanations of certain words and verses included in it. In Aishah's copy the verse "*hafizu ala salawat wa salat al-wusta*" (be punctual with your daily prayers, especially the middle prayer) was written as: "*hafizu ala salawat wa salat al-wusta wa hiya al-asr*" (be punctual with your daily prayers, especially the middle prayer – and it is *asr* prayer). This would seem like tempering with the text of the *Qur'an*, and it was for this reason that a copy of the *Qur'an* which did not contain any interpretations was later prepared. The interpretations and the reasons for revelation were not destroyed, as claimed by some orientalist writers, but were collected and compiled separately and came to constitute what became known as the *hadith* (sayings of the Prophet). Thus from the very beginning the study of the Qur'anic text, *tafsir* and *hadith* went hand in hand.

After the demise of the Prophet the Islamic empire grew to include non-Arabs who had little or no knowledge of the Arabic language and the Arabs themselves started losing the fluency and eloquence of the language. Problems pertaining to the correct recitation of Qur'anic Arabic [*qira'at*] started arising and at the same time legal situations for which there was no injunctions from the *Qur'an* or *Sunnah* (*imitatio Muhammadi*) began to emerge. In their need to find the answers, the Companions started referring the questions to the specialists and intellectuals among them, among whom were Ali, Aishah as well as other wives of the Prophet, Umm al-Darda a female Companion who was described by Bukhari as *faqihah* (highly learned), Abu Bakr, Umar, Uthman, Ali, Ibn Mas'ud, Ibn Abbas to mention just a few. It was during this period that differences started arising among the Companions regarding the meaning of the Arabic words in the *Qur'an*, the correct recitation [*qira'at*] as well as the interpretation of law in Islam. These "readings" carried important differences of meaning, and they appeared mostly at the morpho-phonological and morpho-syntactical levels. Although it was generally accepted that more than one reading could legitimately exist for a given verse, it was also considered necessary to distinguish between "acceptable" and "unacceptable" readings, and, among the former, between "current" and "rare" [*shadh*] ones. Because of these differences, the main preoccupation of the Companions became the text of the *Qur'an* and this was also generated by an urgent desire to find solutions for concrete problems in Muslim society. This determined all their efforts to get a grip on the phenomenon of language study in Islam which saw *tafsir* together with Arabic linguistics developing into a sophisticated science. It became important for a *mufassir* (exegete) to be one well versed in the Arabic language as well as the *Sunnah*.

Today, we also feel that knowledge of the classical Arabic language, grammar, rhetorics, syntax, linguistics, contemporary theories of language etc., is essential for anyone attempting to engage successfully in the interpretation of the *Qur'an*. Just as any reader who, for example, wishes to interpret Shakespeare's text today must have competence in the style of English language in which Shakespeare wrote, a reader who attempts to interpret the Qur'anic text must understand Qur'anic Arabic. Without such linguistic competence or with only limited competence, the dialectic between reader and *Qur'an* cannot adequately get under way.

This is mainly because it is important that each word should be explained within its semiotic range, where the objective of the word is considered as constraining its meaning. This step requires knowledge of Arabic linguistics and grammar. Each word should also be explained within its context and the context of the entire revelation as well as within the context of what the Companions understood, as the Companions were present during the divine revelation and had it interpreted for them.[2]

The word *tafsir* comes from the Arabic root *fa-sa-ra*, which means to make clear, to show the objective, or to lift the veil. When the Arabs say, "*fasara al-shay'a*", they mean, "he disclosed something."[3] *Tafsir* therefore means, "to disclose the meaning of a text."[4] It is through *tafsir* that the Book of Allah and its divine guidance are to be understood. Thus at the outset, we see that *tafsir* is concerned with divine truth and with making that truth manifest and precise so that it can be understood. Therefore, *ilm al-tafsir* (Qur'anic Hermeneutics) may be defined as the science and art of the interpretation of the *Qur'an* which is held to contain divine truth.

Another word related to *tafsir* is *ta'wil*, which is derived from the word *awwala* [*awwal ilayh ta'wilan*] which literally means "to return something". When the Arabs say, "*wa awwala allah alayka dallataka*", they mean "may Allah return your lost property to you."[5] In the Arabic linguistic tradition *ta'wil al-kalam* means to change the literal meaning of a text [*sirf al-kalam an ma'nahu al-dahir*] to another meaning considered suitable [*ma'anan yahtamiluhu*].[6] In Qur'anic studies it means to apply a verse to a given meaning. The condition for the permissibility of this exercise when studying religious texts is that the new meaning should not be against the general spirit of the *Shari'ah*. The following was given as an example of *ta'wil*:

> It is He who brings out the living from the dead' (30:19). If we say here that the meaning of this verse means that Allah brings out a bird from an egg it will be considered good and correct *ta'wil*.[7]

According to some Arabic lexicologists, there is no difference between *tafsir* and *ta'wil*, both mean to interpret and the *Qur'an* has used the words interchangeably.[8] However, according to al-Raghib al-isfahani (d. 502 A.H.), the famous Arabic lexicographer, *tafsir* is the study of the meaning of words while *ta'wil* is the study of the contextual meanings of words. In other words *ta'wil* is the study of a whole sentence or of the text as a unity. Arabs have traditionally differentiated between the two terms and have always referred to the interpretation of dreams as *ta'wil al-ru'ya* and rarely *tafsir al-ru'ya*.[9]

Conventionalist Theories of Qur'anic Hermeneutics

The *Qur'an* is seen in Islam as the highest authority and as the final court of appeal in all theological and legal disputes. The schools of Islamic thought must not determine what the *Qur'an* must say (engage in eisegesis) but the *Qur'an* must determine what the schools should teach. In order to avoid eisegesis, there are written and unwritten principles that underlie Qur'anic hermeneutics.

Two early scholars of the *Qur'an*, al-Zarkhashi in *al-Burhan* and Suyuti in *al-Ittiqan*, correctly identified the *Qur'an* as the foremost commentary on the divine revelation. Imam Zarkhashi (d. 794 A.H.) wrote in his *al-Burhan fi ulum al-Qur'an*, which served as the basis of Suyuti's *al-Ittiqan fi ulum al-Qur'an*, another important source book in the field of *tafsir*: "It is said that the best way of exegesis in explaining the *Qur'an* is with the help of the *Qur'an* itself."[10] This means that one part of the *Qur'an* may be interpreted and elucidated by another part. Examples are abounding, but we may consider a few from the very first chapter [*surah*], the Opening, or *Fatihah*. The phrase "Guide us onto the straight path" (1: 6) has a concept of straight path that may not be immediately understandable. But the rest of the *Qur'an* provides many descriptions of what the "straight path" is. The phrase "The path of those on whom you have showered your bounties" (1: 7) is elucidated by the rest of the *Qur'an* which describes the lives, felicity, and examples of many prophets and messengers and believers.[11]

Similarly, one statement may be inconclusive [*mujmal*] in one part of the *Qur'an*, but explicit [*mubayyan*] in another part. When we read in the *Qur'an* "Permitted to you is the beast of the flocks, except that which is now recited to you," (5:1) we must consider its clarification from another part of the *Qur'an*, namely "Forbidden to you are carrion, blood, and the flesh of swine..." (2: 173).

Moreover, a command with an absolute meaning [*mutlaq*] may be explained by reference to a restricted [*muqayyad*] command, and a general [*amm*] injunction may be elucidated by reference to a particular [*khass*] injunction. The context of the occasions of revelation [*asbab al-nuzul*] also must be considered, since by virtue of being revealed over time, the *Qur'an* displaces earlier commands by later ones. The principle that the *Qur'an* interprets itself [*al-Qur'an yufassir ba'duha ba'dan*] is similar to the principle "*Scriptura Scrupturae interpre*" used by the Christian reformers of Biblical Hermeneutics in the period between 1483 and 1564.

Thus, after the *Qur'an* itself, we have records of the blessed Messenger of Allah explaining the *Qur'an*. For instance, the verse "it is those who believe and confuse not their beliefs with wrong [*zulm*] that are (truly) in security, for they are on (right) guidance" (6: 82) bothered many of the Muslims, who were concerned that everyone does some harm [*zulm*] to their spiritual life. But the Messenger of Allah explained to them that the wrong doing here [*zulm*] was the act of putting one's trust and faith in something besides Allah [*shirk*], and this wrong doing [*zulm*] is connected with the passage in the chapter of Luqman: "Indeed *shirk* is a great *zulm*." (31: 13).

Similarly, the verse "And eat and drink, until the white thread [*al-khait al-abyad*] shows clearly to you from the black thread [*al-khait al-aswad*]" (2: 187) was also a cause for some confusion. While the Prophet was teaching Adi ibn Abi Hatam how to fast and perform *salah*, said to him, "fast and drink until..." (repeating, evidently, the words of the Qur'anic verse). Later on, Adi, who was the son of the famous Hatam Ta'i, took two pieces of thread, white and black, holding them before his eyes, yet he was unable to distinguish between them. He imagined that what the Prophet meant was that one could eat and drink until one could distinguish between a black and white thread in the dawn twilight. When the Prophet heard Adi's account of the episode he laughed and said to him: "O son of Hatam you are indeed dim-witted." He went on to explain that the white and black thread figuratively mean the light of the day and the darkness of the night. "Do you not see that the verse says *min al-fajr*?"

The famous collections of *hadith* include sections on Prophetic explanations, or *tafsir al-nabawi*. The occasions of revelation [*asbab al-nuzul*] were explained by the Prophet thoroughly to the Companions, who were taught to understand the verses that were superseded [*mansukh*] by others. In fact, this role was stipulated in the *Qur'an*:

And we have sent down unto you (also) the Message, that you may explain clearly what is sent for people, and that they may give thought. (16: 44)

In this way the Companions were thoroughly instructed in understanding and applying the divine revelation, and they in turn passed this knowledge on to the Successors, the generation which followed their own. Many of the Companions had committed the entire text of the *Qur'an* to memory, and large portions of the *Sunnah*, and they were thereby able to pass on the vast oral and written literature to the Successors.

The care with which the Companions treated the *Qur'an* is evidenced many times. Abu Abd al-Rahman al-Sulami al-Tabi'i (d. 82 A.H.) remarked that the Companions like Uthman ibn Affan and Abdullah ibn Mas'ud would learn the *Qur'an,* ten verses at a time, never advancing until they were sure of their exact recitation.[12] We know, for instance, from Imam Malik's *al-Muwatta'* that Abdullah ibn Umar took eight years to learn the second, very large chapter, *al-Baqarah.*

By extension, we may also say that the first four leaders of the community of believers after the death of the Prophet were themselves prominent interpreters [*mufassirun*] of the *Qur'an*. These "rightly guided *Caliphs*" as they are called were therefore in a position of being able to apply what they had learnt directly from the Prophet to the new circumstances which arose during their rule. Other interpreters included:

Abdullah ibn Abbas (d. 68 A.H.)
Abdullah ibn Mas'ud (d. 32 A.H.)
Ubayy ibn Ka'b (d. 20 A.H.)
Zaid ibn Thabit (d. 45 A.H.)
Abu Musa al-Ash'ari (d. 44 A.H.)
Abdullah ibn al-Zubair (d. 73 A.H.)

Of these commentators, Abdullah ibn Abbas has pre-eminence. His titles included "interpreter of the *Qur'an*" [*mufassir al-Qur'an*] and "the Ocean" [*al-bahr*], as his knowledge was considered vast. One of the arts that Ibn Abbas included in his vast repertoire was an extensive grasp of the Arabic language. When Nafi ibn al-Azraq once asked Ibn Abbas a number of questions about the *Qur'an* in front of a large audience, Ibn Abbas proceeded to offer corroborative evidence for the meaning of two hundred words in the *Qur'an* from ancient Arabic poetry. Ali ibn Abi Talib himself gave Ibn Abbas great praise. He commented about Ibn Abbas' knowledge of *tafsir* saying, "It is as if he were looking at the unseen through a thin veil." And also, Ibn Umar said: "Ibn Abbas is the most knowledgeable person of the community about what was revealed to him."

Another great scholar among the Companions was Abdullah ibn Mas'ud. Ali ibn Abi Talib praised Ibn Mas'ud highly, saying, "he knows the *Qur'an* and *Sunnah*, and his knowledge is the best." After Ibn Mas'ud and Ali, we may rank Ubbay ibn Ka'b as a leading commentator of the *Qur'an*. Other Companions whose interpretations survive in the *hadith* literature include Aishah, the wife of the Prophet (d. 58 A.H.), Abu Hurairah (d. 57 A.H.), Abdullah ibn Amr ibn al-As (d. 63 A.H.), Abdullah ibn Umar ibn al-Khattab (d. 73 A.H.), Jabr ibn Abdullah al-Ansari (d. 74), and Anas ibn Malik (d. 91 A.H.). Among the four *Caliphs*, Ali is considered the most knowledgeable and is also the one who reported most of the traditions on *tasfir* by virtue of having lived longer than his predecessors. While describing Ali's profound knowledge of *tafsir*, Ma'mar ibn Wahab ibn Abdullah reported the following narration from Abu al-Tufail:

> I once witnessed Ali addressing a gathering saying, "ask me whatever you wish to ask. By Allah! You will not ask me about any issue for which I cannot provide an answer! Ask me regarding the Book of Allah. By Allah! There is no verse in the *Qur'an* except that I know whether it was revealed during the day or during the night, whether it was revealed on the valley or on the mountain!"[13]

Among the second generation of early Muslims [the *tabi'in*] there existed also a group of scholars who had immense knowledge of the *tafsir* science. Sufyan al-Thawry would always advise Muslims of his time saying, "learn the science of *tafsir* from four scholars: Sa'id ibn Jubair, Mujahid, Ikramah the former slave of Ibn Abbas and Dahhak."

As with the growth of the schools of *fiqh*, orientalist scholars believe the growth of hermeneutical sciences during the second and third generations of the *ummah* indicates that the Companions went back to their business with the death of the Prophet, much the same way they assume Jesus' companions forgot him soon after his "crucifixion". Anyone with a less hostile perspective on Islam sees clearly that the growth and development of the hermeneutical and legal sciences took place two or three centuries after the death of the Prophet because the Companions and their Successors were so imbued with the spirit and essence of Islam, which was cultivated in them by the Messenger of Allah himself that the writing down and codification of these sciences was utterly unnecessary for them. In other words, the spirit of the law was more important to them than the letter of the law.

However, once the people who had been trained in the application of this message to their daily and spiritual lives died, it became necessary to codify and make explicit what constituted the methods of applying the divine message. These methods, which assumed second nature to the Companions and their Successors, were developed to make the divine message for those who had only heard about these wonderful days as much relevant and applicable as to those who actually saw the event of revelation.

Three schools of Qur'anic hermeneutics emerged by the first half of the first century *hijrah*. The school cantering around Makkah had as its leader Abdullah ibn Abbas, and its students included Mujahid ibn Jabr al-Makki (d. 104 A.H.), Ikrima (d. 105 A.H.), Tawus ibn Kaisan al-Yamani (d. 106 A.H.), and Ata ibn Abi Rabah (d. 114 A.H.). The Iraqi school had Ibn Mas'ud as its master commentator, and included as students Alqama ibn Qais (d. 102 A.H.), al-Aswad ibn Yazid (d. 75 A.H.), Masruq ibn al-Ajd (d. 63 A.H.), al-Hamdani (d. 76 A.H.), Amr al-Sha'bi (d. 105 A.H.), al-Hassan al-Basri (d. 121 A.H.), Qatadah al-Sadusi (d. 117 A.H.), and Ibrahim al-Nakha'i (d. 195 A.H.). The school cantering around Madinah, which was the first capital of the Caliphate, was led by Ubayy ibn Ka'b, with students such as Abu al-Aliyah (d. 90), Muhammad ibn Ka'b al-Qarzi (d. 117), and Zaid ibn Aslam (d. 130), as well as his sons Abd al-Rahman ibn Zaid and Malik ibn Anas.

The *Tafsir* genre

In response to the growing distance perceived between the contemporary and the prophetic period, the latter half of the first century *hijrah* saw increased efforts at making the commentaries more extensive, and more comprehensive. The second generation of the Successors, also set themselves to the task of writing down commentaries. Perhaps as a gesture of respect, these Successors attributed most of their work to the founder of their particular school, although they did not hesitate to collate information from other schools, too. Some of the outstanding scholars of this period included Isma'il al-Suddi (d. 128), al-Dahhak ibn Muzahim (d. 105), al-Kalbi (d. 146), Muqatil ibn Hayyan (d. Before 150), and Muqatil ibn Sulaiman (d. 150).

After the second generation of Muslims (Successors), diverse genres of *tafsir* started appearing. An exegete would deal with the interpretation from the perspective of his field of specialization. Four distinct types of *tafsir* literature were thus produced during this period:

1. The grammatical *tafsir*, which dealt mostly with the rules of Arabic grammar derived from the *Qur'an* but which failed to deal with the real interpretation of the *Qur'an*. The most prominent scholars in this field were al-Zujaj the Arabic scholar, al-Wahidi who wrote al-Basit, and Abu Hayan the author of *al-Bahr* and *al-Nahr*.

2. The *akhbari* (historical) *tafsir* produced by historians whose main interest lay in the historical study of the *Qur'an*. Apart from the many fabricated narrations, stories and traditions compiled in these kinds of *tafsir* books, the compilers helped to provide certain valuable information on the history of peoples and nations before the advent of Islam. Al-Tha'labi was one of the leading figures in this school of *tafsir*.

3. The *fiqhi* (legal) interpretations produced by legal pragmatists [*fuqaha*] who were particularly interested in deriving laws from Qur'anic verses or were looking for those verses in the *Qur'an* which would substantiate their schools of jurisprudence. Like the works produced in the field of jurisprudence, these interpretations too, strated with the chapter of purity [*taharah*]. Moreover, number of issues that had little, if anything, to do with the verse being interpreted were discussed at substantial length. The most famous book produced in this area was that of al-Qurtubi.

4. The rationalist *tafsir* written by scholars who dwelt on philosophy and dialectic scholasticism [*ilm al-kalam*]. An example of this *tafsir* genre is the *Mafatih al-ghaib* of Fakhr al-Din al-Razi, the *al-Lubab fi ma'ani al-tanzil* by al-Khazin, and the *Kashaf* (book that explains) of al-Zamakhshari. A Mu'tazilah, al-Zamakhshari's ideas have often been rejected out of hand, but many of his insights on the linguistics of the *Qur'an* are nevertheless considered valuable and sound.

While the above mentioned four schools of *tafsir* contributed tremendously to their respective fields of knowledge, they did very little to advance the field of Qur'anic hermeneutics.

Another category of *tafsir* that later developed was the analogical *sufi* (spiritual, mystical) interpretation where the *sufi* claimed to have been directed by Allah through *ilham* (inspiration) to the correct meaning of the Qur'anic verses. The *sufi* divided interpretation into esoteric[*batin*] and exoteric [*zahir*] and claimed that the esoteric was the real intention of Allah and the correct meaning. Regarding the "mystical letters" [*huruf al-muqatta'at*] of the *Qur'an* such as "*ha mim, ain sin qaf*" (42: 1-2) whose meaning had not been provided, not even by Muhammad, had made the Companions and their successors to say, "only Allah knows their meaning." However, these were later explained by *sufi* writers as follows:

> *Ha* refers to *harb ali wa mu'awiyyah* – the war between Ali and Mu'awiyyah. *Mim* means *wilayat al-marwaniyyah* – the rule of Marwan. *Ain* means *wilayat al-abbasiyyah* – the rule of the Abbasid. *Sin* refers to the Safavid rule, and *Qaf* refers to *qudwat al-mahdi* – the leadership of the Mahdi.[14]

The methodology of *Sufism* led to stagnation and the death of intellectual thought in Islam and was met with strong opposition and criticism from almost all *tafsir* scholars who felt that the *Qur'an* must be interpreted and not be destroyed through reading pious meanings into it. It was felt that *sufism* as well as other *Muslim* theologies were attempting to silence the *Qur'an* by imposing their own doctrines on it instead of properly studying the *Qur'an*. Imam Suyuti wrote in his famous *al-Ittiqan*:

> Regarding the interpretations of the *Sufis*, they cannot not be considered as *tafsir* since they claim that the meaning of the Qur'anic text is not exoteric but there is another esoteric meaning which is not known even to a scholar!

The situation has not changed much in our /present day societies. *Tafsir* must stop being nothing more than verification of a particular set of doctrine. In other words, the dogmatic reading of the *Qur'an* must give way to a truly /analytical reading.[15]

Since the field of *tafsir* originated with the Messenger of Allah, it is inappropriate to try to identify the first commentary. Also, since the need to commit the sciences of Islam to writing was not felt until the "time space" or chronological distance separating the prophetic period increased, so trying to pinpoint the first commentary is a futile exercise.

The oldest extant written commentary is that of al-Tabari (d. 310 A.H.). This is the estimation of the classical scholars such as Muhammad al-Dhahabi in his work on commentaries and commentary writers and also twentieth century scholars such as Ahmad Amin. Nevertheless, while that of al-Tabari is rightly famous, earlier commentaries are those of Mujahid ibn Jabr al-Makki, Zaid ibn Ali, Ata al-Khurasani, Muhammad al-Kalbi, and Muqatil ibn Sulaiman al-Khurasani, which are still extant and available.

The Imams of the schools of *fiqh* also worked in the field of commentary. Although we will examine this below, it is appropriate to remark that the science of *usul al-fiqh* developed by these Imams required a thorough development of linguistic evidence and criteria, which although applied ostensibly to the evaluation of the *hadith* literature, nevertheless, considerably advanced the systematization of *tafsir*.

In fact, al-Tabari's massive work, in thirty volumes, treated the issue of authenticating and evaluating the *hadith* literature together with the examination of Qur'anic hermeneutics. Thus, he saw the intimate relation of the information disseminated by the Companions in the form of *hadith* literature with that information disseminated in the form of explanation and commentary.

The *isra'iliyyah* were another sub-topic of the commentaries and were based primarily on historical traditions from Jewish sources. One of the characteristics of the *Qur'an* is that the events of the past are treated normatively. This meant that one event might offer a number of morals, or a few events might offer the same moral. In other words, the *Qur'an* discusses events not from some "objective" or coldly descriptive standpoint, but rather historical events are described for their normative and exhortatory value. Thus we have in the *Qur'an* stories about previous prophets and messengers, and naturally the Muslim community was interested in hearing more about these events. Jews who had recognized Muhammad as the messenger of Allah would often provide the community with information about the events that the Jewish people had preserved.

However, the Muslims soon found out that the stories preserved by the *qussas* (storytellers) were often grossly inaccurate and corrupted.

33

This is not surprising because it is the nature of people to embellish their traditions according to distorting interests. The early community took the following *hadith* to mean that, making inquiries into the events of the Jews was perfectly acceptable: "convey from me even if it is one single verse and narrate from the Israelites and there is no harm. Whosoever attributes a lie to me intentionally, he has prepared his seat in the fire of Hell."

While it is noble and justified to ask questions and make inquiries, according to the *Qur'an*, much of the questioning of the Israelites was prompted by very petty and trivial interests. Is it really important to discuss as to how many and who the "people of the cave" mentioned in the *Qur'an* were, the name of their dog or its colour? Is it not more necessary and significant to understand the moral of that story? People seemed to forget the following verse:

> (Some) say they were three, the dog being the fourth among them; (others) say they were five, the dog being the sixth, doubtfully guessing at the unknown; (yet others) say they were seven, the dog being the eighth. Say you: My Lord knows best their number; it is but few who know their real case. Enter not, therefore, into controversies concerning them, except on a matter that is clear, nor consult any of them about (the affair of) the Sleepers (18 : 22).

One other unintended result of this kind of frenzy for explaining everything to its tiniest and most insignificant detail only appeared with the orientalists and most recently with the *Satanic Verses* of Salman Rushdie. In an effort to explain *sura* (chapter) *al-Najm, al-Tabari, Jalalain* and others put up the most superficial sophistry to explain that the idols *Lat, Uzza, and Manat* were worshiped during the prophetic period by Muslims. Unfortunately some Muslim scholars of *tafsir* did preserve these spurious traditions believing them to be authentic and when orientalist scholars got hold of them they begin to weave the most absurd theories imaginable about Islamic law and theology. And of course Rushdie used this tradition as the basis for his book *The Satanic Verses*.

When we consider the *hadith* that states the nations before the Islamic *ummah* destroyed themselves because they bickered among themselves about things that they did not know[16], we remember that Islam brings out the overriding commitment to work for the benefit of justice and the society. We are free to explore and try to gain insight into the text: but when this exploration is published so as to provide gist for the mill of disagreement and divisiveness, then we are no longer working for the sake of Allah and the cause of Islam. Far from being anti-intellectual, this *hadith* reminds us that some questions are academic, to be discussed and debated dispassionately, but not to be used as springboards to schism and pettiness.

One of the Traditions restricting sophistry in commenting on the *Qur'an* is the following: "Whosoever says anything in the matter of the *Qur'an* according to his own thoughts or anything about which he does not know, he is making his seat in the fire of Hell." Because of this *hadith*, the Companions were very careful in their explanations and would not proffer any unwarranted views. Whenever asked about the commentary of any verse from the *Qur'an*, Sa'id ibn Musayyib would say, "we do not say anything in the matter of the *Qur'an*." From the *Qur'an* itself we learn that there are different levels of interpretation. Some words or phrases admit of a clear and basic meaning [*muhkam*], while others give derivative or allegorical meaning [*mutashabih*]. The verse is as follows:

> He it is who has sent down the Book: in it are verses basic and fundamental; they are the foundations of the Book; others are allegorical. But those in whose hearts is perversity follow the part thereof that is allegorical, seeking discord, and searching for its hidden meanings. But no one knows its hidden meanings except Allah. And those who are firmly grounded in knowledge say: "We believe in the Book; the whole of it is from our Lord;" and none will bear this in mind except those with understanding (3:7).

What has been prevalent and considered accepted doctrine since early Islam is that explicit verses [*muhkamat*] are those whose meaning is clear and there is little room for error in understanding them. The duty of every believer is to have faith in them and to execute their commands. The implicit [*mutashabih*] verses, however, are those whose real /interpretation is known only to Allah and not accessible to human beings. It is only those with perverted hearts and minds who follow and interpret the implicit verses to deceive and encroach on other people.

Contemporary *Tafsir*

Contemporary Islamic scholarship has not contributed much to Qur'anic hermeneutics. This has been mainly because the contemporary discourse of post-modernity is one that takes place in very hostile territories. With theories such as Deconstruction, it means that the *Qur'an* will not receive any special privileges as a divine scripture, but will be treated just like any other work of literature. According to this theory everything is considered to be a text whether it is a fragment of language, advertising poster, a movie, the *Qur'an* or the *Bible*, and it is the text that gets deconstructed. It is a strategy of reading texts which works within the text's own system of beliefs and values. The text itself provides the tools for the process of deconstruction. Employing devices from within the text to be used against the text, the deconstructionist attempts to prove how the text eludes understanding, how its unity disintegrates and how its declared central concerns serve to conceal more vital manoeuvres involving the suppression of unwanted rhetorical "skeletons in the cupboards."[17] He attempts to demonstrate how the text is grounded in incoherence, paradox and contradiction and to achieve this he employs the following strategies:

1. Employing the language of the text under deconstruction.
2. Parodying the style of the text by deliberately imitating and distorting its language.
3. Inventing new terminology to express concepts, issues, relations etc., that are otherwise suppressed within the text.
4. Encouraging the reader to see as metaphorical a term which the text assumes to be literal.[18]

This attitude towards texts has drawn much suspicion and criticism from the conservative Muslim scholars who see such an exercise as heretic.

The traditionalist atomistic view of the *Qur'an* will, without any doubt, condemn and reject any suggestion of looking at the *Qur'an* from the perspective of modern theories of interpretation. From the position that we occupy, we see no problem in regarding the *Qur'an* as literature and using principles of literary criticism in the study of the *Qur'an*. The *Qur'an* was revealed in a world and time when the Arabs had developed some of the highest principles of literary criticism which they tested on the best Arabic poems during the annual fair of *suq ukaz*. Moreover, to prove the inimitability of the *Qur'an*, Allah challenged them to apply the same test on the *Qur'an* or to produce a similar text. The underlying idea was that the literary merit of the *Qur'an* could be appreciated by them as well.

Because we believe that the *Qur'an* is literature (like no other), and there is a degree of coherence and unity in it, we have no problem or objection to anyone subjecting it to any standard of literary criticism. The traditionalist *ulama's* disregard of the unity or coherence within the chapters of the *Qur'an* makes them feel insecure regarding the challenges of modern hermeneutics. This attitude, however, has been a great obstacle to the advancement of Qur'anic studies in the contemporary century. Moreover, the contemporary century is one that has been dominated by the human and social sciences and those *ulama'* trained only in the traditional sciences find it difficult to participate in this sophisticated discourse. This has caused a civil war of ideas within Islam by generating a bipolar reaction of the utmost importance for the interpretation of Islamic sources. It has caused a radical division between the "progressive" element schooled only in the contemporary sciences at Western universities while lacking even rudimentary knowledge of the traditional sciences, and the "conservative" element educated in the traditional universities and seminaries in the Middle East and Indo-Pakistan subcontinent while not familiar with the contemporary sciences. The "conservative" attitude towards the contemporary discourse has been one of total rejection and nostalgia while on the other hand the liberal's attitude has been one of uncritical allegiance. Fortunately, a generation of scholars is emerging, schooled in both the traditional and contemporary sciences, and it is these scholars who have been attempting to seek a *modus vivendi* between the two extremes. They realize that a reader of the *Qur'an* who grew outside of Islamic life, attending a state university, is more likely to see the *Qur'an* as a *din* of conflicting theological claims than a reader who grew up with frequent participation in worship, attending an Islamic college.

Perhaps the main criticism against post-modern thought is that it makes thinking difficult by questioning the habits to which we have grown accustomed. At the same time, this is what makes post-modern thought so important since not all habits are good. As we will see in the next pages, in the name of Islam, we have become accustomed to some habits that violate justice and human dignity. Perhaps this again is the most important lesson of post-modern thinking: we cannot guarantee either the correctness or the soundness of our thinking by merely adopting the right method, or by starting from the right point.

What traditionalist scholars fail to recognize is that Qur'anic Arabic, its vocabulary, idiom, style, and syntax is the language of pre-Islamic and Prophetic milieu, well known and understood by the Arabs of that period. The *Qur'an*'s primary discourse is directed at the Qurayshites of Makkah and it is for this reason it has been reported in *hadith* that it was revealed in the dialect of the Qurayshites.[19] This language represents Arab culture and society at the dawn of Islam, a culture and society far much different from contemporary Arabic because our language keep on evolving due to social changes. We need to acknowledge that there is a time space gap not only between us and the classical interpretations, but just as much between us and the *Qur'an* itself. We cant just read the *Qur'an* and understand what we see, because of the gap that divides past and present. Understanding linguistic communication from a different time and social context obviously requires some set of interpretive tools to carry off the task of cross-temporal and cross-cultural inquiry. Unfortunately, classical Islamic scholarship and Arabic linguistics do not provide us with such tools. The social sciences can provide us with the tools that enable us to bridge the gap between past and present.

Although we believe in the supra-historicity of the *Qur'an*, we need to understand that the revelation of the *Qur'an* is an event that took place within human history, and the message of the *Qur'an* was revealed in human language since language is a human and social phenomenon. This is not the place to discuss, even at rudimentary level, whether language is of divine or human origin, our position is that Allah created in a person the ability to make speech and taught him or her how to do so but language or meaning *per se* is a product of human efforts, and humans are linguistic beings.

If we accept that language is a human phenomenon, and that it is human beings who determine the relation between noun and object or signifier and signified, in that case we must accept that names pertain to things within the realm of human knowledge and that it is human beings who set them by convention. It is not possible to think of, or try to imagine, something that does not exist and has never existed and try to assign a name to it. It is humans who fix names for what they know and for that of which they have some kind of comprehension. Such named things are most certainly finite and changing. Consequently, if we say that Allah translated His divine message into human language, we must accept that revelation came within the confines of human concepts. What this means, therefore, is that revelation cannot state anything other than human concepts, and that it contains nothing that cannot be understood by reason.

The *Qur'an* speaks of Allah having sent every Prophet in the language *of* his people [*lisan qawmihi*] confirming that humans are "creators" of their own language and meaning:

> And we never sent a messenger save with the *lisan* (translated "language") of his people, that he might make the message clear for them. Then Allah sends whom He will astray, and guides whom He will. He is the Mighty, the Wise. (14: 4)

The *Qur'an* is also said to have been revealed in the language *of* the Qurayshite. If the Prophet Muhammad, upon whom be peace, is a universal messenger sent as a mercy to all mankind as the *Qur'an* clearly states, why then was the *Qur'an* sent only in *lisan al-arab* (Arabic) and not in Mandarin, Zulu, Shona, to name just a few of the languages of the Prophet's people [*lisan qawmihi*]? Does *lisan* in the above mentioned verse mean "language" e.g., Zulu as opposed to English? In order to get answers we are forced to deal with issues pertaining to language, meaning, and re-interpretation. We have no choice but to engage in the re-interpretation of the *Qur'an* so that its message is accessible to the Prophet's Xhosa, Swahili, English and Persian peoples. Translation, although it is a form of interpretation, is not sufficient. We already see how difficult it is to translate from one language to another. This is mainly because when translating you not only translate words but also you attempt to translate a society, history, culture, concepts, and feelings. How are you to translate the word "snow" to a desert dweller that has never seen snow in his life and may not even have a word for snow in his vocabulary? All human languages do not have all the words to describe every single existing entity. There are languages where you will not find a noun for dates simply because there are no dates in those areas and a need was never felt to *create* a noun that refers to dates. Therefore, these realities force us to engage in the re-interpretation process, failing to do so would put us in a situation where we find it hard to justify the *Qur'an*'s claim to universality.

The *Qur'an* we have before us is a written text of the revelation that was brought to the Prophet in a period of twenty three years, and like any written text it has ceased to be a *direct* dialogue between Allah and His creation. While the Prophet was alive the dialogue between Allah and His servants took place. If anyone had a misunderstanding regarding a particular issue or verse, he or she had the opportunity to engage in "dialogue" with Allah (through the Prophet). There were occasions when a person would say something that was against the will and *intention* of Allah, and Allah would reveal a verse or chapter answering the person's question and problem. The following verse was revealed following a dialogue between a Muslim lady and the Prophet:

> Allah has heard the saying of her that disputed with you (Muhammad) concerning her husband, and complained to Allah. Allah hears your dialogue. Lo! Allah is most hearing most seeing. (58: 1)

It was customary for the Arabs to say to their wives "you are like the back of my mother" or "you are like my mother" when intending divorce. Saying such a statement would break a marriage. A lady whose husband had uttered this statement to her came to the Prophet pleading that her husband had not intended any divorce, and since she loved him so much, she wanted permission to continue staying with him. The Prophet told her that by saying these words their marriage had been broken. She could not accept this decision and kept on appealing until she complained to Allah. It was at that occasion that the verse was revealed.

The demise of the Prophet marked the beginning of a new chapter in Islam and the end of revelation. For people, it meant that the opportunity to engage in a direct dialogue with the creator no longer existed. All that was left was the written text of the *Qur'an* and the *Sunnah*. The Prophet himself was reported to have said in his final sermon: "I leave you with two things, you will never go astray as long as you hold fast onto them: The Book of Allah and my *Sunnah*."

Two things happens when discourse passes from speaking to writing, first is fixation which will shelter the event of discourse from distraction, and writing also renders the text autonomous with respect to the intention of the author. What the text signifies no longer coincides with what the author intended. In contrast to the dialogical situation, where the meaning is determined by the very situation of discourse, written discourse creates an audience that extends in principle to anyone who can read.[20] In oral discourse, the Prophet, representing Allah, was talking to his people about realities that were common between them, and this is what Allah meant by sending a Prophet in the language of his people. When he spoke of a "*jamal*" (camel), they knew what he was talking about because the camel was grazing a few yards away. If for some reason someone did not know what a *jamal* was, he was able to point to him. With writing, things already begin to change even for the first readers of the text (those who read it in the time when it is written). There no longer exist a situation common to the speaker or writer and the reader, and concrete conditions of the act of pointing no longer exist. To read a text, as Ricoeur says, "is to consider its author as already dead and the book as posthumous." [21] Post-modern thought celebrates the death of the author. The slogan, "every author is a dead author", is an example of the denial of original meaning, because it denies that the meaning of a text can be authoritatively disclosed through reference to authorial intentions. An author's intentions are no more relevant to understanding the text than any other set of considerations; they are not the origin of the text and so have no privilege over other factors.

The Muslim, however, believes that Allah is the author of the *Qur'an* and that the *Qur'an* is His word, which means, like all His other attributes, it is eternal [*sifat al-azaliyyah*]. It exists with Him from eternity [*al-azali*] and will exist with Him till eternity. The meaning of the *Qur'an*, therefore, must also be perpetual. The Muslim rejects the death of the author with reference to the *Qur'an*, even metaphorically, and argue that it is still possible to understand what Allah's intention is when reading the text of the *Qur'an*. The understanding of the Companions of the Prophet of the Qur'anic text, by virtue of having learnt interpretation directly from the Prophet himself is considered as the true and final meaning of the text, and hence Allah's intention.

This emphasis on the understanding of the Companions of the Prophet [*Sahabah*] or the community to whom the text was first read or revealed as a hermeneutical model is what is now known in the field of interpretation as "historical criticism." The historical critical model calls for a radical contextualization of the text. Such a task is broadly conceived, involving extensive knowledge of the period and area under consideration, for example, historical framework and social institutions. For this model, therefore, the meaning of the text reside either in the world represented by it or in the intention of the author, in the case of the *Qur'an*, in what Allah wants to convey to his servants. The task of the contemporary reader is to search and recover the original audience of the Qur'anic text, along with its original message and intention. This kind of reading is informed by an operative though implicit theological principle to the effect that what comes earlier is better.

The model of historical criticism has a strong positivistic foundation and orientation. The understanding of the Qur'anic text derived from the Companions of the Prophet is regarded as univocal and objective, and thus it can be retrieved if the proper methodological tools, scientific in nature are rigorously applied. The meaning disclosed is for all times and cultures. In other words, the meaning of the text, properly secured and established, can dictate the overall boundaries or parameters of the Muslim's life everywhere and at all times. The proper task of the exegete [*mufassir*] is to engage in *exegeses*, not *eisegesis* – a reading and interpretation of the Qur'anic text, and not a reading into the text; allowing the text to speak on its own terms rather than inserting one's words into the *Qur'an*.

This model presupposes and entails a very specific and universal pedagogical model: all readers, regardless of ideological persuasions and socio-cultural moorings, can become such informed and universal exegetes if the right methodological tools are disseminated and acquired. This is a pedagogical model of learned impartation and passive reception, highly hierarchical and authoritative in character, with strong emphasis on academic pedigree (who studied under which scholar or *shaikh*) and schools of thought.

The problem with the historical critical model, however, is that its methodological development fails to successfully address the emerging new questions, concerns, and challenges – challenges and questions such as those arising under the rubric of religious pluralism, the role and rights of Muslim minorities when in non-Muslim states, etc. Classical Muslim scholarship did not address the role of Islam in a pluralistic state or how

Muslims should live as minorities in non Muslim states since it had been perceived that Muslims will always be in a majority and that Islam would always be the dominant force at all times and in every place [*al-islam ya'lu wala yu'la alaihi*]. The reality of the situation, however, is quite the opposite. Muslims today have to flee from tyrant rulers in their Muslim countries to seek shelter and refuge in Western societies most of which are predominantly non-Muslim. Apart from the Muslim refugees, twentieth century Islam has been the fastest growing religion in the United State and Europe, among the African Americans, and the British Afro-Caribbean communities. How do Muslims who have become citizens of these non-Muslim states remain faithful to their religion and yet at the same time participate with fellow citizens from other cultural and religious groups in nation building? While a non-Muslim under the protection of an Islamic government [*dhimmi*] is expected to obey all the laws of the Islamic state, is a Muslim under the protection of a non-Muslim state expected to obey all the laws of the host country most of which conflict with the *Shari'ah* law? These are questions whose answers are absent from classical or medieval Islamic literature or from a historical critical reading of the *Qur'an* and *Sunnah*.

However, in a world of social injustice and discrimination against the racial, religious, and gender other, the historical critical model remains a very important model for interpretation for liberation. It guarantees security against racist and sexist violence on the Qur'anic text. We see how the *Qur'an* is often abused to justify all kinds of un-Islamic attitudes such as the legitimating of sexual relations with female domestic servants in contemporary Muslim societies as a direct result of a misinformed and uncritical interpretation of the verses revealed regarding female slaves. We also see how these poor servants are treated like slaves by their Muslim employers, which again is a consequence of such *eisegesis* or misinterpretations

Interpretation for liberation

Before discussing Islamic liberation theology, it is important that we have a general perspective on liberation theology as a whole. Liberation theology can be defined as a theology of protest against oppression and social injustice. It is that form of reflection that attempts to discern the religious significance of the socio-political struggles in which the poor, women, and people of colour are engaged as they free themselves of their present state of socio-political oppression and economic exploitation.[22] It originated out of the unique experiences of the people of colour in North America and Africa. Many scholars have seen anticipations of the characteristic elements of liberation theology in writings of Latin American theologians in the early and middle 1960s. However, the clear manifestation of a new chapter in the theology for liberation has been in the writings of Gustavo Gutiérrez. The contribution of liberation theology over the years has been precisely in raising the questions of the relevancy of the reading of religious texts in the light of social, political, and economic situations of the oppressed people of the world.[23] It contributed to the development of a hermeneutics of reading from the perspective of colonialism, poverty, underdevelopment, economic exploitation, and cultural victimization. The other positive contribution of this theological genre has been an emphasis on both theory and praxis rather than mere metaphysical theorisation.

Though liberation theology is said to have originated in Latin America, there were parallel developments in other part of the world and in other religions such as Islam. The very suggestion of a theology for liberation in Islam has always been met with suspicion and criticism from the conservative Muslim scholars who argue that Islam is itself liberating and therefore there is no need to engage in any other discourse of liberation. While it is true that Islam in its pristine form as propagated and practiced by the Prophet and his Companions is liberating, it is not true that the "Islam" we have today can offer any solutions to the problems of racial, gender, or class discrimination. Unfortunately after the demise of the Prophet, through the influence of Greek Philosophy, like Christianity, Muslims came to view Allah as outside of human history. Little, if anything, was said about His role in history. The fact that the expression found in the *Qur'an*: "*rabb musa wa harun*" (the Lord of Moses and Aron), confirms that Allah revealed himself by acting in history to bring liberation and justice to the enslaved *bani israil* (the children of Israel) was overlooked. The verse (8:17): "*wa ma ramayta idh ramayta walakin allah rama*", meaning, "you did not slay them, but it was Allah who slew them; nor did you shoot when you did shoot, but it was Allah shooting", which tells us that Allah intervened in the battle of Badr to deliver victory to the Muslims is again ignored. As a result, the revolutionary Islam was transformed into a status quoist "Islam" and the received "Islam" is an ally of the establishment and the theologian benefactors of the *status quo*. In his book, *Islam and Liberation Theology,* Asghar Ali Engineer observed:

> They wrote more on the ritual practices and spent their energy on subsidiary matters [*furu'at*] of the *Shari'at* and completely played down its elan for social justice and its active sympathy with the weak and oppressed [*mustad'afin*]. They came to identify themselves with the *mustakbirin* (the powerful and arrogant).[24]

The main objection against liberation theology has been what is seen as the uncritical use of Marxist theories of interpretation by some liberation theologians, which has resulted in it being described as a "Marxist theology". Moreover, theology of liberation is also considered by Muslims as being of Christian origin. It is important to understand right at the outset that liberation theology seeks to address social problems and in order to fully understand the situation of racism, poverty, gender discrimination, and those suffering under them to escape from them, an analysis of these problems from the sociological perspective becomes increasingly important, and requires recourse to the relevant disciplines.[25] The social sciences are a means to gain accurate knowledge of our society as it really is. Marxism also approaches the same problems from a sociological viewpoint and makes use of the tools provided by the social sciences. The connection, therefore, is not between liberation theology and Marxist Philosophy, but between liberation theology and the social sciences. Moreover, it is not true that Islamic liberation theology was born out of Christian experiences. Islam in its original form is a theology for liberation.

We see in the lives of Companions such as Abu Dharr al-Ghifari (d. 32 H) a strong protest against the hoarding of wealth, the exploitation of the poor, the emergence of a bourgeoisie class indulging in luxury and high life and the misappropriation of public funds on the part of the provincial governors and lesser officials, who built splendid palaces, acquired vast holdings of land and owned huge flocks of camels and sheep while others became poor and poorer.

The radical economic and social change that took place during Uthman's Caliphate resulted in open criticism against the political establishment and Abu Dharr al-Ghifari was the most outspoken critics of the Mu'awiyyah and Uthman's policies.

It was during Uthman's predecessor, Umar, that Islam gained territorial and economic success as a result of military expeditions and conquests. However, Umar realized that dividing the conquered lands among the warriors would have disastrous consequences on military administration, economic and social justice. He, therefore, forbade the distribution of land among the *mujahidin* [warriors] and, instead, nationalized the rent for the benefit of the whole community [*masalih al-mursalah*]. The land, he ordered, was to be left in possession of the original owners who were in turn expected to pay a stipulated tax, i.e., the *kharaj*, direct to the State fund [*baitu al-mal*]. In this way he safeguarded against multiplication of unearned income through the institution of landlordism. It also meant that there was to be no accumulation of wealth in a few hands, no unemployment and no sense of exploitation among the lower income groups.

Uthman, however, abolished Umar's policies; he allowed the privatization of lands and strongly encouraged landlordism. The system of Umar collapsed at the point where it had the most salutary economic effect. We see in the time of Uthman the development of an entirely new relationship between the landlords and the tenants and the introduction of a virtual *latifundismo*. Soon the rich became richer and the poor, poorer. Moreover, there was an increased misuse of political power and misappropriation of funds by the greedy and corrupt Umayyad government officers.

It was during this period that Mu'awiyyah built the famous green palaces for himself, and the Umayyads were accused of appropriating huge sums of money for this purpose. Marwan ibn al-Hakam and al-Harith ibn al-Hakam ibn Abi al-As appropriated sums amounting to three million dirhams with the concurrence of the Caliph Uthman. Abu Dharr al-Ghifari angrily objected to the construction of the "Green Palaces" by Mu'wiyyah and openly told him, "If the palaces are built with the money belonging to Allah (i.e., from the public funds) then it is but *khiyanah* (misappropriation); otherwise if it is built with your own money then it amount to *israf* (wasteful extravagance)"[26]

Abu Dharr al-Ghifari's hermeneutics has been down-played by status quoits Islam and has been presented as an isolated view when historical documents show that many other senior Companions such as Ali as well as others supported his interpretation of the verses of *Zakah*. Abu Dharr taunted the rich class with the *ayah al-kayy* or *ayah al-kanz* (the verse of branding):

> They who hoard up gold and silver and spend it not in the way of Allah, unto them give tidings of a painful doom, on the day when it will (all) be heated in the fire of hell and their foreheads and their flanks and their backs will be branded therewith (and it will be said unto them): Here is that which you hoarded for yourselves. Now taste of what you used to hoard (9: 34-35).

Abu Dharr would now augment the verse with one or two Traditions from the Prophet in the same vein: "They are in great loss indeed who have plenty of wealth except those who show generosity on all sides. But how few are such people!"[27] Abu Dharr's interpretation evoked tremendous response and support from the common people. They flocked around him wherever he went voicing their support for him. They also became bold and booed and jeered at the members of the ruling and privileged wealthy class. The "verse of branding" cited above became the slogan of those protesting against social, political, and economic injustice during that period. Abu Dharr al-Ghifari can rightly be described as the first Muslim liberation theologian.

The classic meaning of theology is an intellectual understanding of the faith [*iman or aqidah*] - that is, the effort of human intelligence to comprehend revelation [*wahyi*] and the vision of faith.[28] Faith in Islam also does not mean only truths to be affirmed, but also an existential stance, an attitude, a commitment to Allah [*huquq allah*] and to human beings [*huquq al-ibad*]. Islamic faith is not limited to affirming the existence of Allah [*wajib al-wujud*]. No, it tells us that Allah have mercy upon us and demands a merciful response. This response is given through mercy for human beings, and that is what we mean by *huquq al-ibad* (the rights human beings). The Prophet said: "for the merciful people, Allah shall show His mercy upon them. Be merciful to those on earth, and the One in heaven shall show mercy upon you."[29]

In yet another tradition recorded in Muslim's *Sahih* he said: "Allah says, 'indeed I have prohibited oppression upon myself, and I have made it unlawful upon you, so do not oppress others'".[30] Islamic theology has always emphasized on praxis [al-a'mal juz' al-iman], meaning, actions are part of faith).[31] When we speak about theology, therefore, we are not talking about an abstract and timeless truth, but rather about an existential stance, which tries to understand and see this commitment in the light of the Qur'an and Sunnah.

The reason why liberation theology is viewed as Christian theology maybe due to the language of its discourse which is widely believed to be a Christian language. The language of liberation, however, did not emerge from within Christianity. It is thoroughly socio-political language, the language of the oppressed people, and freedom fighters everywhere in the world disregard of their theological background. It was only when Christians committed themselves to the struggle for liberation alongside the oppressed that they began to discover the language of liberation.[32]

There are questions and problems that can only be addressed through a critical theology of liberation. Questions such as those pertaining to Muslim members of royal families who spend millions of dollars on prostitution, gambling, alcohol, and drugs when millions of Muslims are living below the poverty line across the world, and Muslim scholars who adopt a quietist attitude and choose not to speak out against such corruption and injustice. We also have the problem of parents who force their daughters into marriage or kill them in the name of family honor, and the scholars who look the other way when wives suffer abuse from their husbands?

We also find problems in the interpretation of certain legal texts that appear to be sanctioning one form of discrimination or another. While writing on the qualifications of an Imam (the leader of prayers), Al-Sharambulali (1069 H.), one of the Hanafi's leading scholars wrote in his book, Nur al-idah (a famous Hanafi book on jurisprudence) that the one among the believers who is the most learned in Islamic sciences should be appointed as the Imam, and where the level of learning, piety, and age is at par among all the worshippers, then in such cases the one who is "the most good looking should be appointed, and then the one with the most aristocratic genealogy". He further writes that, "It is discouraged or disliked [makruh] for a slave, a blind person, or a child born out of wedlock to lead the prayers."[33] Needless to say that this is contrary to the normal practice of the Prophet and Companions whom we know appointed the blind and those considered "not so good looking" to high offices and to the position of *Imamah*. Moreover, this statement and view also perpetuate prejudice and discrimination against the blind and people who are not considered good looking or aristocratic. Beauty and ugliness are relative terms –what is beauty in one society may not so in another. There are no universal standards for measuring physical beauty. The Mosque is not a "beauty pageant" but a place of worship and Allah accepts prayers led by any Muslim, irrespective of how he looks or what family he comes from. Muslim *hadith* scholars and historians have reported how, on two occasions, the Prophet appointed Abdullah ibn Umm Maktum (a blind Companion regarding whom chapter *abasah wa tawalah* of the *Qur'an* was revealed) to be his deputy [*Khalifah*] during his absence from Madinah.[34] Needless to say that on both occasions some of the most prominent Companions of the Prophet were also present. This meant that Abdullah was to be the leader of all the prayers as well as the chief administrator of Madinah. Ibn Hajar writes, "from these incidences (the appointment of Abdullah) we derive proof for the permissibility of the leadership of a blind person."[35] Historians and *hadith* scholars are of the opinion that this happened twice while others say it happened thirteen times, and on one occasion even Ali was present in Madinah.[36]

Ata ibn Abi Rabah (d. 115 H.), was a black Successor [*tabi'i*] who was well known for his piety and extensive knowledge of jurisprudence and Traditions. He was also known for lacking in good looks and was described in *Mishkat* in the following words:

> He was black, had very thick hair, was cross eyed, and later became blind, and yet he was the most eminent jurist and scholar as well as the most respected *tabi'i* of Makkah. Awza'i reported that "he died while he was the most celebrated person on earth." Regarding the looks and knowledge of Ata', Imam Ahmad said, "Knowledge is a treasure which Allah grants to whomsoever He loves. If knowledge was to be granted to people for their good looks, then the daughter of the Prophet (Fatimah) would have been more deserving." Salamah also said, "I have never known anyone in my life who was chosen by Allah for knowledge more than those three: Ata', Tawus, and Mujahid...A large number of scholars were his (Ata's) students".

49

It was this same Ata' who was appointed as the grand *Mufti* of Makkah during period of *hajj* and a law was passed that prohibited any other scholar and jurist to answer questions pertaining to pilgrimage while Ata' was alive.

Unfortunately, a racist and oppressive "Islam" replaced this liberating Islam. Evidence of this is present in the Arabic as well as English interpretations of the *Qur'an* as well as other law books. The following is just one of such examples. Allah said in the *Qur'an*:

> The day when *tabyaddu wujuh* (was translated as "some faces will be white"), and *taswaddu wujuh* (translated as "some faces will be black"). To those *iswaddat wujuh* ("whose faces will be black"), it will be said to them: "Did you reject faith after accepting it? Taste then the penalty for rejecting faith. But those *ibyaddat wujuh* ("whose faces will be white"), they will be in Allah's mercy, they shall dwell therein forever. (3: 106).

This grave mistake cannot be contributed only to the interpreter or translator's ignorance of classical Arabic and linguistics, it is also a mistake which has to do more with the world and history of the interpreter, one that is dominated by prejudice and racism. 'Abdullah Yusuf 'Ali, one of the leading translators of the *Qur'an* into English, wrote in his commentary:

> The "face" [*wajh*] expresses our personality, our inmost being. *White is the colour of light; to become white is to be illumined with light, which stands for felicity, the rays of the glorious light of God. Black is a colour of darkness, sin, rebellion, misery; removal from the grace and light of God (emphasis is mine). These are the signs of heaven and hell.*[38]

Another interpreter of the *Qur'an*, Maulana Muhammad Ali, writes:

> By faces turning white is meant their being expressive of joy, and by turning black, their being expressive of sorrow...you say a man is white [*abyad*] when you mean that he is free from dross and defects.[39]

What the above commentaries and translations seem to be suggesting is that when a man has defects and "dross" you say "a man is *aswad* (black)", hence, being black is a defect. The meaning of the above verse has been misunderstood by Arabic and non-Arabic interpreters of the *Qur'an* who have treated it as either metaphorical when or have uncritically considered the superficial literal Arabic meaning. This further emphasizes the need for a thorough knowledge of classical Arabic language, culture, semantics, and contemporary theories of language study as a pre-requisite for anyone intending on studying the *Qur'an* in order to avoid such gruesome errors.

In South Africa it was common to hear the *alim* (Muslim scholar) expounding on the benefits and advantages [*fazail*] of the Apartheid system. The Group Areas Act (by which people were forced to relocate according to their racial groups e.g., Indians in Lenesia; Blacks in the Townships; Whites in the city Suburbs), he would argue, was a blessing from Allah since it enabled the Muslims to organize themselves into Muslim communities away from the *kuffar* (infidels) and establish their own schools, Mosques, and businesses. The welfare of the Black Muslim who was thrown in the ocean of "infidels" in Soweto was never considered. Can such an *alim*, or any Muslim benefactor of status quoist Islam, who regards blacks and women as less human "created by Allah to serve us" be expected to participate in the *jihad* (struggle) against poverty, racism, gender discrimination, and other injustices?

And again in South Africa, the name "Bilal" has become synonymous with inferiority and black. Every Mosque in South Africa has its own Bilal who calls Muslims for prayers, clean the toilets, and get wages that are below the minimum. If during the absence of the *mu'adhdhin* (the one who calls for prayers) if it was suggested that any Muslim brother can call for prayer, you were likely to get answers such as, "I cannot do that, I am not a darkie (racist term for blacks)!" Every Black who embraces Islam in South Africa today is likely to be re-named "Bilal".

During the time of the Prophet the position of the *mu'adhdhin,* which was occupied only by Bilal, was a very respectable position[40] so much so that some Arab Muslims were jealous of him and complained why the Prophet had to appoint a Black man to such a high position. Bilal, apart from being the special *mu'adhdhin* of the Prophet, was also his financial advisor and treasurer.

The discourse of liberation therefore is one that we may have to engage in without the assistance of such *ulama'*. Issues that are central to any liberation discourse such as pluralism and women's rights are challenges that we may have to tackle alone. There can be no such a thing as a "Muslim's perspective", "feminist's perspective" or even "Christian's perspective" of liberation, by confirming the "us" versus "them", or dominant versus "other" in the liberation process serves to confirm the *status quo* which we seek to remove. We cannot expect the average *alim* who grew up in an ocean of Muslims to understand the significance of these issues. The experiences and contribution of the Muslim who was thrown in the ocean of non-Muslims are becoming increasingly invaluable in our endeavor to establish pluralistic societies.

The *Qur'an* and *Sunnah's* perspective of the oppressed and poor is very clear. The Prophet is known to have asked Allah for him to be resurrected among the poor on the day of judgement. When asked by his wife Aishah the reason for such a request, he explained that "because they will be resurrected and admitted into Paradise thousands of years before the rich".[41] He also was heard saying, "Fear the prayer of the oppressed, for indeed between him (her) and Allah there is no barrier."[42]

Fighting against poverty and other social evils is one of the greatest forms of *jihad*. We can never hope to establish a just society unless we uproot poverty. According to the Prophet, there is a thin line between poverty and disbelief [*kada alfaqr an yakum kufran*], what this means is that poverty may be regarded as one of the root causes of evil and disbelief.

How does one help the poor or uproot poverty? Is it by giving out *zakah* (charity) to the needy or is it by removing the system or regime that is causing poverty? If we only rely on *zakah* as the only tool of uprooting poverty, as *status quo*ist Islam would have us believe, the problem will never be solved and the poor will always return for more. We need to change the systems within our society that make it possible for others to fall ill due to excessive eating while others fall ill due to hunger or starvation. Is our fasting during the month of *Ramadan* or our standing in prayers close to each other; the rich next to the poor and the king or queen next to the commoner, enough evidence of Islam's solidarity with the poor? The standing of the poor next to the rich or the king next to the commoner in prayers will only exacerbate disunity and hatred among the Muslims. How can we ever hope for any form of unity to be established when the poor can note the contrast between the tattered clothes he or she is wearing and the expensive garments that the rich is donning? Should we, for the sake of Muslim unity, separate the rich from the poor in the Mosque?

We have usually considered fasting as "a way of experiencing how the less fortunate feel" and after *Ramadan* the Muslim always consider himself as having experienced first hand the difficulties that the poor go through. Can fasting from dawn, after having eaten a meal fit for two and breaking fast at sunset with another meal fit for three, be equated to the hardships of the poor? While the fasting Muslim knows that he will be eating a dozen *samoosas* and dates at sunset, the poor never knows when he is going to have his next meal. While after the month of fasting the Muslim will resume eating, the poor will still be "fasting" until he leaves this world. *Ramadan* is the month when most of Muslims gain weight!

Is poverty only about food? Why is it never suggested that the Muslim must, in solidarity with the poor, also go half naked or in tattered clothes, sleep on the pavements, live in the squatter camps, and deprive himself of the basic needs such as medicine, education, etc., during the same month of fasting?

Fasting is an *ibadah* (act of worship) prescribed by Allah and certainly not a way of showing our solidarity with the poor. It is the duty of every Muslim, therefore, to show his solidarity by taking part in the struggle against social injustice and poverty. People do not simply happen to be poor; their poverty is largely a product of the way society is organized. Liberation theology critiques structures that enable the *zakah* collectors to live in a life of luxury while the poor on whose behalf they are collecting *zakah* continue to live in poverty. Today only a very small percentage of the *zakah* money that is collected for the poor is distributed and the rest is spent on "administration", phones, cars, and salaries of the collectors. It is not strange to find one giving up his business to start a Muslim charity organization – a lucrative venture! No wonder, hundreds of Muslim charity organizations mushroom every time there is an earthquake, drought, flood, or war in any part of the Muslim world. Liberation theology is a need to speak out against such corruption practiced in the name of Islam, to speak out directly and less and less through intermediaries. This can only be achieved within the historical process of liberation, which seeks to build a truly egalitarian, fraternal and just society, and this is the *maqasid al-Shari'ah* (aims of Islamic law).

Liberation theology, therefore, is *Shari'ah* in practice and we should stop seeing it as a new theology, but a new way of putting into practice this theology.

Islamic liberation theology calls for the involvement of a flesh and blood *mufassir* socially located in the process of interpretation and doing *tafsir*. *Tafsir* should cease to be an exclusive task of the benefactors of the *status quo* and should involve the women scholars, activists, the poor, and the oppressed if any meaningful social justice and liberation is to be achieved. Such a way of reading will ultimately look upon all interpretive models whether traditional or contemporary. It means challenging the system that we may have become accustomed to, particularly when we have found those systems to be oppressive and exclusivist.

Thus, each person should interact with the text. In the words of Professor Amina Wadud, "The assertion that there is only one interpretation of the *Qur'an* limits the extent of the text. The *Qur'an* must be flexible enough to accommodate innumerable cultural situations because of its claims to be universally beneficial to those who believe. Therefore, to force it to have a single cultural perspective – even the cultural perspective of the original community of the Prophet – severely limits its application and contradicts the stated universal purpose of the book itself."[43]

The universality of Islam is in its being open, dynamic and subject to re-interpretation. It is important to understand that we are not dealing with a closed text, *tafsir* is contingent upon the historical context, the cultural situation and level of development, and the philosophical presuppositions of the period in which the *tafsir* is effected. It is not static, but is in constant state of flux, change, and development. What all this means is that there is nothing such as the "final and absolute" interpretation, what we may consider to be the correct meaning of Allah's word may be contingent upon numerous factors. What was a correct *tafsir* in the classical period may be incorrect and dated in the contemporary period and what we may regard correct today may be incorrect in the future. For example, Qur'anic verses pertaining to natural and scientific phenomena were not sufficiently interpreted by classical scholars due to the limited scientific knowledge of that time and today with the technological revolution a *mufassir* is likely to produce a totally different and more informed *tafsir*.

The *Qur'an* praises the true believers as "those whose hearts are filled with awe at the mention of Allah, and whose faith grows stronger as they listen to His revelations [*zadat hum imanan*]" (8: 2). This verse may be read as a direct command from Allah to His servants to engage in reinterpretation since the verses of the *Qur'an* can only increase one's faith if he understands their message, and as we have mentioned above some of these verses discuss issues pertaining to natural and scientific phenomena the understanding of which require some knowledge of the natural sciences, too. Classical interpretations do not deal with such verses in detail.

However, this does not mean that *tafsir* is relative for there are certain *usul* (principles) that carry over from one era to another and each era adds to our basic knowledge and understanding. The Prophet also illustrates this point in a tradition recorded in the chapter of knowledge in Tirmidhi's *Jami'*, Abu Dawood's *Sunan* and authenticated by al-Dhahabi that "many a times the person who transmits knowledge may not be that knowledgeable [*rubba hamil fiqh laisa bi faqih*] and yet he may transmit it to someone who is more knowledgeable than him [*wa rabba hamil fiqh ila man huwa afqah minhu*]." In yet another tradition he equates his *ummah* to rain, it is never known whether the first part or the last part of the rain is better.[44] Thus, each period is not just an isolated time slot cut off from both, the past and future. From the position that we occupy, contemporary *tafsir* must build upon the *tafsir* of the past and at the same time points toward a *tafsir* for the future. It is extremely important for us to realize this point, otherwise we risk the danger of being caught in the conservative-liberal dualism in which the conservatives look to the past and disregard the present and future while the liberals look to the future and disregard the past. Islamic scholarship must be able to conserve from the past that which is vital to its tradition and yet at the same time be moderate enough to be open to new insights so that Islamic scholarship has a past, present, and future. Qur'anic *tafsir* of today must act as a bridge between the past and future.

The *Sunnah* as the Second Primary Source of Law

The word "*Sunnah*" literally means "a clear path or a beaten track", "a normative tradition", "habitual practice", "customary procedure or action", "or an established course of conduct". The *Sunnah* of a person, therefore, is his normal conduct whether it may be good or bad. The Prophetic tradition: "whosoever sets a good practice [*Sunnah hasanah*], he will get the reward for the practice as well as reward for anyone who will emulate him until the day of resurrection; and whoever set a bad conduct [*Sunnah sayyi'ah*], he will carry the burden of its blame and also of those who will follow him until the day of resurrection" suggests that not every *Sunnah* is good *Sunnah*.[45]

The term "*Sunnah*" has always been in use among the Arabs even in *jahiliyyah* (pre-Islamic period) to mean "past traditions" and exemplary behavior. In Labid ibn Rabi'ah's famous *mu'allaqat al-sab'ah* (a collection of pre-Islamic poetry) the term was used to refer to a normative behavior:

Min ma'shari sanat lahum abauhum
wa likulli qawmin sunnatun wa imamuha

He comes from a tribe for whom their ancestors have left a normative tradition; every people have a *Sunnah* and its founder.[46]

Discontinuity from the established traditional behavior [*Sunnah*] was condemned by the pre-Islamic Arabs and any form of departure from customary practice was known as *bid'ah* (novelty). To them, *bid'ah* was the antithesis of *Sunnah*. The term *Sunnah*, therefore, is a pre-Islamic term, which was used even in Islam to denote the normative practice of a community but later, like *hadith*, was used only for the practice of the Prophet.

The word *Sunnah* has been mentioned sixteen times in the *Qur'an* to refer to an established practice or course of conduct. In its juristic usage, *Sunnah* refers to the nomartive practice set up by the Prophet of Islam as a model; his sayings, doings, and tacit approvals which were later established as legally binding precedents in addition to the law established by the *Qur'an*. The basis of the *Sunnah* is the normative activity of the Messenger of Allah, who was the prime interpreter of the divine revelation of the *Qur'an*. When Aishah was asked about the life of the Prophet, she replied that his life was the *Qur'an*. Indeed the practice of Muhammad was shaped, guided, and molded by the *Qur'an* to become normative and a living interpretation of the *Qur'an*. The *Sunnah*, therefore, cannot be separated from the *Qur'an* and it is for this reason that we consider the *Sunnah* as a "second primary source of law". This is not

56

to mean that the *Sunnah* like the *Qur'an* is infallible, on the contrary, as we will argue further, we believe that the possibility exists that a lot of traditions regarded as authentic may be of very doubtful origin.

Another term closely connected to *Sunnah* is *hadith* which means "new", "speech" or "oral tradition". The term *Hadith* was used by pre-Islamic Arabs to refer to any oral discourse or tradition and since with the advent of Islam it became customary to refer to the speech of the Prophet as *khair al-hadith* (the best speech) its meaning was later confined only to the orally transmitted traditions containing the teachings of the Prophet. Even though the two terms have been used interchangeably, their meanings vary. *Hadith* is the narration of the behavior, sayings, doings, and tacit approvals of the Prophet while *Sunnah* is the law deduced from the *hadith* or the actual saying, doing, or tacit approval of the Prophet. In other words, *Sunnah* is the content of the *hadith*. *Hadith* may be described as the index and vehicle of the *Sunnah* and it was common to hear the Companions or early scholars talking about "the *Sunnah* derived from the *hadith*". Today we do the same when we teach *hadith*, we are always looking for laws and "*Sunan*" (plural of *Sunnah*) to be derived from this or that *hadith*.

The Compilation of *Hadith*

The science of *hadith* passed through three main phases: The first phase was that of *kitabat al-hadith*, the period in which the Companions and the early Successors wrote down their collections in the *sahifahs,* as we discussed in the chapter of Qur'anic *tafsir*, these were mostly notes relating to the interpretation of various Qur'anic verses as well as other sayings or doings of the Prophet. The second phase was the collection of those notes [*tadwin al-hadith*], during the last quarter of the first century and first quarter of the second century. One of the eminent figures and *hadith* scholar at that time was al-Zuhri (d.124 A.H.). The third stage was that of the compilation of hadith, arranged according to subjects [*tasnif al-hadith*] in the works that became known as the *musannafs*. This was a phase that started from about 125 A.H. onwards, and important scholars of this period included Ibn Juraij (d.150 A.H.), Ma'mar ibn Rashid (d.153 A.H.) and the famous Sufyan al-Thawri (d. 161 A.H.).

During the first centuries of *hijrah* almost no scholar published his teachings as an independent book. In some cases authors wrote down their lectures for use within a specific and restricted society such as the *risalat abi dawud ila ahl makkah* (the letter of Abu Dawud to the people of Makkah) now known as the *sunan abi dawud* which was written initially as a reply to the letter received from the people of Makkah. Ibn Ishaq (d.150 A.H.), for instance, put his famous *Sirah* in some form of pre-publication at the Caliphal court. Most *hadith* scholars left the transmission and publication of their works to their students [*ruwat*]. Imam Malik is one such scholar who was not responsible for the publication of his work *al-Muwatta* which he left in manuscript form. It was only during the third century of *hijrah* that scholars started publishing their own works personally instead of leaving them to their students [*talamidh*].

The *Sunnah* of the People of Madinah

Let us now consider the *Sunnah* and the living traditions of the emergent schools of law. During the period of the rightly-guided *Caliphs* most of the new problems were solved with recourse to consultation [*shura*]. One of the advantages of the use of consultation was that the gathering of people meant that anyone who had a *hadith* or had seen a particular action could report to those present and thereby help adjudicate the case. In fact, the Caliph Umar made sure people stayed in Madinah as much as possible for this reason, so that *ahadith* could be collected and the collective memory and efforts of the community could be directed to meet the influx of new challenges. Madinah, therefore, became the centre for *hadith* activities which helped new problems to be easily solved by referring to Prophetic precedent. The concentration of tradition scholars in Madinah later led to the emergence of a school which became known as *madrasat ahl al-hadith* (the partisans of tradition) which advocated a rigid application of tradition and frowned at any attempt to use reason or personal opinion [*ra'y*].

The people of the city of Madinah, being the first seat of Islamic government, the home of most of the Companions, and the cradle of Islamic civilization, naturally received great admiration and respect, making the practice of the people of Madinah extremely influential in later legal discussions. If a "lone" *hadith* [*khabar wahid*], i.e., one transmitted with a single narrator, was found to contradict the well-established practice of the people of Madinah, scholars very often ruled in favor of the Madinan practice. This is because the people of Madinah, who were greatly devoted to the Prophet and very much conversant with his practices, were assumed to have preserved his exemplary actions in greatest possible detail.

However, even the practice of the people of Madinah had grades of authenticity. The most authentic of course were practices which originated during the time of the Prophet, and this grade of authenticity came to be unquestionably and universally accepted. But practices which sprung up during the period of the four *Caliphs*, or later in the second century *hijrah*, were not accepted automatically or by default, even by luminaries such as Imam Malik, who was a close observer of the practices of the Madinians.

The power and authenticity of the first category stems from the fact that as the community of people most involved with the day to day affairs of Islam and closest in time and place to the decisions and interpretations of the Prophet, the practices of the people of Madinah would as a matter of course resonate with the *Sunnah* of the Prophet. Although some orientalists try to prove otherwise, no Muslim scholar ever put the practice of the people of Madinah above Prophetic *Sunnah*. This would be tantamount to denying the authority of the Messenger. Instead, what happened was that if a Prophetic tradition was unclear or not securely transmitted, a scholar would certainly prefer to rely on the practice of the people of Madinah, assuming that they would have been most able to preserve the correct solution to a particular arisen problem.

The policy of keeping people in Madinah as much as possible was discontinued under the Caliphate of Uthman. After Madinah, Kufah became a major centre of culture and learning. During his Caliphate, Umar stayed in Kufah during his campaigns in the area of Iraq and Iran. Fifty-eight of the great Companions who had been in the Battle of Badr lived in Kufah, and the famous scholar and Companion Abdullah ibn Mas'ud was sent by Umar to Kufah to teach. In his letter of appointment, Umar wrote: "O people of Kufah, I give preference to you over myself and I send this person whom I need here most, to you. He is Abdullah ibn Mas'ud, the respected Companion of the Holy Prophet, who is sent to you as your teacher. Do not be negligent in learning from him."

Abdullah ibn Mas'ud was undoubtedly a great *faqih* (jurist), and he taught well his disciples. Among his illustrious students were Alkama,

Ibrahim al-Nakhai, Hammad ibn Abi Sulaiman, and then the founder of the *hanafi* school of jurisprudence, Imam Abu Hanifah.

However, the people of Kufah were not as fortunate as the people of Madinah in having a lot of Prophetic traditions at their disposal, moreover, Iraq saw the influx of people from other religious traditions embracing Islam and also the emergence of new Islamic theologies. As a result of this development more questions pertaining to theology and law started arising for which there was no apparent and clear-cut answers in the *Qur'an* or in the scarce Prophetic traditions available in Iraq at that time. Due to communication problems between Madinah and Iraq, it was impossible to obtain, at short notice, traditions from the Madinah scholars for use in Iraq since the problems arising were of an urgent nature and needed immediate solution. This situation led to a sophisticated development of sound personal opinion [*ra'y*], analogical deduction [*qiyas*], and juristic preference [*istihsan*] as subsidiary sources of law in Islam. The people of Kufah became known as the people of sound reason and common sense [*ahl al-ra'y*], a term which was later misinterpreted by many of their opponents who claimed that the Iraq school or jurisprudence attached more importance to reason and personal opinion over revelation and Prophetic tradition.

During the period of Abu Hanifah and his student Abu Yusuf, Iraq became a beehive of intellectual activities but unfortunately this was short lived. Blind following led to the death of all intellectual activities and the restricted type of qiyas they were applying could not cope with the infinite legal problems that kept on arising from time to time. The intellectual contribution of Abu Yusuf who, while working as a judge dealing with concrete economic and social problems adopted a holistic approach to the sources of law and produced very valuable knowledge, but this got fossilized over time.

Today, even though we may have more traditions at our disposal than the early Iraqi community, we find ourselves in a more desperate situation than that of the people of Iraq since these traditions are proving to be finite sources insufficient to address the infinite social and theological questions. It becomes more imperative that we broaden the sources and principles of Islamic law. This process will include, *inter alia,* the re-introduction of reason and rationality as well as the tools provided by the social sciences in the process of doing *fiqh*. Islamic law aims at establishing social justice and freedom and this cannot be done in a vacuum but in a society and we need to understand the society before we can ever hope to successfully apply the law. Consequently, to understand society we will need the knowledge of the social sciences.

Classical Approaches to the *Sunnah*

Some scholars of Islamic studies have misinterpreted the historical development of the science of *hadith* and assumed that the *Sunnah* of the Prophet only attained importance later, perhaps by the third century *hijrah*. This is an erroneous reading of history. The *Sunnah* of the Prophet has always been entirely normative and applicable. Because the Companions were so close to the Prophet, their decisions arose without the formal process developed later by the scientific or systematic jurists. The reason for the jurists to develop a science of *usul al-fiqh* was precisely because they realized that there was no longer the same kind of proximity to the Prophetic era, and therefore it was crucial that the decision making process be formalized, systematized, and written down.

The respect of Awza'i for Prophet's *Sunnah* is clear from the following case: He argued that the foot-soldier who came upon a horse and entered battle should get the reward of a horseman, and not that of a foot-man. This was in opposition to the practice of the Caliph Umar. Awza'i argued his case on the basis of Prophetic *Sunnah*, reasoning that since there was no registration in his days, the soldier's reward was determined in accordance to the extent of his real contribution to the battle.

Abu Yusuf appreciated the following case decided by the Caliph Umar because he stayed so firmly with the idea of Prophetic *Sunnah*. The Prophet gave the general injunction that people should use land they have been granted or after three years, someone else may take it over. Some people from a tribe were given land by the Prophet but did not use it, and someone started using it. Umar ruled that if he or Abu Bakr had given the land, he would have ordered it to be legally the property of those working on it, in accordance with the Prophet's general injunction. Umar argued since it was land granted by the Prophet, the original owners should keep it. Abu Yusuf liked this decision. Shaibani was another scholar very close to Prophetic *Sunnah*. Imam Shafi'i commented that for Shaibani, "no one has any authority when placed alongside the Prophet."[47]

It was not strange that they should attach so much importance to the *Sunnah*. The Prophet himself encouraged the transmission of *ahadith*. He said, "Pass on information from me, even if it is only one verse" and at his farewell pilgrimage he was heard saying, "Let those who are present convey the information to those who are absent."[48] Furthermore, the Prophet made several arrangements for the diffusion of *ahadith* and his *Sunnah*, repeating important things three times, teaching his Companions and asking them to repeat what they had learned. Delegations coming to Madinah were entrusted to the Companions so that they would take care of them and instruct them in the *Qur'an* and *Sunnah*.

The Companions learnt the *Qur'an* and *Sunnah* from the Prophet in the mosque, and thus their centre of learning was the mosque. After his death, the *Caliphs* continued the work of dissemination. We have already mentioned that 'Umar kept the Companions in Madinah in order to help him in administering the community of believers, but he and the other *Caliphs* also sent delegations to disseminate Islamic teachings. We also saw that Umar sent Abdullah ibn Ma'sud to Kufah. The memorization of the *Qur'an* and *ahadith* was praised and strongly enjoined, and many people took up the challenge to learn as much as they could.

The first recordings of *ahadith* were the letters and decisions of the Prophet which his sixty-five scribes produced. Even during his lifetime several Companions kept written records. While the *Qur'an* was safe from any transmission problems, the *ahadith* did have some troubles in transmission, and so in order to make sure the *ahadith* was authentic, scholars developed the most stringent and comprehensive criteria imaginable. Two categories of criticism emerged. First is the evaluation of the chain of narrators [*sanad*]. Second is textual criticism of the versions available as well as internal text criticism. Let us consider them in more detail.

1. The chain would be considered authentic [*sahih*] if it was uninterrupted (it must be *muttasil*) and every reporter in the chain had to be just [*adl*], accurate [*dabit*], one of strong retentive memory [*qawiy al-hifz*], and also be of sound theological and moral background. No mater how great a scholar he could be, the person's character had to be of a very high level.

2. A *hadith* would be cross-compared with other *ahadith* by different students of the same teacher, examined in light of statements made by

the same scholar at different times; an orally transmitted *hadith* would be compared with the written version, and finally the *hadith* would be compared with the Qur'an.

Ibn Ma'in (d. 233 A.H.) visited eighteen of the pupils of Hammad ibn Salamah to read their versions of Hammad's book and told them that he did so in order to detect mistakes: if a mistake occurred in the versions in possessions of all the students, it must have been made by Hammad, but if a mistake appeared in some but not all the versions recorded by the students, the fault lay in the students' recording. Corrective action was immediately implemented and the mistakes set right.

Aishah once sent Urwah to Abdullah ibn Amr to ask about *ahadith* of the Prophet. One of the *ahadith* Urwah brought from him was about the way knowledge would be taken away from the earth. Aishah felt uneasy about this *hadith*. After a year, she sent Urwah back to Abdullah ibn Amr to ask about the same *hadith*. When Urwah reported to Aishah that Abdullah had narrated the *hadith* again exactly as he had done before, she said, "I cannot but think him correct, as he has neither added anything to it nor shortened it."[49]

Imam Bukhari commended the practice of checking the oral version of a *hadith* with a written version and writes that Fatimah bint Qais once gave a *hadith* which was later rejected by Umar because it did not conform with the *Qur'an* and he concluded that perhaps she had not clearly or correctly heard what the Prophet may have said.[50]

Aishah also rejected certain *ahadith* because they did not conform to the *Qur'an*. In a tradition recorded by Bukhari and Muslim, a group of Companions were spreading the rumors that the Prophet saw Allah with his eyes when he ascended to the heavens [*mi'raj*], on hearing this Aishah said: "whoever claim that Muhammad saw his Lord he has fabricated the worst of lies! Allah says in the *Qur'an* that no eyes shall see Him!" In yet another Tradition in Bukhari, Aishah rejected the belief that the dead can hear and argued that the Companions had misunderstood what the Prophet meant. To defend her argument she went on to quote from the *Qur'an*: "You shall never be able to make the dead hear."[51] Amra, the daughter of Abdurrahman said that when Aishah was told that Abdullah ibn Umar is telling people that the Prophet said the dead was punished because of the weeping of the living for him, she said, "May Allah forgive Abu Abdurrahman! He has not lied, but he has forgotten, or has made a mistake in narrating the tradition. What happened was that Allah's messenger came upon some people weeping for a Jewish lady and said: they are weeping for her and she is being punished in her grave." She added, "what the *Qur'an* says is enough for you [*hasbukum al-Qur'an*]: No bearer of a burden will bear another's burden." Ibn Abi Mulaika said that when Abdullah ibn Umar heard Aishah's argument he kept silent and did not object.[52]

According to all *hadith* scholars, reasoning [*'aql*] is also applied to *hadith* at every stage, in the learning of them, the teaching of them, and the evaluating of them. Any Prophetic tradition that goes against human reason will be suspected of having been fabricated, and the dictum *idha sahha naql shahida al-'aql* (if a Tradition is authentic, reason will testify or accept it) is one of the main principles of *hadith* criticism.

Ibn Abi Hatim al-Razi says, "The authenticity of a *hadith* is known by its coming from reliable narrators and the statement itself, which must be worthy of being a statement of the Prophet." (Thus internal text criticism was not neglected in evaluating the *hadith*.) Ibn al-Qayyim notes a number of criteria for rejecting a tradition on the basis of internal text criticism as follows:

It is too exaggerated: when it promises severe punishments for insignificant mistakes or large rewards for small good deeds.

- It can be shown to be empirically and rationally false.
- Its attributions are nonsensical.
- It contradicts the well-established *Sunnah*.
- It bears no resemblance to other sayings of the Prophet.
- Its phraseology labels it to be from questionable sources.
- It contradicts the *Qur'an*.
- Its language style is poor.

It claims to relate events during the time of the Companions but no Companion is in fact relating the *hadith*.

If it is biased against any race or tribe such as all those Traditions reported against the blacks or the Ethiopians [*al-habasha*]:

There is no good in a *zanji* (black), in another narration, "there is no good in a *habasha* – Ethiopian or African", he commits adultery when he is satisfied (with food), and steals when he is hungry. There is generosity and a helping hand among them as well.[53]

One need not be a qualified *hadith* scholar to doubt the authenticity of such a tradition because a basic principle was already established by all *hadith* scholars: *al-ahadith al-marwiyyah fi dhammi al-habasha wa al-sudani kulluha makdhubah wa mawdu'ah.*

While *hadith* scholars are unanimous that any Tradition which is biased against the blacks will be classified as spurious [*mawdu'*], there has never been attempts to critically study those traditions that are misogynistic in spite the fact that Aishah was known for rejecting all misogynistic traditions attributed to the Prophet.

The Prophet was reported to have said that three things interrupt prayer if they pass in front of the believer, interposing themselves between him and the *qibla* (direction to face while in prayer): a woman, a dog, and a donkey.[54] On hearing this tradition Aishah rejected it saying, "Are you people equating us to donkeys and dogs? The Prophet used to perform his prayers while I was lying in front of him!"[55] The *fuqaha* also rejected the view that a woman interrupts prayer when she passes in front of the believer. Bukhari, who also does not accept its authenticity, recorded it in his *Sahih.*

The classical Muslim viewpoint is that there is an authentic corpus of *ahadith* which is traceable to the Prophet. Spurious and questionable additions were, no doubt, made to this core in later generations. We even have a number of people admitting to fabricating *ahadith*. However, because they were perfectly aware of the existence of spurious and dubious *ahadith*, scholars were especially careful to accept only the most authentic *ahadith*, those that could be traced with great certainty to the Prophet.

The assumption that the authentic *ahadith* handed down by the Prophet have the force of law is largely based on the *Qur'an*. These *ahadith* came to us from the Prophet through chains of transmission, called *isnad* in Arabic. The *isnad* system then is a cornerstone of Islam. Sufian al-Thawri calls it "the believers' weapon".[56]

Ibn Mubarak states, "*Isnad* is a part of *din* (the religion), and if there were no *isnad* everyone would be free to report what he wants."[57] The system of *isnad* was so developed that it was even used on non-Prophetic literature, such as light-hearted stories and jokes, used by al-Jahiz (163–235 A.H.), al-Mubarrad (210–A.H.), al-Qutaibah (213 – 276 A.H.), Abu al-Faraj al-Asfahani (284–356 A.H.), and Abu Ali al-Qali (288–356 A.H.).

The Companions were in the habit of accompanying the Messenger of Allah in shifts, so that one group would inform the second what had happened. Thus, the practice of *isnad* developed immediately. In this way, the practice of *isnad* arose as one Companion would report what he or she had heard and then relate it to a third party, all the while making the chains of transmission perfectly clear. This meant that the other person could easily check the source, thereby making the *hadith* very secure.

The first spate of spurious *ahadith* arose with the civil strife between Ali and Mu'awiyyah. This conflict brought out the worse passions from both sides, and these passions clouded the judgement of these *ahadith* fabricators. Mu'awiyyah is reported to have paid people to fabricate traditions in favor of the Umayyads and for this reason Bukhari as well as other scholars were very careful before accepting traditions from any person who was known to have held office in Mu'awiyyah's regime. The contemporary scholar al-Shaukani found 42 spurious traditions about the Prophet, 38 about the *Caliphs*, 96 about Ali and his wife Fatimah, and 14 about Mu'awiyyah.[58] This development made people very cautious, and Ibn Sirin reports that in those days of civil war, scholars would say, "*Name to us your people (chains of transmission),*" and those who belonged to the majority group, the *ahl al-Sunnah,* would be accepted but those belonging to the innovators would be rejected.[59]

By the end of the first century *hijrah* the *isnad* system had become a full-fledged science. In their desire to collect and learn the *hadith* of the Prophet, people used to go from place to place to see the Companions and their successors and learn *ahadith* from them. This journey and process even acquired a name in Arabic, *al-Rihlah*, and became one of the most important criteria for scholarship, Ibn Ma'in said that anyone who learned *ahadith* in his own city only and did not journey to acquire knowledge would not reach intellectual maturity.[60] The obvious explanation for the increase in the number of *ahadith* from the first century is clearly a result of the phenomenon of *al-Rihlah,* where people scoured the Islamic world to find every last Companion and get as much *ahadith* as he or she had.

There is no need to postulate that all the previously undisseminated *ahadith* are spurious. Certainly, we have seen that spurious *ahadith* did exist, and the scholars were well aware of their existence. But, it must be borne in mind that the increase in the number of known *ahadith* owes more to discovering previously unreported *ahadith* than to fabrications or falsifications.

In addition, the scholars started the process of verifying the authenticity of every *hadith* and did not reject outrightly a *hadith* on the plea that it differed in the slightest wording from another. But before doing so, checked and cross-checked every source of the *hadith* before 'certifying' it as authentic. Thus, in order to preserve the exact meaning of the *hadith*, the collectors of *ahadith* would keep every variation they received, to prevent the arbitrary rejection of a *hadith* which might later turn out after further research to be the most authentic.

One scholar would always say at the end of a *hadith* he transmitted, 'or something like that' [*aw kama qala*], to avoid any accusation of passing on something as authentic in every detail which might not be the exact original wording. Also, the preservation of both the context and variant readings of a *hadith* meant that when a ruling came up, it was more likely that the real gist of the *hadith* would be preserved.

The *isnad* system had a very great sweep. One *hadith* from the Prophet that the leader [*Imam*] ought to be followed in the *salah* (established prayer) was reported by at least ten Companions. It has been recorded 124 times by dozens of scholars from different localities. It is reported by 26 third generation authorities. Thus, the number of transmitters went on increasing generation after generation. The *hadith* is found in the same form in ten different locations, namely, Madinah, Makkah, Egypt, Basrah, Hima, Yemen, Kufah, Syria, Wasit and Taif.

Another *hadith* of the Prophet which states the need to wash the hands after waking up from sleep was transmitted by five Companions. There are 16 transmitters in the second generation and 18 in the third. It has been recorded 65 times by dozens of scholars. It was found in Madinah, Kufah, Basrah, Yemen and Syria in the second generation and Makkah. Khurasan, and Hims in the third generation. These two examples show how the knowledge of *ahadith* spread throughout the Islamic world, how the number of transmitters multiplied in every succeeding generation, how the transmitters of a *hadith* disseminated it to different geographical areas, how the *isnad* system made its appearance in the earliest days of the *ummah*, and how it grew with the passage of time.

The importance and value of the examination of the *isnad* is obvious. By impugning the *bona fides* of a narrator through the process known as *jarh* or *ta'an*, i.e., disparaging or wounding the reputation, thousands of untrustworthy traditions were eliminated from the canonical collections. On the other hand, this emphasis on *sanad* criticism led to total negligence on *matan* criticism so much that if the subject-matter [*matan*] contained an obvious absurdity or anachronism there was no ground for rejecting the tradition if the *isnad* was sound. The result of this negligence is that a few traditions which conflict with the teachings of *Shari'ah* found their way into the canonical collections.

Imam Muslim reported a tradition on the authority of Anas ibn Malik who said: "I saw one day on the finger of the Prophet of Allah a silver ring, so the people also got silver rings made and wore them. Then the Prophet discarded his ring, and the people also discarded their rings."[61] Various interpretations have been put forward in elucidation of this tradition. When it is known that the Prophet permitted the use of silver rings, one fails to understand why he discarded it. In order to resolve this paradoxical situation, some doctors of *hadith* are of the opinion that it was not a silver ring but a gold ring which the Prophet discarded. It was an omission or mistake [*waham*] on the part of one of the narrators (Ibn Shihab) that, instead of mentioning a gold ring, he mentioned silver ring.[62] The fact that the *matan* (subject-matter) of this tradition contradicts the teachings and general practice of the Prophet did not stop Imam Muslim from including it in his *Sahih* on the basis that the chain was acceptable and authentic. On the other hand, this may be viewed as his high intellectual integrity and honesty that he chose not to correct the tradition and recorded it as he received it in spite of being aware about the defect in the text.

As we have seen from the above traditions and many others corrected by Aishah, narrators of traditions, even the Companions, were human beings who could forget and make mistakes. The mere fact that a narrator's character and personality is beyond reproach is not enough to render a *hadith* authentic, the need still remain to critically study the *matan* (subject-matter) of the *hadith*. Abdurrahman ibn Abza reports the following *hadith*:

> While I was with Umar, a man came to him and said: We live at a place where water is very scarce for a month or two, what should we do when we are sexually defiled? Umar said: So far as I am concerned, I do not pray until I find water. Ammar who was also

present said to Umar: Commander of the faithful, do you not remember when I and you were tending the camels? There we became sexually defiled, I rolled down on the ground in an attempt to purify myself. When we came back to the Prophet and informed him what I had done he said: 'It was enough for you to do like this' he then struck the ground with both hands, blew them, and wiped his face and both hands. Umar said: O Ammar! Fear Allah in what you say (meaning that he could not remember the incident). Ammar then replied: Commander of the faithful! If you wish I will never narrate this *hadith*. Umar then said, "Nay, by Allah! You may do so but you are fully responsible for it [*nuwallika min dhalika ma tawallaita-do not involve me*]."[63]

It is not our intention to discuss whether Umar was right or wrong in his view, what is of concern to us here is that Umar failed to remember an incident that was being attributed to him and refused to be responsible for its transmission. It is, therefore, possible that some traditions were later attributed to the Companions of which, if they had been present, would have rejected them. Moreover, such traditions when transmitted today through reliable sources, are considered authentic and binding.

The collectors of the six canonical texts, even Bukhari and Muslim, never claimed to have collected all the authentic traditions, nor did they ever claim that all the traditions in their collections were authentic, rather, they said that they collected most of the traditions they found fulfilling their conditions. It was for this reason that later scholars of *hadith* came to supplement on the works of the two with what became known as the *Mustadrakat* (plural of *mustadrak*) or collections of those traditions that fulfilled the conditions of Bukhari and Muslim and yet the two did not, for various reasons, include them in their *sahihs*. Other scholars such as al-Bayhaqi also went on to criticize those traditions they thought to be weak or unauthentic and yet were collected by the two in their *sahihain*.

Later it was felt that an *ijma'* had to be reached on the status of the two collections. Therefore, we can say that the authenticity of the traditions in the *sahihain* is not only due to the scientific process adopted by the two scholars in their evaluation of traditions, nor is it intrinsic authenticity of the meaning of the text, rather, it is a result of the reinforcement achieved by the *ijma'* process even though Muslims are still not commonly agreeable as to which of the two *sahihain* (the two *sahihs*) is more authentic. While majority of Muslims are of the view that Bukhari's collection is the most authentic book after the *Qur'an*, some argue that Muslim's *sahih* is more authentic than Bukhari's. Therefore, if one questioning the authenticity of any *hadith* in the two collections is to be condemned, it should not be because he has doubted a true tradition from the Prophet, but rather, because he has attempted to revise *ijma'* [*kharq al-ijma'*].

Legal Approach to the *Sunnah*

The *Sunnah* of the Prophet may be divided into three categories and not all his actions or sayings are legally binding:

1. His actions and behavior as an ordinary human being: he was not ordered by Allah to propagate them to his followers, such as his eating habits (favorite foods), his manner of walking, talking, sitting, etc. It is not necessary to emulate him in these actions even though the Companion Abdullah ibn Umar was known to imitate the Prophet in every aspect of the Prophet's life. It is also not obligatory to follow the Prophet in matters he expressed out of his personal opinion. Iman Muslim has recorded a tradition on the authority of Rafi' ibn Khadij who said that the Prophet came to Madinah, an agricultural city, and found that the people of Madinah had been grafting the date palms. The Prophet, being from Makkah which is not much of an agricultural area, stopped them from doing this practice and told them that they should put their trust in Allah. After abandoning the practice they began to yield less fruits and came back to the Prophet complaining, whereupon he said, "If I command you about issues pertaining to religion, do accept it, but when I command you about a thing out of my personal opinion, remember that I am only a human being." In yet another narration, he said, "You have better knowledge in the affairs of the world."[64]

The *Qur'an* and Prophetic *Sunnah* have examples of incidences where the Prophet was corrected or reprimanded by Allah after having erred in his personal judgements [*ijtihad*]. This of course does not affect his infallibility, if the doctrine of infallibility is properly and correctly understood.

2. For actions and practices that were specifically for the Prophet alone [*khasais al-nabi*] then in those cases, it was not for any of his

followers to emulate him in such actions, on the contrary, doing so would be violating the Islamic law, such as marrying more than four wives, continuous fasting, etc.

3. All actions, and things the Prophet said, as one divinely inspired and ordered by Allah to propagate them, then such actions constitute the *Shari'ah*.

However, Muslims' approach to *hadiths* today may be classified into four categories:

1. Those who outrightly reject the authority of the *hadith* and *Sunnah* and claim that the *Qur'an* is sufficient as a source of law. This is an approach that is characteristic of the modernist Muslim scholars such as the movements of Sir Ahmed Khan of India and Mahmdud Abu Rayyah of Egypt.

2. Those who accept only those traditions that synchronize with their theological beliefs and positions, and reject any *hadith* that contradicts their schools of thought either claiming that it contradicts the *Qur'an* or that it is merely unauthentic. This is the approach adopted mostly by non-conformist sects primarily due to their lack of knowledge of the science of *hadith*. What is very strange about this group is that while they reject even authentic Prophetic traditions alleging that they contradict the *Qur'an*, they do not hesitate to use spurious traditions to corroborate their beliefs and theological positions.

3. Those who accept the authority of the *Sunnah* but misinterpret the meaning of any *hadith* which they find contradicts their theological or legal schools of thought. This has mainly been the attitude of the followers of the schools of jurisprudence [*madhhab*] as well as the scholars of *sufism* and other Muslim movements.

4. The fourth group consists of those Muslims who accept the authority of an authentic *Sunnah* and try to derive or develop their schools of thought around it. In other words, they believe that it is their schools of thought and theologies that should conform to the *Sunnah*, and that the *Sunnah* and *hadith* should not be twisted to conform with theology and law. Unfortunately, very few Muslims fall under this category as majority of the Muslims around the world subscribe to any one of the first three categories.

While the *Sunnah* is an interpretation of the *Qur'an*, it is also in need of an interpretation. Like the *Qur'an*, where reasons of revelation [*asbab*

71

al-nuzul] are important to determine the meaning of a verse, *asbab wurud al-hadith* (the reasons why a particular *hadith* was said or why an action was done) of a *hadith* are also very important to avoid mistakes such as those committed by other narrators who quoted traditions out of context and were often corrected by Aishah as well as by other scholars of their time.

We should also avoid literalism when engaging in the interpretation of the *Sunnah* and try to acknowledge the gape between the Prophet's community and us. The *Sunnah* of the Prophet was a response to situations that are obviously different from ours. For example, traditions reported concerning Muslim and non-Muslim relations should be understood in that context. Imam Muslim reports a tradition in which the Prophet instructed Muslims not to return the greeting [*salam*] of non-Muslims, the Muslim should just say *wa alaikum* (and upon you) in response.

What had happened was that a group of Jews came to visit the Prophet and upon entering his house they said, "*assam alaikum*" (may death be upon you) instead of "*assalam alaikum*'" (may the Peace be upon you). They said it in such a way that to the listener it would sound as if they actually said "*assalam alaikum*". However, the Prophet was not fooled and he responded simply saying, "and upon you". Aishah who was also present angrily retorted saying, "may the death and curse be upon you, too!" The Prophet went on telling her that what she had done was not polite, she asked him if he had not heard what they said and he told her that he had heard them and had responded saying "*wa 'alaikum.*" He then instructed his Companions, saying: If the people of the Book convey *salam* to you, your response should be "*wa 'alaikum*" for indeed some of them say "*assam*" instead of "*assalam*".[65]

This Tradition was said in a very hostile historical context when the non-Muslims were looking for every opportunity to attack the Muslims, and we can understand why the Prophet instructed the Muslims not to give them any way as a show of strength since any show of weakness on the part of the believers would present an opportunity to the non-Muslims. He also instructed them not to respond to their *salam* as they would to a fellow Muslim and not to greet them at all until they greet the Muslim first.

One living in a completely different environment and context will have a problem trying to follow these instructions. Most of the non-Muslims today are not as hostile to the Muslims as the Jews were in Madinah during the Prophet's era. Moreover, we now have traffic laws that make it illegal for a person to deliberately bump into another car or even for pedestrians to do so to others, for whatever reasons, religious or otherwise. There is also a very large number of Muslims staying with non-Muslim family members (brothers, parents, sisters, wives, etc.) who are not "enemies" at all. How then is one expected to interact with them in light of the above tradition? Should one greet them first in the mornings and evenings, or should one just come in the house and sit down without greeting anyone?

The *Sunnah* should enable us to live in this world peacefully and for that to happen, a new reading is urgently required. Fortunately, contemporary scholarship has been very active in making the *Sunnah* an integral part of a Muslim's life here and now. Today, the International Institute of Islamic Thought (IIIT), located in Virginia, USA has always considered the understanding of the *Sunnah*, its comprehensive, exhaustive analysis and proper approach to using it as a source of knowledge and culture to be among the most important matters of concern to Muslim social scientists today.[66] Many books which deal with the *Sunnah* from a contemporary perspective have since been published by IIIT. The book by the late Shaikh Muhammad al-Ghazali (d. 1996), *al-Sunnah bayna ahl al-fiqh wa ahl al-hadith* (The Concept of *Sunnah* between Legal Pragmatists and the Partisans of Tradition) was one of such great contributions to the contemporary field of *hadith* studies. Unfortunately, so much criticism was generated by conservative scholars concerning the book that the main message of the work was either overlooked or diluted.

Notes

1. The Prophet first banned the Muslims from visiting the graves fearing that, as a people who were new in faith, they may return to idolisation and veneration of graves. After he was satisfied that their faith in one God had become strong, he lifted the ban and said, 'I had prohibited you from visiting the graves, you may now visit them for they remind you of death.' Today we find

Muslims in India, Pakistan, and some parts of Africa idolizing and even worshipping graves, there is no doubt that any one who will suggest that the ban should be re-imposed on these Muslims will not be violating the Islamic law since the reasons and circumstances that caused the Prophet to impose the ban during the early period of Islam are very similar to what we see in India, Pakistan and Africa.

2. Al-Zarkashi, Badr al-Din, *Al-burhan fi 'ulum al-Qur'an,* Beirut: Dar al-fikr, 1980, 157-160.

3. Ibid., pp. 146-147.

4. This definition of al-Raghib seems to suggest that there is a meaning 'hidden' in the text which needs to be 'exposed', this is an issue that has become one of the central problem of modern hermeneutics. See *al-Raghib's al-Mufradat,* Beirut: Dar al-fikr, (s.a.).

5. Al-Zubaydi, Muhib al-din, *Taj al-'arus min jawahir al-qamus,* Beirut: Dar al-fikr, 1994, vol. 14, p. 32.

6. Ibid.

7. Ibib.

8. Al-A'sha was once heard reciting the following poem: *'ala annaha kanat ta'wwalu hubbiha ta'wwulu rib'iyyi al-siqab fa asbaha.* While Abu 'Ubayd was commenting on this verse he said, *'ay tafsir Hubbihi annahu kana saghiran fi qalbihi falam yazal yathbut hatta sara kabiran kahadha al-saqab al-saghir lam yazal yashibbu hatta sara kabiran mithla ummihi wasara lahu waladun yas habuhu'.* The commentary of Abu 'Ubayd here seem to suggest that *ta'wil* and *tafsir* are one and the same thing. See the *Diwan of Al-A'sha,* Beirut: Dar al-fikr, p. 8; & al-lisan wa al-sihah.

9. Al-Zubaydi., op.cit.

10. Al-Zarkhashi, op.cit., p. 125. It is noteworthy that both Zarkhashi and Suyuti do not make this statement themselves but ascribe it to the scholars in general. Most probably, their source in this regard is the explicit statement of Ibn Taymiyyah (661-728 A.H.), in a small book entitled *Fi usul al-tafsir,* which is similar to what Suyuti and al-Zarkhashi state. No one has mentioned this principle before Ibn Taymiyyah. The origins of this statement can be traced in the *Nahj al-Balaghah* and has been attributed to 'Ali. See the Persian Translation by Dr. Sayyid Ja'afar Shahidi (p. 132).

11. Ibid., pp. 175-176.

12. Suyuti, Jalal al-Din, *Mukhtasar al-ittiqan fi 'ulum al-Qur'an*, Beirut: Dar al-Nafais, 1987, p. 130.

13. Ibid., p. 131.

14. Ibid., p. 129.

15. Ibid.

16. Abdullah reported Allah's Messenger as saying: "Ruined, were those who indulged in hair-splitting. He (the Holy Prophet) repeated this thrice." See, *Sahih Muslim, Kitab al-ilm, hadith no: 6450.*

17. Parker, Stuart, *Reflective Teaching in the Postmodern World*, Philadelphia: Open University Press, 1997, p. 69.

18. Ibid.

19. *Sahih al-Bukhari*, Kitab al-manaqib.

20. Ricoeur, Paul, *Hermeneutics and the Human Sciences,* (trans. Ed. Thomson, T.B., Cambridge: University Press, 1995, p. 139.)

21. Ibid.

22. García, Ismael, *Justice in Latin American Theology of Liberation*, Atlanta: John Knox Press, 1987, p. 7.

23. Kiogora, Timothy. G, *Black Theology (Initiation into Theology: The Rich Variety of Theology and Hermeneutics)* ed. Maimela, Simon and König, Adrio, (Pretoria: JL van Schaik, 1998, p. 337.

24. Ali Engineer, Asghar, Islam and Liberation: *Essays on Liberative Elements in Islam*, New Delhi: Sterling Publishers, 1990, p. 6.

25. See Gutiérrez, Gustavo, *Essential Writings*, New York: Orbis Books, 1996, p. 47.

26. Al-Baladuri, *Ansab al-ashraf,* Jerusalem, vol. 5, p. 53.

27. Sahih Muslim, *kitab al-zakah.*

28. Ibid. p. 24.

29. See Sunan Abi Dawud, *kitab al-adab; & Sunan Tirmidhi,* Bab al-birr.

30. *Sahih Muslim*, kitab al-birr.

31. *Sahih Bukhari*, kitab al-iman.

32. García, Ismael, op. cit.

33. *Maraq al-falah sharh nur al-idah,* Beirut: Dar al-nu'man, 1990, pp. 301-302.

34. See the *Sunan of Abu Dawud.*

35. *Mishkat al-masabih,* Karachi: Qadimi kutub khana, p. 100.

36. Ibid.

37. Ibd., p. 611.

38. See Yusuf Ali's commentary to the verse in his translation of the *Qur'an.*

39. See his commentary of the *Qur'an,* Lahore: Ahmadiyyah Isha'at Islam, 1973, p. 160.

40. In a tradition recorded by Abu Dawud in his *Sunan,* the Prophet instructed his Companions saying, 'the one with more knowledge of the *Qur'an* should lead you in prayers and the best one among you or most respected (*khiyarukum*) should call the *adhan.* See *Kitab al-salah.*

41. *Muslim & Tirmidhi,* kitab al-zuhd

42. *Tirmidhi,* Bab al-da'wat.

43. Wadud Muhsin, Amina, *The Qur'an and Women,* Kuala lumpur: Bakti Sdu. Bhd., 1992, p. 6.

44. *Sunan Tirmidhi,* Bab al-adab.

45. *Al-Amidi, Al-ihkam fi usul al-ahkam,* vol.1, p. 87; also see *Sharh al-jalal al-mahalli 'ala jam' aljawami',* vol.2, p.83; and *Al-Shawkani, Irshad al-fuhul,* p. 33.

46. *Al-mu'allaqat al-sab'ah,* Cairo, 1315 H., p. 102.

47. Imam Shafi'i, Treatise VIII, *Kitab al-Radd 'ala Muhammad ibn al-Hasan,* 13; Umm, n. 75, 292.

48. Sahih al-Bukhari, *Kitab al-i'tisam: Bab ma dhukira fo dhammi ra'y wa takalluf al-qiyas.*

49. Bukhari, *Raf' al-Yadain;* see also Ibn abi Hatim al-Razi, *al-Jarh wa al-ta'dil,* p. 337.

50. *Al-Tamyiz,* pp. 68-9.

51. *Bukhari,* vol. 5, p.9.

52. *Mishkat,* p. 152; also Bukhari and Muslim.

53. Al-Albani, Muhammad Nasir al-din, *Silsilah ahadith da'ifah wa al-mawdu'ah,* Beirut, 1384H., vol. 1, p. 50.

54. *Sahih al-bukhari,* vol. 1, p. 99.

55. Bukhari, *Bab istiqbal rajl al-rajl wa huwa yusalli.*

56. Imam Muslim, n. 356, 15.

57. Imam Muslim has recorded all these traditions in his introduction to his *Sahih.*

58. Muhammad ibn 'Ali al-Shaukani (1960) *al-Fawa'id al-majmu'ah fi al-ahadith al-Mawdu'ah* (editor al-Yamani) Cairo, pp. 320 - 428.

59. Imam Muslim, n. 356, 15; or his introduction to *Sahih.*

60. See *al-Rihlah,* n. 24, 89.

61. *Sahih Muslim,* kitab al-albas wa zina (chapter on adornments and beauty).

62. See Imam Nawawi's commentary on *Muslim,* vol. 14, p.70.

63. *Sunan Abi Dawod,* chapter on *tayamum*; & *Ibn Hajar, Fath al-bari,* Cairo: Dar al-diyan li al-turath, 1986, vol.1, pp.528-529.

64. *Muslim,* kitab al-fadail.

65. See *Muslim,* vol. 7, p. 146.

66. Al-'Alwani, Taha Jabir, *The Qur'an and Sunnah: the time space factor,* Virginia, IIIT: 1991, p. 30.

Chapter Three
Ijma': General Consensus

Soon after the death of Prophet Muhammad, an urgent need arose for the Muslim community to find his successor. The turn of events led to the formation of the *ijma'* doctrine which was a consolidated effort involving the use of speculative reasoning and analogical deduction [*ijtihad and qiyas*]. Contrary to common view, the election of Abu Bakr to the office of Caliphate was not accomplished through the *ijma'* process, it was an urgent election done by a small group of the Muslim community in what has been interpreted as an attempt to avoid the feelings of disunity and pre-Islamic Arab tribalistic prejudice which were about to re-emerge. Due to the problems of communications at that time, it has been argued, that it was not possible to expect all the Muslims to be present for the election event. Moreover it took days or even months for Muslims from other parts of the then Muslim world to reach Madinah, and given the circumstances, it would have been hazardous for the Muslims to be without a leader for that period of time. When people started to question the legitimacy of Abu Bakr's Caliphate, the *ijma'* was used to justify his election even though some senior Companions were absent during the election and were a bit upset for having been left out. This later on contributed to schisms in the Muslim *ummah* between what became known as the shi'at ali (the supporters of Ali) and the other Muslims of that time. The people who originally proposed Abu Bakr for election were later on considered the *ahl al-hall wa al-aqd* (people of loosing and binding) in medieval Islamic political theory, and it was also later agreed that correct *ijma'* was the *ijma'* done by the *ahl al-hall wa al-aqd* or the *fuqaha* ignoring the historical circumstances that led to the development of this exclusivist *ijma'*.

The *ijma'* doctrine passed through four main phases of development:
1. The first was the *ijma 'al-sahabah* or the consensus of the Companions, the example of which we have discussed above. Due to the political authority of the Caliphate, this *ijma'* was effected with almost minimal difficulty or strife.

2. The *ijma' al-tabi'in* or consensus of the Successors. *Ijma'* during this period was complicated by the fact that there no longer was a legitimate Islamic government to unite all the Muslims on one view. Moreover, many scholars who had been staying at Madinah dispersed throughout the Arabian peninsula and as a result many diverse theological and legal views emerged as a result of social interaction and acculturation making it almost impossible to solve them through the process of *ijma'*.

3. The period of *ijtihad*: as a result of the disunity and diverse views they inherited from the Successors, the jurists of that period adopted a rigid application of the *ijma'* of the Companions in order to avoid further disunity and isolationism. This was a period when the Muslim world was intensely divided and ones orthodoxy was being judged by his or her allegiance to the *salaf* (the Companions). However every jurist was influenced by his location. Imam Malik gave importance to the *ijma'* of the people of Madinah while Abu Hanifah considered the *ijma'* of the people of Kufah as more reliable. The Hanbali scholars, on the other hand, accepted the consensus of only the first four *Caliphs*.

4. The period of blind following [*taqlid*] of the schools of jurisprudence: this was the period when blind following emerged among the students of the Imams and every one started buttressing the *madhhab* of his Imam with claims of *ijma'*. According to the *Shafi'i* jurist Abu Ishaq al-Isfarayini, more than twenty thousand cases were solved through *ijma'*.[1] This claim cannot be true unless if taken to mean the various claims to *ijma'* that emerged during the post-*ijtihad* period. During this period any claim to *ijma'* was no longer trusted and the only *ijma'* upon which there was a general agreement was that of the Companions. Moreover, the need to be identified with the *sawad al-a'zam* or the majority of Muslims due to diverse heretic views that existed at that time still remained, and the importance of the *ijma'* of the Companions got re-emphasized. It was then that the view of *ijma'* as a conclusive and unequivocal source of law [*hujah qati'ah*] was firmly established. The jurists began to frown at anyone who opposed the views of the *salaf*.[2] The following Traditions were used to support this view: "What the Muslims see as good, surely it is good in the eyes of Allah, and what the faithful think is bad, it is also bad in the eyes of Allah."[3] "The hand of Allah is over the entire group"[4] and "My people would never agree on something that leads them astray."

80

The need to keep the Muslims united after the civil wars that divided early Islam saw medieval Islamic political thought using *ijma'* as a political tool. The leader [*waliy al-amr*] was to be obeyed in all circumstances since he had been elected or approved by *ijma'*. The *ijma'* which approved or elected the leader was that of the *ahl al-hall wa al-aqd* who were themselves appointed by the political establishment. According to Ahmad Hasan, "Al-Ghazali, Ibn Jama'ah, and some medieval traditionists justified the rule of usurpers and tyrants on a religious basis for fear of anarchy and civil disturbance. People were allowed to depose them only in case they were guilty of disbelief. This resulted in quietism and acquiescence and ultimately undermined popular sovereignty, democratic spirit, and freedom of the individual in the community."[5] Imam Muslim recorded in his *Sahih* an incident which serves to expose the quietist attitude of scholars during the Umayyad rule. Abdurahman ibn Abd rabb al-Ka'bah reports that one day he entered the mosque when Abdullah ibn Amr ibn As was seated in the shade of the Ka'bah and the people were gathered around him listening to his discourse. He (Abdullah ibn Amr ibn As) went on to narrate that the Prophet said the following *hadith*:

"He who swears allegiance to the *Caliph* by taking his hand and sincerely with his heart, he should obey him to the best of his capacity. If another person comes forward as a claimant to the *Caliphate* or disputing his authority, then you should all behead the later."[6]

Abdurahman ibn Abd rabb al-Ka'bah says: "I came close to him and asked him: 'Can you say on oath that you heard it from the Messenger of Allah?' He pointed with his hands to his ears and his heart saying, 'my ears heard it and my heart retained it." Abdurahman says: "I then said to him, 'this cousin of yours, Mu'awiyyah, orders us to unjustly consume our wealth among ourselves and kill one another while Allah says: *O you who believe, do not consume your wealth among yourselves unjustly, unless it be trade based on mutual agreement, and do not kill yourselves. Verily, Allah is Merciful to you.* On hearing this, Abdullah ibn Amr ibn As kept quiet for a while and then said, "Obey him in so far as he is obedient to Allah; and disobey him in matters involving disobedience to Allah."[7]

We see here that Abdullah did not instruct Abdurahman to behead Mu'awiyyah as commanded by the Prophet in the *hadith*. This may be interpreted as fear of being accused of inciting rebellion against

Mu'awiyyah's regime. However, this passive and quietist attitude towards the tyrants and authoritarian leaders could not bring about any significant change and revolution which was needed to eliminate the corrupt and evil leadership and build a just and healthy society headed by worthy persons. The political role that the *ijma'* of the *ahl al-hall wa al-aqd* played was to maintain the *status quo,* and anyone challenging the leadership was condemned for attempting to abrogate *ijma'* [*kharq al-ijma'*] *sawad al-a'zam* and for causing chaos [*fawda*]. Traditions and Qur'anic verses were easily available to support this attitude:

"But whoever break from the Messenger after the guidance has become clear to him and follows a way other than that becoming to men of faith, We shall leave him over to what he has chosen and We shall land him in the fire of hell – an evil refuge"(4: 115).

Also,

"O believers, obey Allah and obey the Messenger, and those in authority among you. If you dispute regarding any issue, refer it back to Allah and his Prophet." (4:59)

The Islamic political discourse changed into an accentuation of *laissez-faire* position of abstention from political struggle that turned into the *ulama'* (with notable exceptions) forever, becoming the kings party, strenuously advocating absolute obedience to the empire or the ruling elite.

Irrevocably linked with consensus is the mode of consensus. Thus, the coming together of the affected parties, their discussions and debates, are all prerequisites to an authentic consensus. As we have seen above, the early community began to use the third source of *Shari'ah* with the demise of the Prophet. We also have seen how the election of Abu Bakr as the leader of the community of believers was accomplished through a *quasi-ijma'* which required strong arguments from the *Qur'an* and *Sunnah,* as well as calm and dispassionate arguments about how the interests of the community would best be served. While, as we will see later, speculative reasoning and analogical deduction [*ijtihad* and *qiyas*] can attain validity over a limited range of time and space, no independent judgement will ever be universally valid until it is transformed into a decision agreed to after consultation as marking the consensus of the community of believers.

A clear and detailed definition of *ijma'* is given by Abu Bakr al-Jassas (d. 370 A.H.). He divides *ijma'* into two categories, namely *ijma' an tawqif* (consensus by acquaintance) and *ijma' an istikhraj* (consensus by inference).[8] Although many scholars in the classical period defined '*ummah*' as constituting the scholarly community, al-Ghazali insisted that *ijma'* is the agreement of the entire Muslim community beginning from the advent of Islam to contemporary time.[9] Thus, *ijma'* by this definition is not exclusivist and elitist. Al-Amidi, a famous *faqih*, defined *ijma'* as an agreement between the people of "binding and loosing" [*ahl al-hall wa al-aqd*], it being impossible to bring on a common platform the entire community on one issue.

According to Imam al-Haramain (419-478 AH), the process of *ijma'* requires a certain number of people.[10] The crucial number, whatever it is, is called *tawatur*, which might be translated as "Quorum". Some scholars argue that it is as small as three, while others say a sufficiently large number of people whose number is so large as to preclude error, a somewhat circular argument.[11] While it is not clear what number constitutes *tawatur* to legitimate *ijma'*, it is clear that in early Islam, due to reasons we mentioned above, complete agreement by every Muslim was not considered as necessary for *ijma'*, as is demonstrated by the decision of Abu Bakr to fight the tribes who refused to pay *zakah*, as well as the election of Abu Bakr to the office of Caliphate.

We could also consider *ijma'* as having three categories, namely, verbal consensus [*ijma' al-qawl*], consensus by action [*jma' al-fi'l*], and consensus by silence [*ijma' al-sukut*]. Now *ijma'* on matters of *ibadat* (worship) is considerably more difficult to get than *ijma'* on *mu'amalat* (transactions). Thus, an *ijma'* concerning business transactions can proceed as valid if the *ummah* generally agree and no one speaks up, but if even a non-scholarly Muslim speaks out against a potential *ijma'* concerning acts of worship, that potential *ijma'* is invalidated.

One of the most neglected, but important, concepts in Islam is that of mutual consultation, or *shura*. The principle of *shura*, mutual consultation, has been established unequivocally in the *Qur'an* and *Sunnah*. It is widely held, erroneously, that *shura* means that the supreme single leader is required to consult with a few of his cronies, whose advice he may or may not accept. This view is false. The *Qur'an* states in no uncertain terms that one of the characteristics of the believers is that *"they decide their affairs by a process of mutual consultation"* (42: 38). The Arabic is *amru-hum* (their matters or affairs are decided), *shura baina-hum* (by a process of consultation among them). The construct of this injunction, and the interpretation by the Prophet in the *Sunnah*, affirm that this process is one of mutual discussion where the believers are on an absolutely equal footing.

The fact that the above verse of *shura* mentions *al-mu'minin* (believers) and not the *ahl al-hall wa al-aqd min al-mu'minin or fuqaha'* is ignored by the advocates of an elitist *ijma'*. The verse explicitly states that *shura* requires participation from all believers. The sentence *"amruhum shura bainahum"* is a nominal clause [*jumlah ismiyyah*], and is similar to the Prophetic instruction: *"al-hajj arafah"* (pilgrimage is attending the rituals at Arafat). The characteristic of such a sentence in Arabic linguistics is that it denotes interdependence of one part of the sentence on the other. Muslim scholars have always recognized this point and ruled that *hajj* depends on Arafat. If there is no *hajj* there shall be no Arafat, and in the same way if one decides to leave out the rituals at Arafat, his pilgrimage will be null and void. Therefore, what the verse of *shura* means to us is that if there is no participation from all believers [*mu'minin*] there shall be no *shura*, hence no *ijma'*.

The traditions used to prove the authority of *ijma'* also refer to *"muslimi"*, *"jama'ah"*, *"sawad al-a'zam"*, and *"ummah"* and these are all terms that refer, not to a selected few, but to all believers or those truly representing them. The people should have the freedom to elect a representative council of whomever they wish to participate on their behalf in all consultation and decision-making [*shurah* and *ijma'*]. There are no fixed arrangements in the *Shari'ah* for the representation of the community, other than the general injunctions of justice, democracy, charity, and brotherly compassion. The early *ummah* accomplished representative *shura* by spontaneously appointing delegates or spokesmen who would represent the desires of the entire group. This explicit, spontaneous, and temporal authorization was called *aqd taukil dimni* in Arabic.

The question regarding whom we should trust to decide who qualifies for *majlis shura* (legislature) or *ahl al-hall wa al-aqd* is very important. We have seen thus far that other humans have a relatively poor track record for ascertaining what counts as humanity; at various points in history other humans have considered blacks, women and the poor to be insufficiently human. Our position, therefore, should be that in a society where women or blacks are considered inferior and less human they should be given full rights to decide who represents the entire country in the *majlis shura*. The political process of liberation can achieve this. Experience has shown us that blacks and women are likely to be left out of important decision making processes even though they may be equally or even more qualified academically than those supposed to be representing the entire community. In December 1999 the Kuwaiti's all male parliament narrowly rejected a law granting women full political right to vote and stand in elections. A similar form of discrimination has led to attempts by black Muslims of South Africa to establish what they call an "African Council of Muslim Theologians" since they feel that the present organizations do not represent the black Muslims even though there is at present a lot of qualified African Muslim theologians. Moreover, qualified Muslim women theologians in the world are still not represented at high levels needless to say that women of early Islam participated in *shura* and *ijma'*. The general feeling among the marginalized Muslims is that organizations such as *Majlis al-ulama'* or *Jam'iat al-ulama'* (Council of Scholars) need to be replaced by *Majlis al-sha'ab, Majlis al-ummah*, or *Majlis al-muslimin* (People's or Muslims' Councils).

Abu al-A'la al-Maududi, a twentieth century Muslim scholar of Pakistan, held that the *majlis al-shura* is to be appointed by the head of state rather than being elected.[12] This is completely wrong. Even according to the classical sunni theory of state, which is demonstrably acquiescent to *status quo* power, the people of loosening and binding [*ahl al-hal wa al-aqd*] have to put forward a head a state, and they therefore pre-exist him, rather than being appointed by him. We do recognize of course that when power shifted from the people to the rulers during the Umayyad rule, the king would appoint his own *majlis al-shura*. We are also aware that this is still the practice today in countries such as Saudi Arabia that claim to rule on the basis of *shura*. This has resulted in the ulama members of the *majlis al-shura* excluding women participation in *shura* and also taking sides with the oppressive regimes in human rights abuse. Underlying this misconception is a very pernicious view of the average person. The elite would like to keep the government mystical, they would like to mystify the masses in everything they do, so as to continually convince them that they could never do what the experts can do, and thereby keep them perpetually under control.

The doctrine of *ijma' al-fuqaha* or *ijma' ahl al-hall wa al-aqd* as opposed to the *ijma' al-ummah* is an attempt at the monopolization of knowledge and power, typical of modernist thought. The *ulama'*, though not realizing it, think in typical modernist fashion by emphasizing that *ijma'* is specialized knowledge, which is fully accessible only to certain selected experts. Modernist thought argues that appropriately educated experts have privileged authority to interpret texts, and that they conduct their researches without biases of any sort from their particular theological or political standpoints.

An *ijma'* done only by the *fuqaha'* or the *ahl al-hall wa al-aqd*, even when it claims to be supported by the *Qur'an* and *Sunnah*, is certainly not binding on anyone and will not constitute law until it has been approved by the whole *ummah*. We saw how an *ijma'* was passed by the Gulf *ulama'* soon after the Iranian revolution and during the Iran-Iraq war to declare the Shi'ites as non-Muslims. We also heard allegations of how they had another *Qur'an* different from that of the rest of the Muslims. The war of Iraq with Iran was declared, through an *ijma'*, as a *Jihad* between Islam and Zoroastrianism, a *Jihad* between Sunni and Shi'ite, and a Jihad between the Arabs and Persians. In 1999, Iran's growing political power and influence in the region and on international level, and the Iranian President Khatami's visits to Saudi Arabia and other Gulf countries, had the same academics referring to *Shi'ites* as "fellow Muslim brothers" and to *Shi'ism* as "just another school of Islamic jurisprudence. This proves that some *ulama'* are not always interested in pure and flawless search for truth, but are often swayed by the political and financial consequences of various research programs and *ijma'*s. The *ulama'* and Islamic scholarship have always been locked in a delicate power struggle for identity, balancing the importance of "sincerity" against the exigencies of financial and political support.

Islamic scholarship and the Islamic judiciary systems need to be liberated from the influence of the political establishment. We no longer have the excuses that early communities of *ijma'* had to advocate an exclusivist *ijma'* because of the benefits of globalization. Rapid developments in communications technology, transport and information which bring the remotest parts of the world within easy reach makes it possible for the people in Zimbabwe to participate in an *ijma'* that is taking place in another part of the world, if it is an *ijma'* that affects all Muslims of the world.

It is surprising that while the world is supposed to be in a post-modern era, even countries which claim to be the custodians of democracy, continue to function in purely modernist ways. Noam Chomsky has one of the most powerful voices speaking out against the abuses of government. He demonstrates repeatedly how the government and the experts portray themselves as the only people able to make decisions on behalf of everyone else. In the following passage, Chomsky deflates the idea that the common person cannot understand the supposed complexities of political life. It is a sad commentary on the apathy and passive acceptance of this principle in the United States when we see the lack of political awareness evidenced by the typical United States citizen. In contrast, the supposedly undeveloped nations often reveal far more political savvy and participation. Here is what Chomsky has to say about the mystification of politics:

> If such (critical) analysis is often carried out poorly, that is because, quite commonly, social and political analysis is produced to defend special interests rather than to account for the actual events. Precisely because of this tendency one must be careful not to give the impression, which in any event is false, that only intellectuals equipped with special training are capable of such analytic work. In fact, that is just what the intelligentsia would often like us to think: they pretend to be engaged in an esoteric enterprise, inaccessible to simple people. But that's nonsense. The social sciences generally, and above all the analysis of contemporary affairs, are quite accessible to anyone who wants to take an interest in these matters. The alleged complexity, depth, and obscurity of these questions is part of the illusion propagated by the system of ideological control, which aims to make the issues seem remote from the general population to persuade them of their incapacity to organize their own affairs or to understand the social world in which they live without the tutelage of intermediaries.[13]

Thus, the populace is made passive and apathetic, completely sure that they are incapable of regulating their own lives. And when the history of brutal and total repression of labor unions in the United States is examined, it becomes clear that even the slightest bit of independence and endeavors to regulate one's work life are suppressed by a government trying to be the sole force of control. When it comes to the United States controlling other nations, the same process is at work.

Edward Said also insightfully shows how the 'experts' interpret our world:

> When the experts venture into the public eye it is as experts, brought in because an emergency has caught 'the West' unprepared ... They are viewed as technicians with a 'solid set of 'how-tos' to present to the anxious public. And the public takes kindly to them, for they are an answer to what Christopher Lasch has called 'an unprecedented demand for experts, technicians, and managers (for the post-industrial order).

> Both business and government, under the pressure of technological revolution, expanding population, and the indefinitely prolonged emergency of the cold war, became increasingly dependent on a vast apparatus of systematized data intelligible only to trained specialists; and the universities, accordingly, became themselves industries for the mass-production of experts.[14]

The notion that the average person is unable to arrive at correct decisions concerning public affairs or politics is a devious device to manipulate the masses. It is no coincidence that the issue of the supposed stupidity of the average person is combined with the attitude of paternalism so rampant in politics, but so absent from the early *ummah*. Paternalism is the attitude that the ruler is a wise father, and that what he wants is best for his nation-family, and so the children-citizens should simply shut up and vote for him. Paternalism is clearly seen in almost every government, and more so when a female happens to be at the helm of affairs (like Golda Meir, Indira Gandhi, Margaret Thatcher, Corazon Aquino). It is no surprise that her ruling style is extremely conservative, aligned with *status quo* powers, bearing aggressive hallmarks of paternalism. But occasionally people struggle to get out of paternalistic binds. It is very interesting that the possibly Freudian word "kill" is used concerning the father figure, suggesting that the paternalist dependents can only be free when their father is dead. This kind of stifled structure is indicative of the evil of paternalism.

Similarly, the view that the average person is unable to make moral decisions has led to very serious crimes of the elite. At the heart of the matter lies an acute crisis of confidence in the human intellect and, even more than that, our moral capacities, and it is hard to accept that in all the Islamic world it would be impossible to find sufficient numbers of wise and moral Muslims to help run political affairs. In fact, the closest approximation to what the Muslims should be doing is the Quaker meeting, where the entire local community sits together and discusses important issues. Only when every single last person in the room is convinced does the meeting adjourn. Thus, while the majority is important, they have the obligation to persuade the minority, if indeed they think they are right.

It is pertinent that public health practitioners and administrators are slowly discovering that *shura* is the best form of public health care delivery. Of course, they use different words, but the complete rejection of paternalism and elitism and the acceptance of community priorities and community decision-making is telling. It is a shame on the Muslim community that we, who have after all the divine guidance concerning *shura* and community decision-making, should not have been the first people of this century to assert the value of *shura*.

At the Alma-Ata conference in 1978, the World Health Organization agreed that, "each community should decide on its priorities according to the severity and frequency of problems."[15] One of the things that happen when the community decides is that the secular worldview of western scientific thinking is overthrown. The elevated status of scientists and experts has come under serious criticism from many quarters. Paul Feyerabend, almost a lone voice against the scientisation of society where people become so removed from their environment and common sense that they accept whatever the elite tells them,[16] has stumbled on the concept of *shura*.

It is sad to note that the total civil polity based on *shura* lasted only for about two decades after the Prophet. As the Muslims went into distant lands, the new Muslims were not as much a part of governing their own affairs, as they should have been. Some scholars speculate that the Persians were not as involved as they should have been in regulating their own affairs as Muslims brought up feelings of persecution and suffering which led to a revival of early Iranian motifs and the development of Shi'ism as a vehicle for a suffering minority. Suffice to say civil polity based on *shura* was found locally and at different times, but its expression has not been carried over into modern times at a national or international level.

Abrogation of old *Ijma'* by new *Ijma'*

Ijma' reached directly by the whole *ummah* from the *Qur'an* and *Sunnah* has permanent validity. Consensus originating from *masalih al-mursalah*, however, may be overturned when circumstances change since public interests differ and change according to place and time. Exclusivist or elitist *ijma'*, as we discussed above is not binding on anyone and may be abrogated by an *ijma'* of the *ummah* since it is mostly based on individual interpretation. The scholars of a subsequent generation might argue, in all probability, on the basis of a better authority than the scholars of the previous one.[17]

We even feel that *shura* and *ijma'* should not exclude the non-Muslims staying in a Muslim society. We know that the non-Muslims were present and participated in the various decision-making processes during the Prophetic period when it was pertaining to issues affecting the whole society. The Prophet wrote in his celebrated constitution of Madinah:

> The Jews of Banu Aws are an *ummah* alongside the believers...
> Their relationship shall be one of mutual advice and consultation,
> and mutual assistance and charity rather than harm and aggression.[18]

According to the Hanafi point of view, new *ijma'* can abrogate an old *ijma'*. For example, if the *ulama* and *fuqaha* have unanimously given their concurrence on a certain matter, we certainly will accept the *ijma'*, but this does not mean that until the day of Resurrection no one has the right to disagree with it. If a new *ijma'* is reached by the *ulama* of subsequent ages, which has a stronger basis, then the new *ijma'* will abrogate the old *ijma'*. Abul Yasr al-Bazdawi has mentioned this method of abrogation of an old *ijma'* in his book *Usul-al-fiqh*.[19] Bazdawi lived between fourth and fifth century *hijrah* and is considered an authority on jurisprudence. This view expressed by him has made things easier for us because *ijma'* will not be regarded as an inflexible tool. If by any chance, *ijma'* has taken place on some unreasonable issue and if we have not been able to act upon it due to a change in circumstances, then there is room for the change of *ijma'* and through *shura* and *ijtihad* a new *ijma'* is possible to be achieved.

Ijma' as a universal institution

It is unfortunate that after so many centuries, *ijma'* has never been organized as an institution. As a consequence, Muslims in some countries are not in a position to know whether there is *ijma'* on a certain matter or not. There is no organization to look after the interests of Muslims in different continents so that opinions of Muslims could be sent from one continent to another continent. Possibly, it was very difficult in the ancient times, but today due to the quick means of transport, postal and electronic media, it has become possible that a council representing all Muslims can be established in each country while a hub centre can be established either in Makkah or Madinah. If there is some burning issue, it should be referred to the Centre which will enable the secretariat of the Centre to forward it to the council in other parts of the world. The local secretariat of a given country then would co-ordinate and find the consensus or differences of opinion and the replies forwarded to the centre along with all the arguments in favor of and against the concerned issue. When there is a consensus of all branches from different parts of the world, it will be put forward as the collective *ijma'* binding on the entire *ummah*.

The Interpretative Tools of Islamic Sources: *Ijtihad* and *Qiyas*

The sociology of law shows that legal subject-matters are dealt with by two methods: analytical and analogical. The first method i.e., analytical is adopted by the shi'ite school of jurisprudence, while the later, i.e., ana-logical is used by the majority of the sunni schools. Traditional Islamic scholarship has always considered qiyas (analogical deduction) and *ijtihad* (independent reasoning) as sources of law. This is difficult to accept when given the fact that *qiyas* and *ijtihad* are nothing but process-es of interpreting the sources of Islamic law in an attempt to derive laws.

91

The legal decisions reached after the process of *ijtihad* and *qiyas* remain individual opinions not binding on anyone. They will not assume the status of laws unless if they have been sanctioned by *ijma'*. They are designed to help discover the best application of the *ijma'* guidance. We may equate *qiyas* to *shura* which is also not a source of law but an exercise of reaching to a legal decision.

During the Prophetic period, there was no room for differences of opinion in interpretation, all the unjustifiable differences were temporary ones and they were cleared by the Prophet himself either according to the Qur'anic revelation or by way of his *sunnah*, which was in fact the explanation of the Qur'anic verses which were already revealed. Let us be realistic and acknowledge the fact that the Companions of the Prophet, like any other group of people, differed in their individual abilities, approach or emphasis; and eventually in their knowledge, understanding or reasoning. On one occasion for instance, when the Prophet decided to invade the Jewish tribe of Bani Quraizah, he urged his Companions to proceed to the land of Bani Quraizah saying: "He who believes in Allah and the Last Day should not offer the *asr* (late afternoon) prayer except in the land of Bani Quraizah." It happened that the time of the late afternoon prayer approached while they were still on their way to Bani Quraizah. They started arguing whether they should perform their prayer before reaching Bani Quraizah or whether they should proceed and perform upon arrival as understood from the instructions of the Prophet. One group of Companions, realizing that they would not reach Bani Quraizah before sunset, thought that what he actually meant was that they should try to travel fast enough so that they should reach the land of Bani Quraizah before the *asr* prayer. Their interpretation was that the Prophet was just emphasizing on speed and not place, so they went on to perform the prayer.

The other group argued that the Prophet literally meant that the prayer should only be performed at Bani Quraizah and his emphasis was not speed but place, and they decided to perform the prayer in the land of Bani Quraizah upon arrival after sunset. When they returned to the Prophet they reported the incident to him and he told them that both the groups had understood correctly what he actually meant and had acted according to his command.[20]

Ibn Al-Qayyim, the famous Hanbali jurist, commenting on this tradition says that those who performed the prayer before sun-set were the ancestors of the legal pragmatists i.e., advocates of opinion [*ra'y*], and those who insisted on doing the prayer in the land of Bani Quraizah were the ancestors of the literalists, the advocates of the *Zahiriyyah* school of thought. In this way we get the glimpse of the manifestation of personal opinions of the early Muslims right during the time of the Prophet. In some cases, the Prophet encouraged them to think for themselves on their various worldly matter saying: "You know the affairs of your world better". This effort to arrive at certain decisions to achieve the desired aim is called *ijtihad*. Hence, we shall now examine what *ijtihad* really means.

Ijtihad literally means exerting oneself in an attempt to realize a desired objective. In Islamic parlor, *ijtihad* means the use of individual reasoning, i.e., exerting oneself in order to reach a legal decision on matters not explicitly defined or catered for in the *Qur'an* or in the *Sunnah*. In other words, *ijtihad* is an exhaustive attempt made by a jurist [*al-mujtahid*] to reach a legal decision on issues affecting the given community, and which are not clearly decided either in the *Qur'an* or in the *Sunnah* of the Prophet.

However, it must be clearly understood that *ijtihad* draws on the *Qur'an*, the *hadith* and *al-ijma*. Since *ijtihad* means exerting oneself in order to formulate a legal opinion on issues not explicitly defined in *nass* (the text of the *Qur'an* and *Sunnah*), its connection with the principles of Islamic jurisprudence [*usul al-fiqh*] should be seen in terms of compatibility with and conformity to these principles [*usul*]. In other words *ijtihad* must not contradict nass. In principle, *ijtihad*, cannot come up with an activity which is contrary to the direct text of the *Qur'an* and *Sunnah* [*la ijtihad fi muqabalat al-nass*]. It could only be by ignoring the essence of Islam that an *ijtihad* could be developed which would be in contradiction to the direct text.

Taking the above definition of *ijtihad* into consideration, it becomes quite clear that the term *qiyas*, which is very much used in the writings of the sunni *fuqaha*, though slightly different, sometimes can be used to refer to *ijtihad*. The *fuqaha* of all the schools of *fiqh* agree that in all matters which have not been provided for by the *Qur'an* and the *Sunnah*, or which are not determined by the consensus of opinion [*ijma'*], the law may be deduced from what has been laid down in the *Qur'an*, *Sunnah* and *ijma* by the use of *qiyas* (analogical deduction).

The root meaning of the word *qiyas* is "measuring", "accord", "example", and "equal". The famous Imri'u al-Qais was well known for his extensive use of reason and analogical deduction [*li i'tibar al-umur bi ra'yihi*]. *Qiyas* has been defined by Sadr al-Shari'ah ibn Mas'ud as well as the *Hanafi* school as "an extension of law from the original text to which the process is applied to a particular case by means of a common *'illah* (cause) which cannot be ascertained merely by interpretation of the language of the text."[21] To the *Maliki* school *qiyas* is "the accord of a deduction with the original text in respect of the *'illah* or effective cause of its law".[22] In the Shafi'i school, it is regarded as "the accord of a known thing with a known thing by reason of the equality of the one with the other in respect of the effective cause of its law". Hence, in the words of Imam Shafi'i, *qiyas* and *ijtihad* are two terms with the same meaning.[23]

The origin of *qiyas* is still a point of controversy in Islamic legal history. However a detailed study shows that there are parallels in Hellenic thought, particularly the similarities between *qiyas* and certain procedures in Roman juridical theory. There is also a strong possibility that certain principles of *qiyas* were very much influenced by the understanding of *qiyas* in Greek empiricist medicine. Early Arabic grammarians and scholars of linguistics also used these principles.

The function of *qiyas* or *ijtihad* is to discover *illah* (*ratio legis* of law) or efficient cause so that it may be extended to cases of similar nature. The *Qur'an* prohibits *khamr* (wine), and the *illah* for that prohibition is its intoxicating effect, hence prohibition will be extended to all such cases where this *illah* is found such as heroin, cocaine, marijuana, ecstasy, etc.

Ijtihad or *qiyas* is not always universal; instead, *ijtihad* is a method of coming up with something essentially from the sources of Islam to meet a circumstance which had not arisen before in a society. The decision about what to do is therefore, both locally inspired and locally valid. If the circumstance is universal, the issue is one of *ijma'* of the whole Muslim *ummah*, but if it is local, the issue is one of *ijtihad*. However, because it is local, the authority of the decision must only be considered equally local. Time and place limit decisions reached through *ijtihad*. The manifestation of a novel circumstance elicits a novel decision, based on the principles of Islam. Since one person's circumstance may be different from another, the *ijtihad* done by each person will be different and will reflect the time, place, and circumstances under which it is done.

The *ijtihad* of Malik, Abu Hanifah, Shafi'i, or Ahmad ibn Hanbal, therefore, is not binding on others even though all of them cultivated their decisions from the universal essence of Islam.

In this way, *ijtihad* must be seen as operating from the level of the universal essence of Islam to the level of locality and temporality. The opposite is impossible; one cannot make a local and temporary law part of Islam. The one without the other is impossible; one cannot create a decision from the challenge of a particular time and place without getting a decision based on justice and Islamic principles but on the most powerful, influential, and dominant force of that society. All man-made laws suffer from distortion through force, whether that force is the police and army, or "public opinion" or one of keeping up with the times. What people do not realize is that power can be easily made invisible, with the result that laws may appear very just on paper but totally unjust in practice.

Man-made laws reflect the power structures and channels in the society, and justice and truth and other concepts become defined and delimited by the most articulate and powerful sections of the same society. In great contrast to this state of affairs, Islam, as the revelation and tradition preserved by Allah Himself, must and should provide for justice under any circumstance, and also provide the means for liberation and felicity, even if this entails shaking the power channels of society.

Indeed, the early community did witness a tremendous power struggle in Makkah and even in Madinah, as the old order was swept aside for the initiation of justice in the area, which spread in the form of the *Shari'ah* throughout the Muslim world. In this way Islam became the perennial critic of the *status quo*, exhorting Muslims everywhere to bring their affairs under the guidance of Allah and refer matters to the Almighty Allah and His Messenger. Contrary to "fundamentalist" Islam, *Shari'ah* does not necessarily aim at imposing penal law, or establishing an "Islamic state", but it aims primarily at establishing a society (not government) based on equality, peace, justice, and unity. Madinah was an Islamic society long before it became an Islamic state with Islamic penal law. The criminal laws of Islam were revealed after a just and peaceful society had already been established at Madinah.

The Companions were clear in their acceptance of *qiyas* and *ijtihad*. The Caliph Umar directed Abu Musa al-Ash'ari saying, "know the similarities and weigh the cases against them using analogical reasoning."[24] The use of *qiyas*, however, is rejected by the *Imamiyyah* shi'ite and the followers of the External school [the *Zahiris*] such as Daud and Ibn Hazm. The majority of the sunni schools and the *Zaydiyyah* shi'ite have accepted the validity of *qiyas*.

In order to limit the abuse of *qiyas*, Maliki scholars insist that the mere identity of attributes without an identity of causes is not a sufficient ground for the application of *qiyas*. Imam Ahmad ibn Hanbal preferred even the evidence of a weak *hadith*, one without a clear and secure chain of transmission, to the use of *qiyas* or *ijtihad*. Other scholars distinguish between absolute and relative *qiyas*, rejecting the idea of absolute deduction [*qiyas al-mutlaq*].

Imam Daud al-Zahiri started out as a strong supporter of Imam Shafi'i, but later on he rejected the use of *qiyas*. It is not clear whether Imam Daud saw this to be a contradictory position, because he praised Imam Shafi'i effusively for his adherence to Prophetic tradition. However, he did write against *qiyas* in his book *Kitab ibtal al-taqlid* and *Ibtal al-qiyas*. His student, Ibn Hazm, also wrote against *qiyas* in his *al-Ihkam fi usul al-ahkam*.

Ijtihad and Ta'wil

Although similar for most of the part, the terms *qiyas*, *ijtihad* and *ta'wil* cover slightly a different phenomena. In order to understand this subtle difference between *qiyas* and *ta'wil*, we shall attempt to define *ta'wil*. *Ta'wil*, as we explained in chapter two, means "to reach a thing or come to the point", that is, to probe into the inner meaning of the text and discover its intent and purpose. Allamah Bazdawi in his "*usul*" describes *ta'wil* as the interpretation where the possibility of doubtful meaning is dispelled by recourse to some authority or proof.[25] *Ta'wil* is thus an extension of *ijtihad* and has an amazing capacity to cover the growing needs of society, for the text may be interpreted with reference to its words and the meaning implicit therein, its context and the *hadith* of the Prophet on the subject. In this way the text is open to useful interpretations to cope with the situation and to accommodate the various needs and transactions of the modern world. There is no doubt that the answers and solution to most problems will be found through this exercise. And if anything essential is not covered by such interpretation, the principle of *darurah* (the rule of necessity and need) will come into operation.

For any *ta'wil* to be sound, it must be supported by some proof. Hence, one must endeavor to understand not only the words occurring in the text and their meaning but also the circumstances under which the text came into existence. This requires that the reader must be knowledgeable enough to delve into the matter by examining all these aspects before doing *ta'wil*. Ibn Qayyim is of the view that *ta'wil* or interpretation by way of sound analogy is not the business of every person. Only those can do it who are well-grounded or firm in knowledge to which there is a reference in the *Qur'an* itself[26] and who have a deep insight into the main cause or the intention of the Law Giver.[27]

The importance of *ta'wil* may be imagined by the fact that the Prophet himself acted upon it and is said to have prayed to God to give the power of *ta'wil* to his companions. In the case of Abdullah ibn Abbas he prayed: "May Allah give him insight into the religion and instruct him in *ta'wil*."

Again, orientalist writers believe *ta'wil* is just baseless speculation inspired by factional strife. What they try to deny is that when the Companions talked about "their opinion" or exercising their reason, they never meant by it to imply groundless and secular kind of speculation. Instead, using one's reason was encouraged and seen as enjoined within the guidance of the divine revelation. Thus, using one's reason meant working from the essence of Islam; after learning much about Islam through their proximity to the Prophet and their knowledge of the *Qur'an*, they were able to take this grounding and foundation and develop relevant applications for any aspect of the direct text.

It was the common practice of the Companions that if the cause [*illah*] was apparent they immediately acted upon *qiyas tam* and resorted to *ta'wil* only when the cause was not apparent and tried to find out the inner meaning of the text, not according to their own judgement but having regard to the word and meaning of the text, its context and *hadith* of the Prophet available on the subject. We will see in the next few pages (our discussion on *ijtihad* in the period of Umar) how Umar observed the above principle in the interpretation of the Qur'anic Verse: "*Alms are only for the poor and the needy, and those who collect them and for those whose hearts are to be reconciled, and to free the captives and the debtors, and for the cause of Allah and the wayfarer, a duty imposed by*

Allah." Umar refused to give the *mu'allafat al-qulub.* The cause [*illah*] having ceased to exist the text was inapplicable. This is the case where the cause of law was not very clear but Umar argued his case with reference to the context. This has always been cited as one of the finest example of *ta'wil.*

According to some scholars, Umar's judgement was based on *hikmah* (act of wisdom) rather than *illah* (cause) and, therefore, *illah* must be dispensed within worldly affairs. Those who hold this view make a distinction between *illah* and *hikmah* whereas they are both inseparable. *Illah* is the ground of action. If the action is devoid of *hikmah* (wisdom or sound sense) it will amount to folly which cannot apply to the law of Allah, the all wise.

The above is the procedure, most appropriate and best calculated to accommodate the needs of society, preserving at the same time the stability and ideal form of law. Shafi'i, as one of the chief architect of jurisprudence, seems to have propounded his classical theory on the basis of the practice followed by these *Caliphs* and, indeed, it is the right procedure or else the unity of law and the uniformity of society would be undermined if analogy were to depend upon the free use of reason not guided by the aims and intent of law [*maqasid al-shari'ah*]. He recognized, in principle, only *qiyas tam* but he was not opposed to *ta'wil* based upon some clear guidance in the text or its context.

Al-Manat: Basis of *Ijtihad*

It may so happen that a new case may arise in which the legal provision may either be implicit or explicit. An implicit provision may either be in the form of general rules or in the form of permission derived from the absence of any prohibition. The need and method of legal reasoning, both depend on the nature of these provisions. In some cases *ijtihad* may continuously be needed, while in other cases it may not be necessary at all.[31] To justify the validity or invalidity of the new case it needs to be examined thoroughly. This justification is exercised by demonstrating the correspondence of the essential elements in the new case with the basis of the provision in the *nass.* These bases are called *manat.* Some scholars have tried to divide *ijtihad* in reference to these *manat.* Al-Shatib, a Maliki jurist has divided *manat* in the following four categories:

1. *Al-Manat Al-'Amm*: This *manat* is the general verification of basis of the rules of *Shari'ah*. In this case, the rule [*hukm*] in its legal precept [*mudrak*] is already established. The function of the *mujtahid* is to verify the application of these general bases in the subjects of law, but only in a general and universal sense.[32]

In other words the basis of the legal provisions are examined as far as they are applicable to all the *mukallafin* (Muslims upon whom laws are binding). Shatibi explains generality ['*amm*], to mean that this type concerns *anwa'* (species, types) of *mukallafin*, and not the *ashkhas* (persons, individuals).[33] It is called "general" to distinguish it from the second type of *ijtihad*, which is specific. Shatibi illustrates this point with the legal ruling that requires a witness to be *adl* (just). The general and broad meaning of *adl* is known, but to determine the characteristics and qualifications on the basis of which a witness can be typically described as *adil* is the function of a *mujtahid*. In order to evaluate this qualification in case of a particular witness *ijtihad* is required.[34] *Taqlid* cannot solve this problem, because this process of evaluation can never end. In this respect, every new case is unique in itself.[35] Furthermore, Islamic law does not pronounce its rulings to cover all particular cases individually. The rulings of law in Islam are general and abstract so that they can cover new and infinite cases that evolve in a constantly changing society.[36]

It is because of the above reasons that Shatibi regards this type of *ijtihad* as a continuous process. If one admits the discontinuity of this *ijtihad*, one makes the application and extension of the rules of *Shari'ah* impossible.[37] Human acts never happen in the abstract, they always happen concretely and as individual cases. If this type of *ijtihad* discontinues, the obligations of *Shari'ah* will exist only in a person's mind, and not in reality.[38]

2. *Al-Manat Al-Khass*: This *manat* is different from the first one, as it concerns *ashkhas* (individuals) of a rule. This is more detailed and particular. For this a *mujtahid* relies more on *taqwa* (piety) and *hikmah* (wisdom or inner reason).

3. *Tanqih Al-Manat*: The refinement of the basis of the rule. This *manat* concerns those cases where the proper qualification [*wasf*] is mentioned in the text of the ruling but in conjunction with another matter; the task of separating and refining this qualification is done by *ijtihad*.[39] Imam Shatibi says that this type of *manat* is not concerned

with the method of *qiyas*, but is rather a type of *tawil al-zawahir* (interpretation of the literal sense).[40] In a certain sense, it also belongs to what Shatibi calls *al-ijtihad bi al-istinbat* (reasoning by inference).[41]

4. *Takhrij Al-Manat*: Deduction on the basis of the rules – this type refers to the text of a ruling where *manat* are not mentioned. The *manat* are found through the process of *qiyas*. This method is, therefore, called *al-ijtihad al-qiyasi* or reasoning by analogical deduction.[42]

Shatibi is of the opinion that among these four categories the first is ever continuing, but the continuity of the other three is need based. The reasons for the continuity of the first type have already been noted. Shatibi explains the need of continuing the other three as follows:

> The new events which were not known in the past are very few, in proportion to those which have occurred in the past, because of the expansion of the body of rules due to the investigation and *ijtihad* of the preceding jurists. It is therefore possible to accept their decisions in the major part of *Shari'ah*.[43]

The Muslim jurists justified the need for *ijtihad* by arguing on the basis of *khilaf*. In other words, if the opinions of scholars differed on a certain point, the case was considered open for *ijtihad*. For Shatibi this implied *khilaf* in *Shari'ah*, which he vehemently rejected. He maintained that in its basis *Shari'ah* has unity; *khilaf* is neither intended to exist nor to perpetuate.[44] Hence *khilaf* in this technical sense is not sufficient to justify continuity of *ijtihad*.[45] What justifies *ijtihad* is the absence of rules to cover new cases.

It is essential for jurists to go deeper in investigating the circumstances in which he is doing *ijtihad*. He should start with *tahaqquq al-manat* (investigation of the basis of ruling) and second *tahakkum* (decision).[46] Shatibi explains that the method of deduction of conclusion in *ijtihad* is quite different from what is followed by logicians. The premises here do not mean the formulation of propositions in accordance with the figures [*ashkal*] of syllogism known in logic. Nor does *ijtihad* depend upon considerations of syllogism, such as *tanaqud* (contradiction) and *aks* (conversion). If there is found any similarity, it must not be confused with the technical terms of logicians.

The closest logical figures of syllogism to the method of *ijtihad* are *qiyas iqtiran* (syllogism by coupling or combining two propositions) or *istithnai* (syllogism by exclusion).[47] Shatibi quotes the Miliki jurist Abu al-Walid al-Baji (d. 1081) who rejected logicians' claims that there cannot be a conclusion without two premises, and, referring to *fiqh*, argued that it is possible to conclude from one premise only.[48]

It is in the light of this explanation that Shatibi rejects the requirement of a knowledge of the rules of logic for *Shari'ah* purpose,[49] whereas a knowledge of the Arabic language and that of the objectives of law is considered *sine quo non*. As for other sciences such as the science of readings of the *Qur'an*, or that of *hadith*, or *kalam* (dialectic scholasticism), they are not considered absolutely necessary. In fact, a *mujtahid* can justifiably accept the conclusions reached by these sciences as *muqaddimat* (premises or foundations) in *ijtihad*.[50]

The above analysis of *ijtihad* shows that Shatibi saw it as a processor of adapting the legal system to social changes. What distinguishes his treatment of *ijtihad* is his outlook as a jurist. He looks upon *ijtihad* as a necessary process, neither open to everyone nor at all times. It is exercised only when it is needed. *Ijtihad*, therefore, provides a change in Islamic legal theory.

The Development of *Ijtihad*

As already mentioned, neither the *Qur'an*, nor the *hadith* of the Prophet had given all necessary detailed information about law in Islam, thus such details had to come gradually and in accordance with the ever-changing socio-economic conditions under which the Muslim society evolved.

The use of *ijtihad* was not as widely practiced during the lifetime of the Prophet as was the case later. The revelation of the *Qur'an* was still continuing on the Prophet and thus the divine directives were coming to guide the *ummah*. Likewise, the guidance from the *Sunnah* of the Prophet was still available to the early Muslims, making things easy for them in all aspects of their lives. But, still the Prophet approved, and even encouraged the exercise of *ijtihad*. He was known to have approved of Mu'adh ibn Jabal, his *qadi* (judge) to Yemen, when he (Mu'adh) informed him that in case of inability to find solution in the *Qur'an* or in the *Sunnah*, he would have to exert himself to reach a decision based on his own opinion.[51] No doubt this endorsement of *ijtihad* by the Prophet had encouraged the Companions to exert themselves in finding solutions to issues not explicitly decided upon in the Holy *Qur'an* or the *Sunnah* of the Prophet.

Period of Abu Bakr

On the death of the Prophet in 632 A.C., Abu Bakr became the first Caliph. The principles of *ijtihad* and *ijma'*, that is the consensus of the opinion of the Muslim community, became an important practice during his *Caliphate*. Abu Bakr declared that he was not a Prophet of Allah and hence received no revelation. So, whenever a legal issue came up, where there was more than one opinion, he resorted to *ijma'*. He said in his first speech to a public gathering, "I am an ordinary human being. If you see that I am on the right path, follow me, but if I am on the wrong path correct me." Thus, it was necessary to consult the community and arrive at their consensus of opinion. It is narrated in the *Musnad Darimi* that whenever any case came up in the court of Abu Bakr, first he referred to the *Qur'an* and adjudicated according to its injunctions. Otherwise, he would fall back on the *Sunnah* of the Prophet. If he found difficulty in arriving at a decision on the basis of the *Sunnah*, then he would consult Muslims around him. He was very cautious in the application of analogical deduction in any matter concerning juristic opinion. This is the reason why he depended on other Companions to give their opinion based on the *Sunnah* of the Prophet.

Thus, during the early period of Islam, especially the period of the four *Caliphs* and their immediate successors, *ijtihad* was widely used. The *Caliphs* and the Companions were known to have taken many important decisions on matters affecting the welfare of their community – either by means of personal reasoning or through *shura* (consultation) among themselves. Among the unprecedented decisions taken by the use of *ijtihad* was the settlement of the problem of apostasy [*al-ridda*][54]; as well as the collection of the *Qur'an* and its later standardization.[55] One of the most important juristic decisions that Abu Bakr gave and which was based on *qiyas* was in respect to the law of inheritance. If one died leaving behind a grandfather or a brother and a sister, who would inherit the estate in the absence of the father and the children, should it be the grandfather or brother and sister? Abu Bakr consulted other Companions and gave his decision based on the *ijma'* of fourteen Companions, which included Abdullah ibn Abbas and Abu Musa al-Ashari, saying that the grandfather will step in for the deceased father, and thus the brother and sister as lawful inheritors. It was this kind of difference of opinion about which Umar once said: "I wish there were Prophetic precepts in respect of the inheritance of *kalalah*." Abu Bakr based his opinion on the interpretation of verse three in chapter *al-nisa*. Since there was no clear explanation in respect of the father in verse twenty-four of the same chapter, Abu Bakr opines that in the matter of *kalalah*[56] it is not only that the father is dead before *kalalah* inherits, but even the grandfather should be dead before giving the right of inheritance to the *kalalah*. Verse three of chapter *al-nisa* mentions clearly the brother and sister and there is the clear indication that if the deceased leaves behind a father or grandfather, the law of *kalalah* will not operate.[57]

Period of Umar

After the death of the first Caliph Abu Bakr, Umar, his successor, continued the effort to spread the knowledge of *Qur'an*, *sunnah* and *fiqh*. In order to encourage this learning, Caliph Umar fixed stipends and remuneration for the teachers and *huffaz* of the *Qur'an* (those engaged in the memorization of the *Qur'an*). Umar also sent some companions of the Prophet, such as Ubadah ibn al-Samit, Muadh ibn Jabal and Abu Darda, who had also memorized the *Qur'an*, to Syria to teach the *Qur'an*. Umar's effort increased the number of *huffaz* into thousands; at one point Abu Musa al-Ash'ari wrote saying that he had three hundred *huffaz* in his army.[58] Likewise, to spread the knowledge of *Sunnah* he made various copies of the Prophetic *hadith* and sent them to his governors. Scholars of *hadith* like Abdullah ibn Mas'ud were sent to Kufah with a group of scholars to teach *hadith*. He also sent Umar ibn Hasin and Ma'qal ibn Yasar to Basrah, and Abu Darda to Syria for the same purpose. All these great scholars of *Qur'an* and *Sunnah* were approached by people in different areas to seek juristic opinion on various aspects of life and daily living.

In order to find the authentic sources of the narration of *hadith*, Umar also adopted a very strict approach towards those who reported *hadith* without producing other Companions as witnesses for their narrations. When Mughirah narrated a *hadith* concerning the laws of pregnancy, Umar demanded a witness among the Companions, and he accepted it only when Muhammad ibn Maslamah ascertained its authenticity. After being satisfied he said, 'I did not disbelieve you, all that I wanted to do was to satisfy myself regarding its authenticity.'[59]

Umar also used to discuss important juristic points in his Friday sermons and used to send his governors of the provinces various newly recorded juristic problems and their solutions which had come about due to the spread of Islam in far away places. In the appointments of the government functionaries and officials in various provinces and districts, Umar made sure that the *fuqaha* (jurists) were also included among them. Some jurists were appointed purposely to be sent to newly occupied lands to teach theology and jurisprudence. The jurists and teachers were highly paid in the time of Umar.[60]

During his Caliphate, Umar used *ijtihad* so much so that he would at times seem to be going against the direct text of the *Qur'an*. There is a famous incident mentioned by scholars regarding Umar's *ijtihad*. It was the practice of the Prophet to give alms to the former enemies of Islam who were converted *en masse* after the conquest of Makkah as an appeasement act. This was done after a verse had been revealed ordering the Prophet to give them a special portion from the *zakah* even though most of them were very wealthy: *"The alms are only for the poor and the needy, and those who collect them, and those whose hearts are to be reconciled [al-mu'allafat qulubuhu]."* (9: 60) This practice was carried over by Abu Bakr during his reign but when it was Umar's period he refused to give them anything saying, "we are a people whom Allah has honored and empowered with Islam (Islam is no longer in need of your moral support, you either enter into Islam unconditionally or you are free to remain as non-Muslims)"[61] Umar's argument was that the cause and reason [*illat al-hukm*] of the decision to grant them alms in the initial stage was the need to win their moral support at a time when Islam was still weak, and since this reason and need no longer existed in his time, he gave a ruling against the practice of giving alms to non-believers. The *ijtihad* of Umar emphasized on what became known in Islamic law as *illat al-hukm* (cause and reason for a law to be passed). It became a principle in Islamic law that *al-hukm yadur ma'a al-illah adaman wa wujudan, ibahatan wa haraman* (the law is subject to, or will always be attached to the cause and reason. At times when the cause and reason no longer exist, the law will also cease to exist).

After understanding this general principle, it becomes easy to interpret law in Islam. For instance, what was the cause and reason for deciding to grant women less the share of men in the inheritance laws of Islam mentioned in the *Qur'an*? Does the cause and reason [*illah*] still exist? If it does, we will have to continue giving them less, and if it has ceased to exist, we will have to re-interpret the verses of inheritance laws.

Likewise, in the period of Umar, Dhahak ibn Khalifa complained that he requested his neighbor Muhammad ibn Maslamah to allow a water passage to flow through his field, but Muhammad ibn Maslamah refused. Umar too called him and pleaded on his behalf but he again refused. Since, there was no harm, in allowing water to flow from his land and that he too would benefit out of it and there would accrue no harm to his land, Umar ordered that water passage be dug. There was no direct text available but he gave an *ijtihad* verdict acting on the *hadith* "*la darar wala dirar fi al-islam*" (there shall be no harm of the self nor of others allowed in Islam). If there was no harm done to either party, such a provision is allowed in Islam. This verdict was given on the basis of *maslahah* (public interest).[62]

Likewise, if one gave triple divorce to one's wife, Umar considered it as a final divorce in order to stop further occurrence of such divorce by way of *sadd al-dari'ah* (deterrent measure), contrary to the practice of the Prophet and Abu Bakr who regarded triple divorce as a single divorce.[63] If a man married a woman in *iddah* (period of retreat), Umar revoked the marriage, and by way of punishment he did not allow this type of marriage between them, throughout their life.[64] These decisions were basically taken on the grounds that they served the best interest of the community, which was a prime objective of Islamic Law. Thus, in the absence of the textual assertion [*nass*], the *Caliphs* and the Companions felt obliged to use *ijtihad* as the only means left for them to establish a just and orderly society. By this exercise, they had set a precedent for future generations to follow.

Period of 'Uthman

Juristic procedure based on *ijtihad* continued during the Caliphate of Uthman. They are recorded in the books of *hadith* and jurisprudence. One of Uthman's juristic decisions was in respect of Hurmuzan ibn Ubaid Allah ibn Umar in a murder case. Uthman said that if any deceased person had not left any heir behind, the ruler would step in as his guardian. Since Hurmuzan had no heir, Caliph Uthman accepted *diyyah* (blood money, compensation) in place of *qisas* (death penalty) as the guardian of Hurmuzan. In this case he gave the amount of *diyyah* from his personal property to the *baitu-al-mal* (public treasury). His predecessors had already facilitated the mode of payment of *diyyah*, but Uthman said that one could give its value rather than camel if one wished to do so.[65] There were many points in which he in his juristic views where he differed with his predecessors and other Companions but that was seen as part of the process of *ijtihad*.

Uthman considered marriage as unlawful if it was contracted by any person who was in the state of *ihram* while performing *hajj* or *umrah*.[66] Ali differed from him on this issue. Another judgement of Uthman which was contradicted by Ali was regarding the inheritance of a divorced woman who was still observing the period of retreat [*iddah*], he argued that some sort of relationship still continued between the divorced woman and her late husband even though it was a final divorce [*bain*] When some people objected to some of his differences of opinion in juristic matters and to what they saw as a constant departure from tradition, Uthman explained himself saying:

> By Allah we had the opportunity to be in the company of the prophet while on his journey. When we fell sick, he used to look after us; when some of us died, we used to walk together behind the bier; when we went for *Jihad*, we were his Companions; when we were destitute, he shared whatever he had with us. Alas, today, the people who try to point out his *Sunnah* to us, are those who have not seen even his face.[67]

The greatest mastery that Uthman possessed was in the field of the law of inheritance. Since Uthman was a successful businessman before he took over the Caliphate, he was very good in mathematical calculations. Therefore, he gave a great contribution along with the Prophet and other scholarly companions like Ali, and Zaid ibn Thabit in the calculations of the shares of inheritance. Even in the early Caliphate of Abu Bakr and Umar, the cases of inheritance were referred to either Ali or Uthman who solved difficult problems in the light of the *Qur'an* and *Sunnah*. Some people were even afraid that perhaps, after the death of scholars like Uthman, Ali, and Zaid, the knowledge of *mirath* (law of inheritance) would become poorer.[68]

Another important task that was fulfilled during the Caliphate of Uthman was the preparation of the standard copy of the Holy *Qur'an*. He made great effort in compiling and preserving the *Qur'an*, leaving the task of the *Sunnah* to be attended to non-officially, i.e., by the individual Companions. The first copy of *Qur'an* was made at the advice of Umar during the Caliphate of Abu Bakr. This copy was afterwards revised and reproduced by a four-man commission headed by Zaid ibn Thabit, appointed by the Caliph Uthman. The new version was read in the mosque, approved unanimously by all the Companions who were present at that time. Several authentic copies were made and sent to the main mosques in the capitals of the provinces. All this was achieved through the *ijtihad* of the *Caliphs*.

Period of 'Ali

Caliph Ali's contribution to the development of Islamic jurisprudence is well documented.[69] He spent his years of the Caliphate in Kufah where he gave a number of juristic decisions. This is the reason why most of his decisions are incorporated in the Hanafi School of *fiqh* which developed in Kufah.

During the time of the Prophet, Ali gave two judgements in Yemen. Islam had just penetrated there and people still continued to follow old customs and traditions. In the first case a woman had sexual relations with three different persons in one month. After nine months, a child was born to her. A dispute arose between the three men as to who should get the custody of the boy. Ali decided the case as that of *diyyah*, and drew a lottery in the name of the three claimants. The child was given to the man whose name was picked in the lottery. Then, Ali asked him to give the other two claimants the amount of *diyyah* to be divided by them. In other words, the case was decided on the basis of *qiyas* and the boy was treated as a slave child. The child now became the full-fledged son of the person to whom the custody was given while the other two were compensated. When the Prophet heard of Ali's judgement, he smiled and approved it.[70]

In another case, some people had dug a deep ditch in order to capture a lion. When the lion fell into it some people collected near the ditch to see the lion. They started playing a sort of practical joke with one of their friends and took him close to the ditch. Unfortunately, one of them slipped and while falling into the ditch, he unintentionally, caught the hand of another man in order to save himself. While the second man was being pulled into the ditch, he held tight the loin of the third man and the third man tightly held the fourth of them. Eventually, all the four fell into the ditch and the lion killed them all. Their families started quarreling with one another over the incident. Ali pacified them by saying that it was improper to enter into bloodshed in the lifetime of the Prophet. He volunteered to decide the matter between them and told them that if they were not satisfied with his verdict, they were free to go to the Prophet. The people agreed, Ali decided the case by saying that those who were instrumental in digging the ditch in order to capture the lion should pay the *diyyah* in the following order: the heir of the first deceased should be given one third; those of the third deceased should be given half while the heirs of the fourth deceased should be given full amount of *diyyah* for settlement. The heir of the first deceased was given one-fourth share because the incident ranged between culpable homicide and murder and the decision was given on the basis of intention on the part of each deceased. The case in which there was the least intentional pulling of the person into the ditch was given the smallest share of *diyyah*. Where the intention was greater, the greater amount was awarded. A little more increasing degree of intention can be found in the other three persons who dragged each other into the ditch. Then, the case was decided on the basis of *mirath*, law of inheritance. Although there were four persons involved in the incident, the least amount that can go to one of them was one-fourth. When one-fourth was given to the first deceased, the remaining two were allowed half each of the remaining amount. Who should pay the amount of *diyyah* was the next question. The crime was committed by those who dug the ditch near a residential area in order to catch the lion. Since no definite people could be found out of the residents who were responsible in digging the ditch, the *diyyah* was imposed collectively on all the residents. An appeal against Ali's judgement was taken to the Prophet during his farewell pilgrimage [*hajj al-wada*]. But the Prophet, after reviewing the case, confirmed Ali's judgement.[71]

There is yet another interesting judgement given by Ali. Two persons were going on a journey. One carried three loaves of bread and the other carried five loaves of bread. When they sat to eat together a third traveller came there. He was invited to join the meal. When they finished the meal the guest took eight dirhams out of his pocket and gave them to the two hosts as the price for the food and went away. The owner of five loaves thought that he should retain five dirhams. Therefore, he gave the three dirhams to the owner of three loaves of bread. But the latter was not happy and demanded that he be given four dirhams. When the case was brought to Ali, he advised the latter to accept the three dirhams that his friend was giving him. But the latter insisted that strict justice must be done in the case. Thereupon, Ali decided that he should be given only one dirham and his friend should retain seven dirhams. He explained the decision as follows: Since there were eight loaves in all and three persons ate them, it meant that the eight loaves were divided into twenty-four pieces and everyone took eight pieces. Now, the man with five loaves supplied fifteen pieces but ate only eight pieces, thus leaving seven pieces for the guest and the man with three loaves supplied nine pieces but ate eight pieces, thus leaving only one piece for the guest. As the guest had given eight dirhams for the eight pieces he consumed, the man who supplied one piece, in all fairness of logic should receive only one dirham whereas, the man who supplied seven pieces was entitled to seven dirhams.[72]

Apart from these decisions, based on individual *ijtihad*, it is reported that the *Caliphs* used to consult other Companions whenever they felt unable to find solution in the *Qur'an* or the *Sunnah*. The likes of Abdullah ibn Mas'ud, Abu Musa al-Asha'ri, Mu'adh ibn Jabal, Ubayy ibn Ka'ab, Um Darda, and Zaid ibn Thabit were present around them. The decision reached through these consultations was accepted and considered as a form of consensus [*ijma'*] to be respected by the coming generations as long as it served the interest of their communities. The other Companions continued this practice.[73] Thus, being guided by the spirit of Islamic law which is to facilitate and not to complicate, "*Allah desires ease for you and He desires not hardship for you.*" (*Qur'an* 2: 185), the Companions and the immediate generation that followed them [*tabi'un*] exerted great effort in the attempts to find the best solutions to problems encountered by their communities.

The period of the four *Caliphs* covered the thirty years that followed the death of the Prophet, the companions of the Prophet, under the leadership of the Rashidun Caliphs, took the responsibility, of propagating, defending the religion, reinforcing the Muslim state's control all over

Arabia and extending its boundaries beyond the Arab land.

The *Caliphs* who took the place of the Prophet as heads of the state having all legislative, judicial and executive powers, found themselves confronted with new problems coming from Arabia as well as from the newly conquered provinces previously under the control of the Byzantine and the Persians about which the *nass*, i.e., *Qur'an* and *Sunnah*, were either silent or not clear. The Companions of the Prophet were in agreement that reference should be made first to the *Qur'an*, then to the *Sunnah*, and finally their own opinions based on reason. In major issues, the *Caliphs*, who usually gave reference to communal decision, used to hear the opinion of the other Companions in open meetings especially in Madinah, the seat of the Caliphate.

Following this procedure, the Companions thus agreed on several points. Those agreements, taken in the light of the Qur'anic verses ordering the Muslims to keep together and avoid divergence; and in view of the traditions of the Prophet as well as reports from his Companions assuring the infallibility of the Muslim Community as a whole, were considered binding on the generations to follow; therefore the agreement of the Companions was given the name of *ijma'* (i.e., consensus of opinion) which took the third place in the list of the sources of Islamic law. On the other hand, the Companions of the Prophet also differed in several issues. These differences constituted good grounds for the emergence of different schools of law.

Although the Companions never differed about the *Qur'an*, and *Sunnah* as the main sources of law, due to the absence of the Prophet and the termination of the revelation, the differences of opinion could no longer be prevented. From then on, agreement and disagreement featured in the Islamic Jurisprudence.

The Companions were in complete agreement about the authenticity of the Qur'anic text as the word of Allah and the primary source of the religion. Therefore, they only differed in the interpretation of some verses. The *Sunnah* unlike the *Qur'an*, was not a limited collection of authorities, and although some of the Companions at that time were having their own personal compilations of traditions, the bulk of the *Sunnah* remained as reminiscences (in the minds of the Companions) that were usually recalled and narrated whenever they were needed or asked about.

None of the Companions of the Prophet was continuously accompanying him and none of them could give (or claimed to have) full account of his sayings (explanations, orders, addresses, judgements, advises, etc.), deeds (private and public) or his approvals to the official and non-official practices. It could be said that "lack of knowledge" was one of the reasons behind the differences. The four *Caliphs* and the eminent Companions in more than one occasion invited the others to tell what they had heard from the Prophet in relation to a specific issue. And, in many cases, decisions, judgements or opinions were altered because of the *Sunnah* thus obtained. But lack of knowledge of *Sunnah* was not always the reason why differences arose; it was also the lack of authentic *Sunnah*. This is especially true where there is an apparent conflict between a Qur'anic rule and the *Sunnah* narrated on the same issue. It should be mentioned here that by adopting a "consultative approach" in making policies, rules or decisions, the *Caliphs* and their governors and judges reduced to the minimum the legal differences among the Muslim community without depriving the individuals of the freedom for personal opinion or personal practice.

Umayyad Period

The jurists of this period were mainly the young Companions like Abdullah ibn Abbas, Abdullah ibn Umar, Aishah and the successors [*tabi'un*]. Besides some theological differences and the political split in Muslim community, this period could be correctly described as the period of the methodological and scholastic differences among the Muslim scholars concerning (modes and means of receiving and transmitting knowledge, as well as sources and methods of interpretation and deduction of rules). This period is also known as the period of *sighar al-sahabah* (young Companions) which begun in the time of the Caliphate of Mu'awiyyah in the year 41 A.H. and lasted up to the beginning of the second century of *hijrah*.

From the days of the Prophet, till this period, many of the elders and youngsters had been appointed either as governors, judges, teachers, or travelled as visitors or immigrants and had the opportunity to stay in one part or another of the Muslim State. A new generation of the *tabi'un* i.e., those who did not see the Prophet but had met his Companions and who were eager to know as much as they could about him, gathered around

111

the learned Companions of their area receiving the *Sunnah* of the Prophet from them. It was also during this period that the opinions and judgements of the four *Caliphs* and the elder Companions were compiled. Many prominent jurists appeared in the big Muslim towns. Sa'id ibn al-Musayyib, Salim ibn Abdullah ibn Umar followed by Zuhri. Yahya ibn Sa'id and Rabi'ah ibn Abd al-Rahman were some of the great scholars of Madinah. Ata was a famous learned scholar of Makkah, Ibrahim al-Nakha'i and Sha'bi were the great jurists in Kufah, al Hasan al-Basri was famous in Basrah, while Taus and Makhul were highly respected in Yemen and Sham (part of Syria).

Two different jurisprudential approaches dominated the early Islamic society of this period. The first was the *ahl al-hadith* (traditionist) approach represented by the jurists of Madinah. Like Ibn Musayyib, Sa'id and others inherited not only the traditions but also the "spirit of the Companions" in restricting themselves to practical issues. They refrained from answering hypothetical questions and relied mostly on the "received knowledge" i.e., the *hadith* of the Prophet and the opinions and judgements of the Companions, especially those opinions which were enforced as rules or adopted as policies during the era of Abu Bakr, Umar, Uthman, and Ali.

The second approach was that of the scholars of Iraq (that is Kufah), the *ahl al-fiqh* (legal pragmatists), who are at times referred to as the jurists of Kufah. It comprised of scholars like Ibrahim al-Nakha'i and others who used *ra'y* (i.e., opinion) or *aql* (reason) very often, and were also ready to join theoretical discussions and answer hypothetical questions. But we ought to remember that counter attitudes were also found in both regions. Rabi'ah ibn Abd al Rahman was in a way a rationalist of Madinah, while Al Sha'bi was the traditionist of Kufah in Iraq. These two attitudes adopted by Sa'id ibn al Musayyib and his successors in Madinah, and Ibrahim al-Nakha'i and his successors in kufah are referred to as 'the ancient schools of *fiqh*'.

In this era, in addition to the *Qur'an* and the *Sunnah* as the main sources of law, the opinions which were dominantly accepted by the Companions or generally adopted during the era of the four *Caliphs*, were accepted as binding authority and the opinions of the Companions generally were preferred to *ijtihad*. Accordingly, the school of Madinah was said to be based on the opinions of Abdullah ibn Umar, Abdullah ibn

Abbas and Aishah while that of Kufah was thought to be based on the opinions of Abdullah ibn Mas'ud, Ali and Shuraih – the famous judge. However, each of the prominent jurists at this stage was an Imam in his own right.

This period, beginning from the second century till the fourth century, is also known as the period of *tabi'un* and the *a'immah mujtahidun*. The great *tabi'un* of this period include Abu Jafar Muhammad ibn Ali ibn Husain known as Imam Baqir Sadiq, Ali ibn Husain ibn Ali, Said ibn Musayyib, Urwah ibn zubair, Abu Bakr ibn Abd al-Rahman, Ubayd-Allah ibn Abdullah, Salim ibn Abdullah ibn Usman, Sulaiman ibn Yasar, Qasim ibn Muhammad ibn Abi Bakr, Nafi, the servant of Abdullah ibn Umar, Muhammad ibn Muslim who is well known, Ibn Shihab al-Zuhri, Yahya ibn Said al-Ansari, Mujahid, Ikramah, Ata ibn Abi Rabah, Alwamali, the pupil of Abdullah ibn Masud who was known for giving *fatawa* on various *fiqh* issues. The great work done during this period is the compilation of *Sunnah* and deduction based on the *Sunnah* of the Prophet.

Abbasid Period

Though *ijtihad* was an accepted method of arriving at legal decisions on matters affecting the welfare of the Muslim Community, the Muslim jurists of this period were not unanimous in using it as a legitimate means to reach legal decisions. While some used *ijtihad* more freely, others either rejected it or used it only in a very restricted sense.[74] During the early period of Islam, the decisions reached by *al-mujtahidun* (those who exercised *ijtihad*) were mostly in the form of *fatwa* (legal opinions) given as answers to questions raised by some individuals. There was no attempt at this time, to write these *fatwas* down or to systematize them. That was done during the formative period, that is the period of the foundation of the schools of law [*al-madhahib-al-fiqhiyah*]. In this period *ijtihad* was widely used, and decisions reached by the great jurists were collected to form the basic doctrine of these schools.

This marked the beginning of the systematization of the schools of *fiqh*. This development took place between the early second century and the fourth century to the *hijrah*. The period was characterized by the vast expansion of Islamic learning throughout the Muslim world, the collection and the systematization of *hadith*, the emergence of the

Imams or the founders of the schools of *fiqh*, such as Abu Jafar Muhammad ibn Ali ibn Husain known as Imam Baqir the founder of *ja'fari fiqh* and one of the teachers of Abu Hanifah the founder of the Hanafi school, Malik ibn Anas, the founder of the Maliki school, Muhammad ibn Idriss al-Shafi'i of the Shafi'i school, and Ahmad ibn Hanbal, the founder of the *Hanbali* school. Among the learned jurists of this period were those subscribing to the school of *ahl al-hadith* or the *Zahiri* school which based judgements exclusively on the text and would not pass judgement unless there was a text supporting it. Then there were also those who belonged to the *ahl al-ra'y* or *ahl al-qiyas* who conceived *Shari'ah* as a subject of rational thinking, which they believed must operate under general principles based on the *Qur'an* and the *Sunnah*. And to these principles [*usul*] they related all issues which might evolve in the absence of the *nass* and they never hesitated to use *ijtihad* in order to reach a legal solution.

In the exercise of personal reasoning, these people never hesitated whenever they saw something they considered as good and in conformity with the spirit of *Shari'ah* to make use of it. This was called *istihsan* and *masalih al-mursalah*. According to them, whatever was considered good [*hasan*] by the Muslim community must also be good to Allah, the Law-Giver. The purpose of using *al-istihsan* and *al-masalih* seems to have originated from the belief that literary dependence on the *nass* may lead sometimes to deviation from the spirit of the law, which is to make things easy and not to complicate them. This was the reason why the use of *ijtihad* was an accepted principle during the early period of Islam. Caliph Umar ibn al-Khattab and Abdullah ibn Abbas and many other Companions became known as belonging to *ahl al-ra'y*. During the formative period, the writings of al-Shafi'i were the best defense of *ra'y*. The position of the *Zahiris* (literalists) or at times known as *ahl al-hadith* which was represented by the writings of Daud ibn Ali, the leader of the *Zahiri* school which was founded in the middle of the third century does not seem to have gained many supporters among the Muslim scholars. This period was characterized by the emergence of distinguished jurists who made systematic studies of the *Qur'an* and the *hadith* and at the same time they systematized *fiqh*, *qiyas* and *ijtihad*. In the later period, their disciples devoted themselves to organizing legal theories and opinions from the materials handed down to them by their masters. These disciples included the Imams of the four Sunni schools of *fiqh*.

Opening or re-opening of the Gate of *Ijtihad*

In order for us to re-open the doors of *ijtihad* today, we need to reintro-
duce the role of *aql* (reason) and *hissiyat* (senses) as sources of knowledge in Islam along with revelation. We also need to thoroughly study
the social sciences. The dichotomy that exists between the rational,
empirical, and religious sciences needs to be removed. One of the major
problems inherent in contemporary Islamic epistemological thought is the
belief that some types of knowledge are harmful to human beings. Islam
actually does not consider any type of knowledge as harmful. However,
what has been called useless or harmful in the *Qur'an* consist of *pseudo-
sciences* or the lores prevalent in the pre-Islamic period. Islam never
maintained that only theology was useful and empirical and rational
sciences useless or harmful. This concept was made common by the
semi-literate clerics or by the time-server among them who wanted to
keep common Muslims in blind faith so that they would not be able to
oppose unjust rulers and resist clerics attached to the courts of tyrants.
This attitude resulted in the condemnation of science that led to the
decline of Muslims in politics, economics, and technology.

It gave birth to movements which considered elementary books of
theology as sufficient for a Muslim, and discouraged the assimilation or
dissemination of empirical knowledge as leading to the weakening of
faith. The conflict between faith and science only arises when science has
been transformed into a religion; in other words, when it has acquired a
sort of positivistic religion, or at least, philosophy, of its own, and has
transgressed the true form and definition of modern science.

What is known today as modern science, and because of its close
association with Western thought since the Enlightenment, is a science
armed with, or immersed in, a completely materialistic world-view. This
science has allowed itself to transgress its legitimate boundaries, and
whereas it was originally meant to be applied solely to the material world,
it has given itself the authority to pass judgement on every conceivable
subject. And since it is unable to ascertain either truth or the falsehood of
propositions concerning matters within the extrasensory or supernatural
realm, it denies the very existence of such worlds. The blame for this
opposition to, or better to say, denial of the existence of, a world inacces-

sible to the human sense organs lays far more upon the shoulders of materialistic scientists than upon those of experimental science *per se*. Undoubtedly, the science practiced by such persons, burdened by a particular set of intellectual shortcomings and prejudices, would be entirely antithetical to belief in the existence of a spiritual world and a supernatural divine entity; an entity which, obviously cannot be subjected to ordinary scientific investigation.

Exercise of the intellect [*aql*] is of significance in the entire Islamic literature and it played an important role in the development of all kinds of knowledge, scientific or otherwise, in the Muslim world. *Ijtihad* is a dynamic principle in the body of Islam. Much before Francis Bacon, the principles of scientific induction were emphasized by the *Qur'an*, which highlights the importance of observation and experimentation in arriving at certain conclusions. It may also be pointed out that Muslim jurists and exegetes made use of the method of linguistic analysis in interpreting the Qur'anic injunctions and the Prophetic tradition. Al-Ghazali was probably the first Muslim philosopher to make use of the linguistic analytical method to clarify certain legal, theological, and philosophical issues. There are even those who feel that he was maligned than properly understood by both the orthodox and liberal Muslim interpreters of his legal and philosophical thought. We also see that his method of pessimism paved the way for intellectual activities in the Muslim world, but because of historical and social circumstances, it culminated in the stagnation of philosophical and scientific thinking, which later made him a target of criticism by philosophers and other theologians.

Moreover, the gate of *ijtihad* was never closed by the nass, nor by the Companions, *tabi'un or tab'-tabi'un*. Therefore, the call for re-opening of the gate of *ijtihad* may sound out of place. It is a well known fact that the Companions and the majority of scholars during the formative period of Islamic law, including the founders of the schools of law, never put restriction on the use of *al-ijtihad* as those put later by medieval scholars. But whether the absolute *ijtihad* should be extended beyond the formative period of Islamic law, has been a matter of disagreement among the scholars. In fact, the Shafi'i jurists and the majority of the Hanafi scholars did call for the extension of *ijtihad al-mutlaq* to all Muslims. And although the *Malikis* are not in favor of extending *ijtihad al-mutlaq* beyond the formative period, they nevertheless, allowed the restricted *ijtihad* [*ijtihad al-muqayyad*] to function within the framework of the established schools of law. *Ijtihad* in fact is the vehicle for the development of Islamic law. It was through the continuous use of *ijtihad* that the schools of *fiqh* were founded; indeed, *ijtihad* itself in the form of *al-qiyas,* has been gradually recognized as the fourth principle of Islamic jurisprudence. As already mentioned, apart from the *Qur'an* and the *Sunnah,* the two most important principles of law *ijma* and *al-qiyas* evolved out of the exercise of *ijtihad.*

However, our approach to *ijtihad* and *qiyas* today must be universal and holistic. We need to acknowledge that the traditional *qiyas,* with its emphasis on a specific ratio legis of law [*illah*] derived from a specific verse or *hadith* is becoming increasingly lacking in coping with the infinite cases that may not have a specific asl (original case) in the *Qur'an* and *Sunnah.* Moreover, the conditions and restrictions put down on *qiyas* by Muslim jurists are all inherited from the rules of *qiyas* as understood in Greek empiricist medicine. What we need, therefore, is a universal *qiyas* where we study the text of the *Qur'an* and *Sunnah* in order to derive a general theme which will become our *asl* (original case). This general theme will be applied in answering any novel cases. This approach will not be much different from Umar ibn al-Khattab's methodology which was based on *aql,* general public interest as well as the aims of *Shari'ah* [*maqasid*]. Our *qiyas* should, *inter alia,* focus on the *masalih al-mursala* (public interest) as the determining factor in all legal decisions.

New *ijtihad* will revivify the Islamic legal system which has become too theoretical and pedantic, for instance we see how this kind of *fiqh* today rules that a marriage or business contract will not be considered valid if specific words or formulas are not used during the contract. Similarly the laws of *zakah* will only be applicable on the money that has reached "a specific" amount [*nisab*], and only after a "specific period" of time [*hawlan al-hawl*]. Only after these conditions are found will one be expected to pay "a specific amount" (two and half percent of the money). If the money is a penny less upon approaching the period, one may not pay the *zakah.* This has led to people evading paying the *zakah* by means of what is known in Hanafi *fiqh* as "*hilah*" (trick), giving out a small amount from their money to their friends or relatives just before the period when they are expected to pay, only to collect their money back after the date has passed. The general purpose of law in Islam, that of uprooting poverty, is ignored.

Ijtihad should inform us that the socio-economic conditions of a society change with the passage of time. Likewise, the principles [*usul*] utilized to impart justice and a state of equilibrium are subject to change. At a time of class struggle, the wealth is concentrated in the hands of a few rich people; the majority is deprived of the basic needs and suffers from poverty and deprivation. If Islamic law advocates a rigid application of a specific system for the distribution of wealth, its universal character will undoubtedly be jeorpadised. The end of law in Islam is equity, justice, liberality, and balance. Any measure that may be applied therefore will be considered a part of law and not a violation of law.

Muslims need to understand the influence exerted by Islam on social process, and the conditioning imposed by the dynamics of society on the forms and expressions of Islam. The socio-phenomenal dimension present in the received Islam need to be acknowledged, that is, the social motives for religious beliefs, practices, and laws, the real manner in which such beliefs, practices, and laws took shape and developed, and consequently, the concrete effects of such beliefs and praxis on society. Many of the Islamic movements and approaches have outlived their purpose and usefulness. Not so much because they failed in solving the problems of their societies, but because today we are faced with new challenges and new problems that require a new approach and new *ijtihad*. What we have inherited is a museum, and today's *mujtahid* is just an archaeologist scavenging through dead texts, and today's *ijtihad* is nothing more that a cannibalization of the past. The result is a dead *fiqh* which is far removed from the realities of everyday life. *Ijtihad* for us is not an option but an obligation, an urgent need to move from mere theorisation to praxis.

Notes

1. *Fawatih rahmawat sharh musallam thubut,* vol.2, p. 212.

2. Imam al-Ghazali, *Al-Mustafa,* vol. 1, pp. 112-114.

3. Saif al-Din al-Amidi (1347) *al-Ihkam fi Usul al-Ahkam* (Cairo) I: 112.

4. Al- Suyuti (1352) *Jami' al-Saghir* (Cairo).

5. Hasan, Ahmad, *The Doctrine of Ijma' in Islam: a study of the juridical principle of consensus,* Islamabad: International Islamic University, 1991, p.23.

6. *Sahih Muslim,* Kitab al-imarah.

7. Ibid.

8. Abu Bakr al-Jassas, *Kitab Usul al-Fiqh,* M.S. Dar al-Kutub.

9. Imam al-Ghazali, op.cit., 110.

10. Zuhaili, Wahbah, *Usul al-fiqh al-islami,* Damascus: Dar al-fikr, 1996, vol.1, p.523.

11. Ibid., 524.

12. Maududi, *The Islamic Law and Constitution,* Lahore: 1960, p. 236; see also Fazlur Rahman (1981) "A Recent Controversy over the Interpretation of Shura" *International Journal of Middle Eastern Studies,* 291 - 301. See Abul Husain al-Basri, *Kitab al-Mu'tamad,* Damascus: 1964, vol., p. 457; & al-Sarkhasi, *Usul al-Sarkhasi,* Cairo: 1372 A.H., vol. 1, 311.

13. Noam Chomsky, *Language and Responsibility,* Harvester Press: 1977, p. 4.

14. Edward W. Said, *Covering Islam: How the Media and the Experts Determine How We See the Rest of the World,* New York: Pantheon, 1981, p. 141.

15. D. Beghin, et al. (1989) "A versatile approach to health system evaluation" *World Health Forum,* 10 : 37.

16. See also the superb work of Jerry Mander (1978), *Four Arguments for the Elimination of Television* (New York: Morrow Quill) who notes that "human beings no longer trust personal observation, even of the self- evident, until it is confirmed by experts." See Winkel (1991). "Is this (fire) a fake?" *Islamic Quarterly,* for comments on this work.

17. Abdul Aziz al-Bukhari, *Kashf al-asrar,* Istanbul, 1307 AH, vol.3, pp. 896, 970, 982.

18. Ibn Hisham, *Sirah,* vol. 1, pp. 178-179; & Ibn Kathir, *al-Bidayah wa al-nihayah,* vol. 3, pp. 224-226; & Haykal, M.H, *The life of Muhammad,* American Education Trust, 1976, pp. 181-182.

19. Al-Bazdawi, *Usul al-Bazdawi,* Karachi, 1966, p.247.

20. *Bukhari*, Kitab al-magazi.

21. *Al-Talwih ala tawdih*, vol. 2, p.52; see also *al-Taqrir wa tahbir*, vol. 3, p. 119; *Kashf al-asrar*, vol. 2, p. 988; & *Fawatih rahmawut*, vol. 2, p.274.

22. *Al-Mustasfa'*, vol. 2, p.45.; Al-Amidi, *al-Ihkam fi usul al-ahkam*, vol. 3, p. 4.; & *Irshad al-fuhul*, p.174.

23. *Al-Risalah*, p. 477.

24. The authenticity of this narration was disputed by Ibn Hazm in his *al-Mahalla* (vol. 1, p. 59) and in his *Mulakhass ibtal al-qiyas wa al-ra'y* as well as by orientalist writers. The problem with the narration, he says is its narrator, Abdul al-Malik ibn al-Walid who is reporting from his father and both of them are not reliable narrators. However this narration was reported through other authentic sources. Dar al-qutni and al-Baihaqi reported it from Abu al-Mulih al-Hudhali. Ibn Abi Shaibah also reported part of it from Amr ibn Shu'aib who is narrating from his father, and his father is narrating from his father ('Amru's grandfather). Dar al-Qutni recorded it again from Ahmad from Said ibn Abu Burdah while al-Baihaqi recorded it again from Abu al-Awam al-Misri. Ibn Jawzi quoted it in his biography of 'Umar, and Ibn Qayyim in his *A'lam al-Muwaqqi'in* (vol. 1, p. 85). See also *Nasb al-Raya fi takhrij ahadith al-hidaya,* vol. 3, pp. 63-81. Ahmad Shakir wrote in his foot-note of Dar al-Qutni's narration from Ahmad ibn Hanbali: "In our opinion the best chain of this narration is that of Sufyan ibn Uyainah from Idris ibn Zaid ibn Abd al-Rahman al-Uwadi who is a reliable narrator (*thiqah*). He says that Said ibn Abi Burdah showed him a book in which this narration was written and read it before him, and this is the best way of transmitting any tradition. Reading from a book is more reliable than narrating from memory."

25. Bazdawi, *Usul*, cf. Muslehuddin, m. *Philosophy of Islamic law and the Orientalists,* Delhi, 1986, pp. 129-130.

26. *Qur'an*, chapter 3: 7.

27. Ibn Qayyim, Al-Jawziyah, *I'lam al-Muwaqqiin an Rab al-alamin,* Cairo n.d., vol. 2, pp. 20-21.

28. Ibid, p. 20.

29. *Qur'an*, chapter 9: 60.

30. Mahmassani, *Falsafah,* op cit., p. 111.

31. Al-Shatibi, Abu Ishaq, *Al-Muwaffaqat,* Cairo, 1969, vol. 4, p. 89.

32. Ibid, p. 90.

33. Ibid, p. 97.

34. Ibid, p. 90.

35. Ibid, p. 91.

36. Ibid, p. 92.

37. Ibid, p. 105.

38. Ibid, p. 93.

39. Ibid, p. 95.

40. Ibid, p. 96.

41. Ibid, p. 162.

42. Ibid, p. 96.

43. Ibid, p. 105.

44. Ibid, p. 118.

45. Ibid, p. 128.

46. Ibid, p. 334.

47. Ibid, p. 337.

48. Ibid, p. 339.

49. Ibid, p. 339.

50. Ibid, p. 110-111.

51. Ibn Abd al-Barr, *Jami al-Bayan*, Vol. 2, p. 56.

52. Ahmad ibn Hanbal, *Musnad*, vol. 1, p. 20; also see *Tarikh al-Khulafa*, p. 68.

53. Darimi, *Musnad*, Bab al-Fitya wa ma fihi min al-Shiddah.

54. The fact that initially the majority of the Companions objected to waging war against those who were involved in *riddah* is sufficient to show that the decision was based on Abu Bakr's *ijtihad*.

55. Ghazali, *al-Mustasfa*, 1st Edition, Cairo, 1323 A.H., p. 242.

56. *Kalalah* is a person who neither has parents nor off-springs.

57. For further discussion of this subject, see *al-Bukhari Sahih al-Bukhari*, Kitab al-Faraid, Chapter on *Mirath al-Sadd ma'al-abb wal ikhwah*.

Islamic Law: Theory and Interpretation

58. See *Kanz al-Ummal,* vol. 1, p. 281.

59. Abu Dawud, see *Kitab al-Diyat al-Janin.*

60. For details, see *Numani, Shibli, Khulafa-i-Rashidin,* Azamgarh, 1973, pp. 151-154.

61. See Ibn Kathir, *Tafsir al-Qur'an al-azim,* Beirut: Dar al-Ma'rifah, 1986, vol. 2, p. 379.

62. Khadri Beg, Muhammad *Tarikh Tashri 'Islam,* Beirut, 1967, p. 102; also see *Muwatta* by Imam Malik.

63. See *Sahih Muslim,* Kitab al-talaq.

64. Ibid, p. 106.

65. Abu Yusuf, *Kitab al-Kharaj,* p. 192.

66. Ahmad ibn Hanbal, *Musnad,* p. 168.

67. Ahmad ibn Hanbal, *Musnad,* p. 29.

68. Shah Wali Allah Dihlavi's work *Izalah al-Khafa'* gives a number of instances of Caliph Umar's *ijtihad* on a number of points.

69. See Ahmad ibn Hanbal, *Musnad,* vol. 1, p. 140.

70. Hakim, *Mustadrak,* vol. 3, p. 135.

71. Ibn Hanbal, *Musnad,* vol. 1, p. 77.

72. See Suyuti, *Tarikh al-Khulafa;* also Shibli Naumani, *Khulafa' al-Rashidun,* pp. 346-347.

73. Al-Khudari, *Tarikh al-Tashri al-Islami,* pp. 115-116.

74. Al Musari, *al-Nass wa al Ijtihad,* p. 201; Abu Zahra, *Usul al-fiqh,* Cairo, 1973 p. 273.

Chapter 4

PART ONE

Al-Masalih al-Mursalah
(Public Good or Public Interest) and Social Change

*M*asalih is the plural of the Arabic word "*maslahah*" which means welfare, interest or benefit. In juristic terminology it is used with the qualifying word, "*mursalah*", meaning unrestricted or undefined interest. It is a juristic device that has always been used in Islamic legal theory to promote public benefit and preventing social evils. Imam Malik approved the idea of "public interest" as one of the sources of *Shari'ah*. *Masalih al-mursalah* corresponds to utility, and it is somewhat similar to juristic equity or preference [*istihsan*].

Masalih al-mursalah is probably the most important hermeneutic option used by the Maliki *fuqaha* to accommodate social changes and to justify the doctrine of *maqasid al-shari'ah*. The Muslim society found a new boost through *masalih al-mursalah* to solve various new problems mainly in trade and commerce. The growing economic activities demanded freedom of contract. The Maliki *fuqaha* found it difficult to respond to such demands. The new forms of contract had become highly complicated. The older framework of contract in Maliki legal theory, which still operated on the legal theory of *shirka fi al-zar'* derived from the early Madinan practice of partnership, did not provide sufficient analogies to new kinds of contract which were different both in form and in nature. The Maliki *fuqaha* tried to solve these problems by adhering to the method of analogy through various devices, but the search for particular precedents to particular cases proved unsuccessful. The *fuqaha*, therefore, were forced to work on the Maliki principle of *maslahah*. They also employed such principles as *adam haraj* but it was difficult to apply such principles indiscriminately to all areas of social and legal change.

The basic components of the Maliki concept of *masalah* have been given as follows:

1. Consideration for the needs of mankind
2. The rationality of legal commands and the responsibility of man
3. Protection from harm, and

4.   Conformity with the objectives of the law giver.

Some scholars have distinguished *maslahah shar'iyyah* from the ordinary concept of *masalih*. The former is abstract and simple, while the ordinary *masalih* does not exist in pure and simple form; it always contains certain elements of *mafsadah* (confusion). Ordinary *maslah* is known by weighing the aspects of good and evil in an action; whichever dominates characterizes the thing in question. *Maslah shari'yyah* is a legal obligation that takes into account only the dominating aspect which is pure and simple, unmixed with any *mafsadah*.

According to the doctrine of *masalih al-mursalah, ijtihad* or interpretation of the *nass* (text) is to consider the underlying or hidden meaning of the revealed text in the light of public interest. *Qiyas*, as we have discussed before, is the primary method of tracing the effective cause or *illah* of the *nass* (text) to be extended to the cases of similar nature. If the cause is apparent, it will also be extended to similar cases, but the difficulty will only arise when the cause is not apparent. The *Caliphs*, in such a case, resorted to *qiyas tam* (sound analogy) or *ta'wil* and tried to discover the cause with reference to the words of the revealed text, exploring its implicit meaning and its context, and the *hadith* of the Holy Prophet. The Maliki scholars resorted to their method of interpreting the text according to their own reason taking into consideration the social utility. This is the main difference between the principle acted upon by the *Caliphs* and the hidden cause and wisdom which the Maliki scholars tried to discover by employing their reason. This value judgement that they applied is known as "*hikmah*" (act of wisdom). In other words, they did their *qiyas* (analogical deduction) based on *hikmah* which is actually the underlying reason behind the text. Thus, the application of their reason in finding out the *hikmah* is the basis of *masalih al-mursalah*.

Shatibi, a Maliki scholar has given an insightful analysis of *adah* (human social habits) and *Shari'ah* which he says are very closely connected. Although Allah wills both, yet the former belongs to the Creative Will and the latter to the Legislative. Except for certain fundamental laws human *adah* may undergo changes, whereas *Shari'ah* insofar as it reflects the divine will cannot change. To find rules for new situations occurring because of changes in *adah* one needs to know the exact rule of the intent of the law. This intent can be known through studying *adah* in combination with the principles inductively derived from *Shari'ah*.

It is here that the doctrine of *masalih* is admirably suited to Shatibi's understanding of social changes and to his views on legal change. According to him the *awaid* (plural of *adah*) or the habits of individuals and social practices alike are stabilized by certain universal laws which do not change. The changes that occur in society happen because of the movements of social customs along with the migration of people. More fundamentally, changes are generally produced by human needs. It is when these social changes go beyond the provisions of the rules of law or when they become too complicated for the existing rules, that a *mufti* or *mujtahid* comes to play his role through the agency of a *fatwa*, to examine the law and legal theory as they relate to the changes in question on the ground of *masalih*.

From this point of view, *masalih al-mursalah* helps to convey the humane side of the *Shari'ah* and emphasize the rational comprehensibility of the *hikmah* and its relevance to the promotion of man's material interest. In this process the distinction between *hikmah* and *illah* is sometimes lost, the latter term being employed to cover the meaning of the former.

Shaikh abdul Wahab Khallaf emphasizes on the social utility of *Shari'ah*. He draws a sharp difference between *hikmah* and *illah*. To him, *illah* must not only be suitable [*munasib*] but also objectively recognizable [*zahir*] and should be very clearly defined [*mundabit*]; *hikmah* lacks these qualifications, yet it represents the true motive for Allah's enactment of the ruling. *Hikmah* is the main thing and the underlying reason without which *illah* will serve no useful purpose. He, thus equates *hikmah* with what Imam Qarafi (d. A.H. 684) referred to as the "promotion of benefit."[1]

In order to elucidate the difference between the *illah* of a ruling and its *hikmah*, Shaikh Khallaf further gives an example of the Qur'anic verse: "*Fasting is for a fixed number of days, but if any of you is ill, or on a journey, the prescribed number should be made up from the days later.*"[2] Relief from hardship, according to him, is the *hikmah*, while travelling or illness is the *illah* (cause).[3] Other scholars say that *illah* covers also *hikmah* and the interpreter has to take into consideration *illah* which is the effective cause of the revealed ruling so as to extend it to similar cases. He is not primarily concerned to identify the *hikman* of the ruling, but to identify the *illah* that becomes the basis of the ruling.

Relying on the *hikmah*, furthermore, would lead to certain legal judgements contradicted by the conclusions of consensus. The prohibition of adultery, for example, might be ascribed to the *hikmah* of the necessity to protect genealogy; but on this basis, it would be logical also to prohibit inter-marriage between persons of unknown parentage, which by consensus is not in fact the case. The *hikmah*, in other words, is an unacceptable criterion for judgement because of its generality and uncertain character; reliance on it is presumptuous and likely to lead to distortion.[4]

Classification of *Masalih* or Interests

The Maliki jurists have classified *masalih* into three categories:

1. *Masalih Mu'tabarah*

Interests recognized in *Shari'ah*, e.g., the protection of one's life, religion, family, reason, property and honor. To them, these are the interests protected by the rules of transactions necessary for life, rules of worship for religion, rules of marriage for family life, punishment for the use of intoxicants to protect the faculty of reasoning, punishment for theft to protect property, punishment for adultery and calumny to protect honor.

2. *Masalih Mulghiyah*

These are interests discarded by *Shari'ah*, e.g., the case of ruler who breaks the *Ramadan* fast and instead of prescribed penance of freeing a slave and distributing alms, a court jurist gives judgement that the ruler should fast for two consecutive months, since the usual penance would be of no great sacrifice for a wealthy man. This is condemned and discarded by *Shari'ah*.

3. *Masalih Mursalah*

Interests not very apparent in *Shari'ah*, e.g., undefined and unrestricted interest which are undefined and unrestricted.

Imam Malik, the advocate of the doctrine of *masalih al-mursalah* has attached the following three conditions for its adoption[5]:

1. The case in which *masalih al-mursalah* is to operate must be pertaining to matters of transactions and other social matters so that interest involved in it may be constructed upon ground of reason. The case must not be related to *ibadat* (religious observances).

2. The *maslahah* should be in harmony with the spirit of the *Shari'ah* and should not be in conflict with any one of the sources of *Shari'ah*.

3. The *maslahah* should be in case of essential and necessary things and not of mere luxury. These essential and necessary things should have a direct bearing on the preservation of religion, life, reason, offspring and property.

As a matter of fact, all the schools of *fiqh* in one way or another use *masalih al-mursalah* even though they may use different terms for it. According to Al-Qarafi, a Maliki scholar, "We (Maliki) use it [*masalih al-mursalah*]; and the truth is that it is generally used in all of the four schools."[6] He is also of the opinion, and it is certainly true, that this doctrine is not only a Maliki device, since it is used, at least unconsciously, by all jurists: "It is commonly said that *masalih al-mursalah* is peculiar to us (i.e., the Maliki school), but if you examine the other schools, too, we will find that when they weigh the similarities and differences between two matters, they do not seek (textual) corroboration for the consideration on the basis of which they compare and differentiate, but rather they are content with sheer suitability [*munasabah*]... Thus, it is found in all schools."[7]

The Doctrine of '*Darurah*' and '*Masalih al-Mursalah*'

The *Shari'ah* allows for stability and change, balanced as it is between the rigidity inherent in a legal system completely obvious and completely determined with the flexibility of a legal system associated with essence and abstract ideas. This *Shari'ah*, then, has the capacity to meet every need, and the concept of its benefit to society means that the *Shari'ah*, is flexible enough to benefit society in every aspect of its existence.

The society which faces hardship, like the individual, is allowed to do whatever necessary to survive, even if in the process some aspect of the *Shari'ah*, is temporarily made inoperative, while a more general intent and injunction is followed. But this emergency action does not change the eternal law; neither does it apply for a moment after the emergency has passed. It also does not apply for the person using this temporary abrogation as a way of challenging the wisdom of Allah.

The definition of the concept of *halal* and *haram*, allowed and forbidden, rests with Allah. As we pointed out, nothing has an inherent good or bad in the sense that we can point out, without divine guidance, something as bad or good. Instead, the real issue is the attitude of the person. In this way swine flesh is not forbidden to the person starving to death with absolutely no other recourse, because in taking a small piece for survival, the believer knows that it is not evil itself. However, the moment some strength has returned, and the emergency has passed, the believer returns to the stipulations of the verse which forbids swine flesh. In this way, the believer recognizes that Allah, for reasons sometimes but certainly not always apparent, has declared some things lawful and some things unlawful.

This Qur'anic verse is pertinent to this argument:

"Say: who has forbidden the beautiful (gifts) of Allah, which He has produced for His servants, and the things, clean and pure, (which He has provided) for sustenance? Say, they are, in the life of this world, for those who believe, (and) purely for them on the Day of Judgement. Thus, We explain the Signs in detail for those who understand. Say, the things that my Lord has indeed forbidden are shameful deeds, whether open or secret; sins and trespasses against truth or reason; assigning of partners to Allah for which He has given no authority; and saying things about Allah of which you have no knowledge."[8]

The basic principle which emerges from this verse is that a thing which is not disallowed is deemed lawful. The well known dictum in *Shari'ah*, is "Lawfulness is a recognized *a priori* principle of all things," in Arabic *"al-ibaha aslun fi al-ashya'"*. In other words, everything is presumed to be lawful unless it is definitely prohibited by law. This dictum arises from the following verses of the *Qur'an*: "*It is He who has created for you all things that are on earth; moreover His design comprehends the heavens, for He gave order and perfection to the seven firmaments; and of all things He has perfect knowledge.*" (2: 29), "*Do you not see that Allah has subjected to your (use) all things in the heavens and on the earth, and has made His bounties flow among you in exceeding measure, (both) seen and unseen? Yet there are those who dispute with Allah, without knowledge and without guidance and without a Book to enlighten them.*" (31: 20)

Furthermore, there is a *hadith* concerning this dictum which runs as follows: "Whatever Allah has declared lawful in His Book is lawful, and whatever He has declared unlawful is unlawful, and whatever He has remained silent about is forgiven. Then, accept those bounties of Allah, who does not forget anything." Then the Prophet recited the verse (of chapter *Mariam*): "*Your Lord never forgets anything.*"

Those things which are made unlawful are enumerated in detail in the *Qur'an*: "*He has enumerated in detail whatever is made unlawful for you.*" (6: 119) Because of the clarity of what is unlawful, and the subsequent lawfulness of everything else, we are not to become involved in disputes which might entail both discord and making something unlawful which Allah wants to be lawful, which is a terrible act indeed.

In a *hadith* it is recorded: "Allah has made obligatory deeds essential, do not waste them, and He has fixed limits, do not cross them. Whatever He has declared as unlawful, do not violate them, and He has kept quiet about certain things; it is a kind of mercy for you, do not enter into unnecessary discussion about them."

Now, besides the lawful and unlawful, there are some things which are doubtful, and these things occupy a space somewhere between the lawful and unlawful. It is wise to avoid ambiguities, as the Prophet has advised.

The lawful is made clear and the unlawful is also made clear, and in between lie the acts which are doubtful about which most people do not know whether it is lawful or unlawful. One who kept away from it in order to safeguard his religion and honor, he will remain in peace. But, if one is involved in doubtful things, it is possible to fall a victim to unlawful things. Like a shepherd who grazes his herds near forbidden ground, it is possible they might enter it

Masalih al-mursalah, therefore, has far-reaching implications for situations which require pragmatic solutions that there is no alternative but to find some solution. The following examples will indicate the degree of necessity in each case:

1. When certain taxes are imposed by the government in order to meet the costs of maintaining the army to protect the country.

2. The punishment of the criminal by depriving him of property if his crime was perpetrated over that property or its equivalent. For example, if a son kills his father in order to inherit property, *masalih al-mursalah* will rule that he should be deprived of the property.

3. In a case of war, if the enemies use prisoners of war as human shield, *masalih al-mursalah* will permit the killing of the prisoners of war in the course of fighting the enemy if such action should be found

essential to contain and ward off the enemy and to protect the interests of the country.

These examples of *masalih* point at some degree of necessity. This is where *darurah* or "the rule of necessity and need" and *masalih al-mursalah* come very close to each other.

Because of the close relationship between *darurah* and *masalih al-mursalah*, Imam Al-Ghazali, a Shafi'i scholar and Al-Tufi, a Hanbali scholar recognize the merit in *masalih al-mursalah* and accept it as a very useful concept to meet the challenges of changing times. Imam Abu Hamid al-Ghazali feels that *masalih* are not the interests of suitability in its unlimited sense:

> If the *Shari'ah* is silent on the use of *masalih al-mursalah* in a particular situation, we must then distinguish between cases of necessity and need [*darurah wa hajah*] and cases in which only improvements and embellishments [*tahsinat wa tazyinat*] are in question. This distinction severely restricts the meaning of *maslahah* for while it basically mean "obtaining benefit and preventing injury", these are human aims, concerned with human welfare only in human terms, whereas what we mean by *maslahah* is conservation of the aims of the *Shari'ah*. The aim of the *Shari'ah*, in regard to a person is fivefold: to conserve his or her religion, life, reason, offspring and material wealth. Therefore, all that secures conservation of these five elements is a *maslahah*, and all that jeopardizes them is *mafsadah* prevention of which is also another *maslahah*. The preservation of these five interests falls within the category of necessities and is amply exemplified in the revealed laws punishing heresy, murder, wine drinking, adultery and theft.[9]

Having considered Imam al-Gazali's view on *masalih al-mursalah,* we shall now examine another view of Najmuddin ibn Abd al-Qawy al-Tufi (d. 716 A.H.) who said that *masalih al-mursalah* is the source of law and that it supersedes even the provision of the *nass* (revealed text). He discusses *masalih* which applies to essential situations and this amounts to *darurah* (necessity) and in fact necessity knows no law. He emphasizes on the *hadith* "*la darar wa la dirar fi al-islam*" which means "there shall be no harming of the self nor of others in Islamic law"[10], and considers this to be the first principle of *Shari'ah*. He says that since *maslahah* is meant for preventing injury, it makes it necessary to provide facilities to those who are confronted with hardships.

His view is that if the text and *ijma'* should happen to conform to the *masalih al-mursalah* in a given case, they should be applied immediately. However, if they oppose it, then "consideration of *masalih al-mursalah* must take precedence over the *nass* (text) and the *ijma'*. This is done through the process of restriction [*takhsis*] and clarification [*bayan*] – not by the process of attacking them – just as the *Sunnah* is sometimes given preference over the *Qur'an* by serving as a means of clarifying it."[11]

The approach of al-Tufi here is very similar to that of the Caliph Umar, and it is one that needs to be tested in the contemporary society. We know that Umar, at one time, suspended the punishment for theft since applying this punishment at a time of famine was against *masalih al-mursalah*. Islamic law has always maintained that before any government decide on cutting people's hands it should provide jobs for people, and if a person steals because he could not find anything to eat, it is the hand of the leader that should be cut and not that of the thief.

PART TWO

Other Subsidiary Juristic Devices

Istihsan: **Juristic Preferences**

> Those who listen to the word, and follow the best that is contained in it, those are the ones whom Allah has guided, and those are the ones endued with understanding. (*Qur'an* 39: 18.)

The commentators have interpreted this verse in two ways. If 'word' in this verse is taken as any word, the clause would mean that good and pious men should listen to all that is said and choose the best of it for general good – as long as that word is according to the spirit of the Divine Message. But if "word" were taken here to mean the Word of Allah, it would mean that they should listen reverently to it, and where permissive and alternative courses are allowed for those who are not strong enough to follow the higher course, those endued with understanding should prefer to attempt the higher course of conduct. For example, it is permitted within limits to punish those who wrong us, but the nobler course is to repel evil with good.[12] We should try to follow the nobler course.

131

Like *masalih al-mursalah* by the Maliki school, *istihsan* has been regarded by the Hanafi school as a basis of law. The jurists of different schools have used different Arabic terms to describe the same concept. The Hanafis call it *istihsan* meaning equitable preference to find a just solution to new problems. The Hanbali scholar Ibn Qudamah as well as the Maliki jurists and Ibn Rushd have also occasionally used the term *istihsan*. *Istihsan* is not very much liked by the *fuqaha* of other schools of *fiqh*. Even a great scholar like Imam Shafi'i wrote a treatise called *al-radd ala al-stihsan* (Refutation of *istihsan*). Possibly Imam Shafi'i has his own reasons to object and reject the principles of *istihsan*. According to Hanafi school of thought, *istihsan* means that only the apparent situation about some juristic issue alone should not be taken into consideration but deeper aspects of it should be looked at before giving any verdict. For example, normally Islamic jurisprudence rules that if one gives something as *amanah* (trust) to a person, the person receiving *amanah* is duty-bound to return the same thing to him when asked to do so. Supposing one gives a check of $500 to be delivered to someone, the same $500 check should be given to the person and one may not decide to give cash instead. But, in our post offices today, when a money order is sent through the post office the amount is mixed with other amounts coming to the post office. According to the working of the post office, the person receiving the money order will receive quite different notes although it will be exactly the same amount. This is acceptable according to the Hanafi point of view. This is called *istihsan* even though it seems to be against the principles of *amanah* to some extent.

Similarly, in a contract for manufacture and sale, where a person requests another to make a certain item for him, such as a boat, the subject matter of the contract is a thing which is not in existence at the time of the contract, namely the item to be manufactured. Thus, it is void by analogy. But since such contracts have been approved by the *Sunnah* based upon the Prophet's deeds and since they have been universally accepted by the people (consensus), analogy had to be abandoned, and contracts for manufacture and sale became permissible through *istihsan*. In actual fact, there is an element of necessity and need in this type of contract in order to provide facilities to those who are subjected to hardships.

While analogy is to protect *Shari'ah* against the free use of reason, *istihsan* and *masalih al-mursalah* stand for freedom in the use of one's own reason. There has been some opposition to this theory by those who hold that there is no place for "preference". According to Ibn Qayyim, there is nothing in the *Shari'ah* contrary to analogy and that which may be thought to contradict analogy is either due to the fact that the analogy is faulty or that the particular rule is not established by a text to be a part of the *Shari'ah*.[13]

Imam Shafi'i has rejected *istihsan* on the ground that "he who practices *istihsan* assumes unto himself, the power of law-making." Imam Shafi'i considers both *ra'y* (one's own opinion) and *istihsan* to mean one and the same thing. Some jurists like Imam Shafi'i argue on the basis of the Qur'anic verse which says that man is not left without guidance, that one who uses *istihsan* acts as if he were left without any such guidance[15] and comes to whatever conclusion he pleases. They also argue that if one were authorized to use *istihsan* one would have to acknowledge that others are free to use another *istihsan*, and there would be several right decisions and juristic opinions on one and the same problem. Imam Shafi'i gives an example:

> Supposing the governor and the *mufti* should say concerning a divine scourge that there is no provision for it either in a text or by analogy, and supposing they should have recourse to *istihsan*, would it not be incumbent upon them to concede to others the right to prefer some other ruling? Consequently, every governor and *mufti* in the various cities would rule according to his preference and there would be many contradictory rulings and opinions on the same case ... If one of those who would wish to discard analogy should claim that people ought to obey his decisions, then, he should be told, "who has ordered that you be obeyed so that people become duty-bound to follow you? If some other person claimed such right from you, would you obey him? Would you not say that you would only obey him whom you have been ordered to obey? Similarly, you have no right to claim obedience from anyone. Obedience belongs only to those who Allah and the Prophet have ordained that they be obeyed. Right is that which Allah and the Prophet have order to be pursued and have pointed to through a text or through deduction."[16]

The Hanafi jurists and other protagonists of *istihsan* also rely on the Qur'anic verse which they often quote:

Who hears advice and follow the best thereof [*ahsanahu*]: Such are those whom Allah guides and such are men of understanding.[17]

Likewise, they quote the tradition of Abdullah Ibn Mas'ud: "That which the Muslims find agreeable [*hasan*] is agreeable to Allah." They argue that this is enough authority for them in support of *istihsan*.

We shall examine some more examples of *istihsan* in order to form a clear view about this juristic device:

1. The *bay' bi al-wafa* or a contract which can be construed as a kind of mortgage was allowed because of the practical need for such transactions in the interest of public welfare.

2. Islam attaches great importance to the proper dress of woman [*satr al-awrah*]. No man except her husband can see certain parts of her body. However, on account of necessity, a physician may be allowed to medically examine and diagnose a woman in the interest of saving her life.

3. Divorce given in sickness or just before death [*mard al-mawt*], even though effected as irrevocable [*talaq bain*], will not deprive the divorced wife from her share in the inheritance. The husband in reality is seen as trying to deprive her of her rights and attempting to shun his obligations. It will be treated like the divorce of an escapee [*talaq al-farr*]. Some Shafi'i and Zahiri jurists disagree with the majority of Muslim jurists on this issue. The Hanafi jurists maintain that the entitlement of the divorced wife lasts during her *iddah* period while the Hanbalis take the view that she will be entitled to participate as long as she has not remarried. The Malikis, however, accord her the right to participate in the inheritance even if she has remarried provided the deceased did not recover in between the "death illness" and his ultimate death.

4. The *hadd* punishment of amputation of hands in case of a theft will not be applied if all the evidence proved that it was committed during the period of a famine when no food was available and that one was forced to steal. Imam Shafi'i says that he will apply this rule simply because Umar decided a case in this way. He does not think that it was done on the principle of *istihsan* or *masalih al-mursalah*.

5. The eating of meat which has not been slaughtered according to the Islamic ritual [*dhabihah*] is permissible where no other lawful food is available.

6. Destruction of lawful foodstuffs is not allowed without any special reason. But Umar ordered the spilling of milk mixed with water as a punishment that would prevent deceit of dishonest persons engaged in the sale of adulterated milk.

7. The second call of the *adhan* (call or announcement) for Friday congregational prayers was not a practice in the time of the Prophet and Uthman bin Affan, the third Caliph, started it as a reminder for the benefit of the public.

Imam Malik bin Anas also gave several juristic decisions (*fatwas*) based on *masalih al-mursalah* (public interests). Some of them are listed as follows:

1. The Muslim ruler may exact additional taxes from the citizens in the period of emergency.

2. A Caliph or a ruler does not have to be the most meritorious claimant, otherwise strife will be inevitable.

3. Imam Malik as well as Imam Ahmad bin Hanbal prohibited the sale of grapes, which is otherwise legal, to a wine merchant as he will use them to ferment wine which is unlawful.

4. The sale of arms during a civil disturbance is prohibited since it may intensify the struggle.

Most of these rules could fit into Hanafi *istihsan* or Shafi'i's *qiyas*. Imam Abu Hamid al-Ghazali calls the same juristic device *istislah* which means "seeking the better option."

The difference between *istihsan* and *masalih al-mursalah* is negligible. *Istihsan* helps the jurists in cases when the analogy of the fixed code clearly points to follow a different course which may make things easy. In acting on *masalih al-mursalah,* under same conditions, one chooses a free course, for the sake of the general benefit to the society. *Istihsan* is almost equivalent to Equity in the English common law concept. *Masalih al-mursalah* is akin to the concept of Utility which forms the basis of legislation in most parts of the world today.

Istidlal and *Istihbab*

It should be noted that the concept of public welfare and general interest can really be helpful particularly in cases which are not regulated by any authority of the *Qur'an*, the *Sunnah* or *ijma'*. In the case, equitable considerations may override the results of strict *qiyas* taking into consideration the public interest. Shafi'i jurists have employed *istidlal* to achieve similar results by avoiding merely the application of strict *qiyas*. *Istidlal* is the process of seeking guidance, basis and proof from the source although its dictionary meaning is merely an argumentation. *Istidlal*, in reality, is expressive of the connection that exists between one proposition and another. For example, sale is a contract and the basis of every contract is consent, therefore, consent is the basis of sale. It is a sort of logical deduction and, more aptly, a striving after a basis for a rule of law.

Istishab: Legal Presumption

Istishab, for instance, relates to the deduction by presumption of continuity which is similar to the principle of evidence. The literal meaning of istishab is "seeking for a friend or seeking for a link" i.e., seeking for some authority or proof. Freedom from obligation, for instance, is presumed until the contrary is established. Even though *istishab* and *istidlal* have been considered sources of law, they are actually used to serve as a means to arrive at sound analogy or *ta'wil*.

As for example, freedom from obligation is presumed until the contrary is established. *Istishab*, in other words, means a rule of evidence or a legal presumption of continuance [*istishab*] of conditions [*al-hal*]. In other words, it is the presumption in the laws of evidence that a state of affair known to exist in the past continues to exist until the contrary is proved. *Istishab* is accepted by all schools of Islamic Jurisprudence as a subsidiary source of *Shari'ah*. There is a presumption of innocence until guilt is established. This presumption, is based on *istishab*. There will be a similar presumption of *halal* (lawful) things in the absence of its specific prohibition. A debt is presumed to subsist until its discharge is evidenced. Likewise, a marriage is presumed to continue until its dissolution [*talaq*] becomes known. In the case of *ibadat*, mere doubt does not vitiate the validity of rituals. Supposing a man after ablution entertains a mere doubt as to whether he still has his ablution to perform the prayers, there is a presumption of purity [*tuhr*] and, similarly, if he thinks genuinely that he has performed the correct number of prostrations [*sajadah*] in his prayer, a mere doubt will not affect his genuine belief. In the case of an ownership title, judge will presume ownership from valid title deeds until the contrary is proved. If a person is missing [*mafqud*], his wife remains his legal wife until the court, after due enquiries, issues a decree presuming the contrary, namely death.

Sadd al-Dharai‘: Locking the ways

Sadd al-dhari‘ah (plural *sadd al-dharai‘*) really means "blocking the ways" even if the method involved is otherwise legal. In fact, this source of *Shari'ah* is not much different from the *masalih al-mursalah*, but it is used by Maliki jurists and some Hanbalis under this name. Most of the rules categorized under *sadd al-dhari‘ah* can conveniently fit into the various subsidiary sources related to public interest or public welfare which we have discussed above.

This doctrine is founded on the idea of preventing evil before it actually materializes.[18] For example, *khalwa* or illicit privacy between members of the opposite sexes is unlawful since it constitutes a means to adultery and fornication whether or not it actually leads to it. Therefore, all sexual overtures which are expected to lead to adultery or fornication are similarly forbidden by virtue of the certainty that the action would possibly lead to sin.[19] When a particular act is deemed to lead to a certain result, whether good or evil, it is held to be the means toward that end and the intention of the doer is not relevant. This is based on a general principle of *Shari'ah*: *al wasail ila al-wajib wajibun wa al-wasail ila al-haram haramun* (the exigencies of obligatory acts will be considered obligatory while the exigencies of unlawful acts will be regarded as unlawful).

PART THREE
Urf, Adat: Usages and Customs

Urf or useful social custom as a legal device has played an important role in the development of jurisprudence as it was accepted as a legitimate ground for interpreting *Shari'ah* on the basis and exercise of *ijtihad*. It is through the use of *ijtihad* that people could decide what was *mustahsan* (good) and what was not good for the Muslim society. Shahrastani has rightly said: "*al-Nusus tantahi wal waqai‘ la-tantahi*" (the text, whether the *Qur'an* or the *hadith* is limited or finite while events which are the subjects of text have no limit and are infinite). Therefore, *ijtihad* is necessary in order to consider the ever changing events within the society in accordance with the spirit of *Shari'ah*, i.e., the spirit of the *Qur'an* and *Sunnah*.

The majority of decisions reached by the Muslim society in the past or even today are usually meant to serve the interest of the society by solving specific problems peculiar to specific periods and specific circumstances and mostly based on specific *urf* (customs) peculiarly known to that community. Such decisions based on *urf* need not always be binding to other Muslim communities living under different socio-economic conditions, unless such decisions can serve the same purpose and render the same services that they were initially designed for, regardless of socio-economic differences. The imposition of such decisions based on *urf* (customs) of a given community at all times will create more problems than solutions.

According to Ibn Abidin, in most legal decisions the *mujtahid* (jurist), simply bases his decision on the prevailing customs [*urf*] in his society to an extent that if he were to operate in a different social set-up or in a different period of time, he would be obliged to reach a different conclusion. That is the reason why a *mujtahid* must acquire a thorough knowledge of all the customs and social norms prevalent in his society. It is usually seen that a certain legal decision suitable to a particular society may not necessarily be suitable to another social set-up. An imposition of such decisions in places and situations with a different social set-up will inevitably result in inflicting hardship on the people in that society. This will be contrary to the spirit of *Shari'ah* which is based on ease and flexibility in dealing with human problems. It should always be kept in mind that decisions reached by other Muslim communities in different times and places can remain binding only to the extent that it serves the same purpose for which it was initially taken.

Some scholars attempt to place *urf*, the general usage, as a fifth *asl* of *fiqh* alongside the four generally recognized *usul*. Once the *urf* does not come in conflict with the *Qur'an* and *Sunnah*, there is no harm in accepting it. *Urf* is categorized as *urf amm* the general usage and *urf khass*, the local custom or a custom observed for a time only. It is *urf amm*, the general custom and usage, that will be acceptable provided it does not go against *nass* and is also required through *maslahah*.

Awaid: Natural Behavior

Imam Shatibi, the Maliki jurist, has given a beautiful exposition of the *awaid* (singular *adah*) and *Shari'ah*. They both originate from one source, Allah. Yet as they represent two different levels of Divine Will and they do not function in the same way. *Adah* represents the level of *al-irada al-takwiniyyah*, the contingent intention, where man has no choice but to obey the rules. In *Shari'ah*, obedience depends on man's choice. Human acts insofar as they belong to *al-irada al-takwiniyyah,* necessarily need man's intention and volition for obedience. *Awaid* which cover habits of an individual and in reference to social practices of the community in conformity with the laws of nature [*kulliyat al-wujud*] resulting from *al-irada al-takwiniyyah*, provide the deterministic element that stabilizes the function of social as well as legal system.

With the exception of universal principles, the *awaid* are, however, subject to change. The *Shari'iah* is based on the unchanging principles that *awaid* which belongs to human beings [*al- awa'id al-jariya bayn al-khalq*] may change. Since *Shari'ah* governs these *awaid* as well, it must respond to these changes. The mechanism of this response to social practices gives strength to the legal systems in the religion of Islam.

In the present day increased mobility and globalization has brought people of different *awaid* to come and live together. When an individual, coming from a different social system, becomes the subject of another legal system, or a legal system is introduced where a different social system is in function, the *awaid* of the incoming people have to be accommodated. Obviously, this change does not affect the fundamentals, as the *awaid* on which *Shari'ah* is based are universal. This social change requires to be accommodated in order to maintain the stability and applicability of the legal system. The second change requires to be accommodated in order to maintain the stability and applicability of the legal system. The second type of change occurs when the old practice no longer satisfies human needs, or when some new elements either from without or from within are introduced. Yet another type of change is introduced when social practices or institutions come into conflict with each other or with the purpose of law; this conflict may arise from a clash of personal interest or because of certain new developments in society. Whatever the cause, the change in a social system takes place in such a manner that it requires the legal system to respond to these changes.

Since the possibility of such change is unending and the rules of law are limited, it is out of this necessity that the legal system is organized on rational basis both in its principles and methods, so that it is manageable by human reason. According to Shatibi, since human reason alone cannot achieve such organization, the *Shari'ah* has provided man with general guidelines. Among these guidelines, some can be tested in social practice and some cannot. Those that cannot be tested are *ibadat* and *aqidah* (faith and observance of religious duties) and they are to be obeyed as such. Of those which can be tested and which are rationally intelligible are *adat*. The *adat* constitute the major area of human acts. Since it is possible to rationally organize the adat, the *Shari'ah* has left the details to be worked out by legal reasoning by the society.

It must be clearly understood that in the Islamic legal system, no innovation can be accepted in *ibadat*, whereas in *adat* changes are possible. Acts of worship belong to that area of *masalih* which is known only to Allah and they cannot be rationally explained. They also cannot be observed and tested by human reason just as they cannot be extended by analogy to similar situations. On the other hand, the *adat* are based on *masalih*. Similarly, the *adat* are observable and they can be tested. This is the reason why they are extendible by analogy and can be the subject of *ijtihad*. The *adat* are also known to the society on the basis of social knowledge and anthropology, but the *masalih* of *ibadat* cannot be known by social experience and hence cannot be prescribed, discontinued, changed or extended by the society.

Hence, *urf,* the known practices and *adat* the customs, are recognized as subsidiary sources by all schools of *fiqh*, although the Maliki school attaches more importance to custom than other schools. The customary rules remain valid as long as there is no provision on a given matter in the *Qur'an* and the *Sunnah*. If any of the customs contradict any other rule of *Shari'ah*, they will be considered outside the realm of Islamic law.

PART FOUR
Masalih and the Ever-changing Society

Masalih of the society and the principle of *darurah* have provided dynamism in the *Shari'ah* and have removed rigidity that had crept into the Islamic jurisprudence since the 3rd and 4th Century of Islam. As we have seen before, Imam Abu Hamid al-Ghazali (d.1111 C.E), Ibn Taimiyyah (d.1328 C.E.), and Shaikh Najm ad-Din Tufi (d.1316 C.E) were the chief exponents of this dynamism. They all had the benefit of going through the former writings of the jurists on Islamic legal thought.

It is true that "good" is only known to Allah, eternal blessings and property may be attained by living according to His Law, with good *niyyah* (intention). The real good cannot be rationally known. Allah, our Creator, has warned us that often we like a thing which is injurious to us and we dislike a thing which is good to us.[20] But the present day modernists believe in the rational determination of good and bad and also agree in principle, with the school of utility according to which pleasure is the good. This is what scholars like Imam Malik, Imam al-Ghazali, Ibn Taimiyyah, Tufi and others greatly disliked. They only used *maslahah* and the principle of *darurah* (necessity and need) whenever the occasion arose. Al-Ghazali has said in his famous book, *Mustasfa:*

> We have restricted use of it [*maslahah*] to implementation of the purposes of the law determined by the *Qur'an*, *Sunnah*, and *ijma'*. Every *maslahah* that does not consist of implementing the under-stood intent of the *Qur'an*, *Sunnah*, and *ijma'* is foreign and inappropriate to the operation of the law. It is, therefore, void and rejected, and whoever has recourse to it is arrogating the power of legislation, just as whoever uses *istihsan* is legislating. Every valid *maslahah* is based on implementing the intent of the Law, which must be determined by the *Qur'an*, *Sunnah*, and *ijma'* and must not fall outside the scope of these sources.[21]

This is an important warning given by al-Ghazali so that at any point in history the Muslim society may not be misguided. Every good thing can be put to good or bad use. A sharp knife can help to chop vegetables but can also be used to inflict injury. If unrestricted use of *masalih al-mursalah* is done by selfish and misguided judges, while giving their verdicts, then there will be oppression and violation of human rights in the Muslim society.

Masalih, therefore, must not be used like an unbridled horse that gallops in whatever direction it likes harming whatever comes in its way. Every faqih and qadi has his own accountability to Allah. Ibn Taimiyyah says in his, *al-Hisbah al-islam* that needs and necessities are the factors which give rise to the principle of *hisbah* (accountability) in public administration. Likewise, Ibn Qayyim confirms the same view in his *al-Turuq al-Hukmiyyah*. Hence, *masalih al-mursalah* must be used carefully and in a restricted sense to find solution to problems under *darurah* (necessities and needs).

A fine example as to how juristic opinions [*fatawa*] will be influenced by *maslahah* is given by Ibn Taimiyyah, which has been narrated by Ibn *Qayyim*, his pupil. Ibn Taimiyyah says:

> I was passing with some of my friends in the days of the Tartars, and saw a group of them (Tartars) who were drinking alcohol. One of my friends wanted to reprimand them, but I prevented him from doing so and said, Allah has prohibited strong drinks as they divert people from Allah and offering *salat*, but strong drinks have diverted these people from committing murder, capturing children and plundering, so leave them alone.[22]

Drinking alcohol in this case was overlooked both as *maslahah* (public interest) and the need of the time in order to save the people from murder and plunder and from creating chaos in the society. According to Ibn Qayyim, when there is *darurah* and *hajah*, even *riba al-fadal* (bank interest) becomes permissible.[23]

Masalih al-mursalah do not call for any change of law at all. The law remains as it is as nobody has power to tamper with the Divine Law. Ibn Taimiyyah allowed the Tartars to continue drinking alcohol going by the principle that one should prefer the lesser of the two evils perpetrated by evildoers. He did not change the Divine Law but only worked on the rule of *darurah* and *hajah* (necessity and need). *Masalih al-mursalah* or *darurah* cannot change the law but helps to accommodate the change.

Under the concept of *darurah* and *maslahah*, any juristic opinion that goes contrary to the texts must be carefully examined. Any admissible customs, and the concession granted because of hardships must be restricted only to matters not provided for in the *nass* (text). This is the view of Abu Hanifah and his pupils, Muhammad ibn al-Hasan al-Shaibani, Imam Shafi'i and Daud al-Zahiri.[24] Ibn Hazm, as we have seen, completely rejects any departure from the *nass* (text).

In recent times, some eminent Muslim scholars have made invaluable contribution to *usul al-fiqh* and its dynamism through the use of devices like *masalih*. The most prominent works are those of Dr. Husain Hamid Hasan[26], Dr. Muhammad Sa'id Ramadan al-Buti[27], and Dr. Mustafa Zaid[28].

According to Dr. Husain Hamid Hasan the theory of *istihsan* and *masalih* is based upon two principles, first, the excellence and superiority of *Shari'ah* lies in this that it provides for the needs of society and interests of the community and secondly, the text contains all the *masalih* or interests and it is incumbent upon the interpreter, in the absence of explicit text, to discover and determine *masalih* or interests by what is consistent with the text and the intention of the law giver. He maintains that all human needs and interests are incorporated into *Shari'ah* and *maslahah* or interest is that which is stated in the text and no *maslahah* can take precedence over the text. This is in consonance with the view of Imam Shafi'i who holds that *Shari'ah*, i.e., Divine Law is a declaration on all matters and provides for every possible eventuality in life and this is the claim advanced by the *Qur'an* itself: "*And We have revealed to you a Book as an exposition of all things.*"[29] "*We have neglected nothing in the Book.*"[30] "*There is nothing fresh nor dry, but is to be found in the revealed Book.*"[31] "*And in whatsoever, you differ, the verdict therein belongs to Allah.*"[32] "*Islam is perfect*"[33], so is its law.

Dr Sa'id Ramadan al-Buti, on the other hand, cautions that *masalih* must not be used at random. He maintains that the effective way to preserve *Shari'ah* in its ideal form is to determine *maslahah* by the needs recognized in *Shari'ah* otherwise it will be exposed to extraneous factors added which are against the spirit of *Qur'an* and *Sunnah*. The following Qur'anic verses guide us in determining the *maslahah*:

And judge between them by what Allah has revealed, and follow not their vain desires, diverging from the Truth that has come to you;(5: 51)

We have sent down to you the Book in Truth, that you might judge between men, as guided by Allah: so be not (used) as an advocate by those who betray their trust; (4: 106)

If you differ in anything among yourselves, refer it to Allah and His Apostle. (4: 59)

If any do fail to judge by (the light of) what Allah has revealed, they are (no better than) unbelievers. (4: 57)

After quoting these verses, Dr. Sa'id gives the following rules in respect of *maslahah*:

1. Nothing of the *Qur'an* or *Sunnah* is permitted to be particularized by independently judged *maslahah*, for a text from the *Qur'an* can be explained only by a similar text or authentic *Sunnah* as *Sunnah* can only be explained by a similar *Sunnah* or a text from the *Qur'an*. A *maslahah* which is not derived from the *Qur'an* and *Sunnah* cannot be regarded as *maslahah*.

2. It is incorrect to take a dictum of certain jurists that "laws change according to the times" on its face value, for what has been proved by the *Qur'an* and *Sunnah* or *qiyas* based on them is ever-lasting. Had it been subject to change, the law would have ceased to exist long ago. What the jurists meant by their dictum refers only to those laws which are based upon customs, for such laws have to change, under *darurah*, according to the changing customs.

3. Every one who tries to interpret the text must take into consideration the important points, referred to above, with regard to *maslahah* in *Shari'ah*, so that he may not confuse *maslahah* with what the protagonists of modernism claim to be *maslahah*.[34]

In other words, he uses the word *maslahah* in the restricted sense so as to mean *hajah*.[35]

Mustafa Zaid also carefully considers the rule of *maslahah* in his thesis. He has listed various examples of *masalih* which are within the framework of *Shari'ah* to show that they touch upon every aspects of life. They are, in fact, needs and necessities of men as provided by *Shari'ah*.[36]

Maslahah certainly provides the basis for dynamism in *fiqh*, but, if care is not taken, a lot of harm can be done to the cause of *Shari'ah*. *Maslahah* or public interest is not merely a vague and uncertain concept. It is a device to help us to shape the future of the society by accepting the challenge of modern times and live as Muslims honorably in the modern world of today. The touchstone to judge the validity of *maslahah* is of course the *Qur'an* and the *Sunnah*.

Notes

1. See Al-Khallaf Abdul Wahab, *Masadir al-Tashri al-Islami*, Kuwait 1972, p. 49.

2. *Qur'an*, chapter 2 : 184.

3. Al-Khallaf, *Masadir*, op. Cit., p. 49.

4. Cf. Kerr, M. H., *Islamic Reforms*, California, 1966, p. 74.

5. Mahmassani, S., *Falsafah al-Tashri fil Islam*, tr. F.J. Zaideh, Leiden, 1961, p. 88.

6. Al Qarafi, *Shihab al-Din*, *Al-Dhakhirah*, Cairo, 1961, vol. 1, p. 122.

7. Ibid.

8. *Qur'an*, chapter 7: 32.

9. Al-Ghazali, *al-Mustasfa*, vol. 1, pp. 139-140.

10. This tradition was reported by Imam Malik as a *mursal* as well as by Shafi'i from Malik, by Ahmad, Abdurrrazaq, Ibn Majah, and al-Tabarani on the authority of Ibn Abbas. The problem with this chain is that Jabir al-Ju'fi, one of the narrators is weak. It has also been reported from other sources: by Ibn Abi Shaibah and Dar Qutni and was classified as *hasan* (good). Other reliable chains include the ones from Abu Sa'id, Abu Hurairah, Jabir, 'Aishah, and many others.

11. Mustafa Zaid, *Al-Maslahah fil Tashri al-Islami,* Cairo, 1954, See appendix, p. 17.

12. *Qur'an*, chapter 16: 126

13. Ibn Qayyim, Al-Jawziyah, *I'lam al-Muwaqqi'in 'an-Rabb al-'alamin,* Cairo, n.d., vol. 1, p. 335; Also see Ibn Taimiyyah, *majnuah al-Rasail al-Kubra*, Cairo, 1323 A.H., vol. 2, p. 218.

14. Al-Ghazali, *Al-Mustasfa,* Cairo, 1937, vol. 1, p. 137.

15. *Qur'an*, chapter 75 : 36.

16. Imam Shafi'i, Mohammad bin Idris, *Al-Umm*, Boulaq 1320 - 25 A.H., vol. 7, pp. 273 - 274.

17. *Qur'an*, chapter 33 - 18.

18. Kamali, M. H, *Principles of Islamic Jurisprudence,* Cambrige: Islamic Texts Society, 1991, p. 311.

19. Ibid.

20. *Qur'an*, chapter 2 : 216.

21. Al-Ghazali, *al-Mustasfa,* op. Cit., pp. 143 - 144.

22. Cf. Mahmassani, S., *Falsafah al-Tashri fil Islam,* tr. F.J. Zaideh, Laiden, 1961, p. 117.

23. Ibn Qayyim, *I'lam al-Muwaqqi'in*, op.cit., vol. 2, p. 273.

24. Al-Shafi'i, *Al-Umm*, op.cit., vol. 7, p. 275. Also see Ibn Qayyim, I'lam, op.cit., vol. 2, p. 208.

25. Ibn hazm, Ali bin Ahmad, *Al-Ihkam li Usul al-Ihkam*, Cairo, 1343, 48 A.H., vol. 5, p. 4.

26. *Nazariyyat al-Maslahah fil Fiqh al-Islam* (Ph.D) Thesis, Cairo University Cairo, 1971.

27. *Dawabit al-Maslahah fil Shariat al-Islamiyyah* (Ph.D Thesis of Al-Azhar) Damascus, 1967.

28. *Al-Maslahah fil Tashri al-Islami wa Najmuddin al-Tufi*, Cairo University masters Degree Thesis, 1954.

29. *Qur'an*, chapter 16 : 89.

30. *Qur'an*, chapter 6 : 38.

31. *Qur'an*, chapter 6 : 59.

32. *Qur'an*, chapter 42 : 10.

33. *Qur'an*, chapter 5 : 4.

34. Al-Buti, Dr Said Ramadan, *Dawabit al-Maslahah*, p. 411 - 413.

35. Ibid, pp. 54-55.

36. Mustafa Zaid Ali, *Maslahah fil Tashri al-Islami*, Cairo, 1954, p. 28.

Chapter Five

The '*Taqlid*' Regime and the Sunni Schools of *Fiqh*

owards the end of the fourth century of *hijrah*, many sections of the Muslim society, particularly the disciples of the four great doctors of Islamic law, became more and more anxious about the ever present tendency of despotic rulers to manipulate *ijtihad* for their own purposes. They were also anxious about the corrosive effects of alien concepts and philosophies which *ijtihad* drew into Muslim thought. Moreover, they feared the divisive effects of *ijtihad* on the unity of the society. All this caused the emergence of the *taqlid* regime which discouraged *ijtihad* and demanded succeeding generations of jurists and lawyers to recognize the authority of the deductions, and interpretations and reasoning of the first generation of jurists as final and binding. In this way a monolithic partisan pattern of jurisprudence and law emerged to dominate the Islamic discourse. Needless to say, this was in direct opposition to the teachings of the early doctors of Islamic law and the founding fathers of the schools of jurisprudence.

Along with despotism, social injustice, economic and intellectual stagnation, the doctrine of *taqlid* was responsible for destroying the inner vitality and purposefulness of the Islamic society, thus preparing it for alien domination in the form of *al-gazw al-askari* and *al-gazw al-thaqafi* (military and intellectual incursion).

Liberalism and secularism in the form of Kamalism, in Ottoman Turkey and its various versions in the Muslim world were philosophies which viewed Islam in terms of the phenomenon of *taqlid* (unchanging and oppressive), and campaigned for its total rejection in favor of a total uncritical allegiance to secularism and occidental thought.[1] The reactionary attitude of the *taqlid* regime may also be blamed for having caused the emergence of various claimants to *tajdid* (reform) and the *Mahdi* across the Muslim world. There is hardly a Muslim country which did not have its own *Mahdi*, even America produced its own *Mahdi* by the name of Fard Muhammad.[2]

What Muslims the world over need to understand is that the system of *taqlid* was established with the purpose of protecting *maslahah* and societal interests and therefore should not be condemned. But then again they also should accept that *taqlid* served that purpose at the cost of spiritual and intellectual initiative and substituting rigidity for flexibility of Muslim social teachings. The condemnation of the *taqlid* regime will be justified if Muslims refuse to accept that it has outlived its purpose and it is now time for change and new progressive approach.

When non-Muslim opinion refers to negative aspect of Islamic fundamentalism, it is the systems of *taqlid* that they have in mind. These systems should be put in perspective and seen as responses to certain historical circumstances. It is accommodation of change rather than its denial which is fundamental to the teaching of Islam.[3]

Blind imitation, *taqlid* in Arabic, is the result of a loss of confidence in one's ability to recognize the essence of Islam, and the falling back on the previous forms of Islamic culture or *fiqh* so as to retain one's life, which dribbles like sand through the fingers the tighter it is held. In a more legal sense, *taqlid* means following the decisions reached by respected and renown scholars of the past.

Let us proffer three traditional definitions of *taqlid* as follows. *Taqlid* is acting on the statement of someone else without any proof.[4] *Taqlid* is the acceptance of a statement of someone else rather than your own, and that too, without any proof.[5] *Taqlid* is the acceptance of a statement without any proof in which mere good opinion about someone has been followed rather than accepting the statement on the basis of knowledge or tested principles [*usul*] or their derivatives.[6] The term is used as a technical term for the uncritical adherence to the doctrine of a school and all its traditions; in this sense it has been translated as "traditionalism", "authority" and "blind following".

Taqlid can also be divided into *taqlid al-mutlaq,* or absolute imitation, and *taqlid al-shakhsi,* or the imitation of an individual. The supporters of *taqlid* justify their position from this verse, which suggests that besides the Prophet, the opinion of people charged with authority is binding:

"If they had only referred it to the Apostle, or to those charged with authority among them, the proper investigators would have tested it from them" (4: 83).

They also point to the *hadith* "Follow Abu Bakr and Umar after me", but this is not correct because the key verb used by the Prophet is derived from *iqtida* instead of *taqlid*.

In order to prove their position, the supporters of *taqlid* again try to show that the Companions actually used *taqlid*. They point to the statement of Abu Musa al-Ash'ari, "As long as Abdullah ibn Mas'ud is present, do not ask me any questions." But clearly this statement is not a justification for; rather it shows how much respect Abu Musa had for Ibn Mas'ud.

One of the negative consequences of *taqlid* has been the assumption that the leaders of the four schools were in some way as distinct and separate as their followers had often become. What is surprising to the person who witnesses in someone the strict observance of one school to the exclusion of others is that the leaders themselves were very much aware and admiring of the work of the other leaders, and on many occasions they frowned at anyone following blindly.

Abu Hanifah

The example of Imam Abu Hanifah (d. 150) in travelling to the main centers of Islamic learning suggests that the discussions of *fiqh* were not at all isolated, even though regional themes and variations did occur. The environment of the early scholars of *fiqh* was conducive to the assimilation of a wide variety of issues and solutions, so that when an Imam decided on a particular solution, it was clear that this preference took place not because diverse solutions were unknown but because one of the many solutions was accepted as more valid. Abu Hanifah learned *fiqh* from quite a number of scholars. In Kufah, he studied under Sha'bi ibn Salamah ibn Kuhail, Manarib ibn Dithar, Abu Ishaq, Aun ibn Abdullah, Amr ibn Murfah, A'mash, Adib ibn Thabit al-Ansari, Samak ibn Harb, and others. In Basrah, he studied under Qatadah and Shu'bah. While in Basrah he possibly had the opportunity to meet the two fathers of Arabic grammar and linguistics, al-Khalil and Sibawayh, and may have learnt from them the use of *qiyas* in Greek empiricist medicine. He then went to Makkah and Madinah, where he studied under Ata ibn Abi Rabah. He also studied under Ikramah, a disciple of Abdullah ibn Abbas. Thus, his background was very much comprehensive and a product of a wide and open environment of learning.

Abu Hanifah's students also attained great fame. In fact, most of the decisions attributed to Abu Hanifah were made by his students. Ya'qub ibn Ibrahim ibn Habib, known as Abu Yusuf and Muhammad ibn al-Hasan al-Shaibani, two of his disciples are known to have differed with their teacher in 85 % of his legal decisions, and today's Hanafi school is based on their teachings. This demonstrates that Abu Hanifah was one who disliked *taqlid*, even if it was imitation of him. He was certainly not authoritarian and was successful in instilling in his students an attitude of independent thinking and use of reason guided by the *Qur'an* and *Sunnah*.

Born in 80 A.H., Abu Hanifah was first raised as a trader, but soon took a great interest in education. One day as he passed the house of Imam Sha'bi, a learned scholar of Kufah, he was asked, "Whose classes do you attend?" "No one's" he replied. "I see sign of intelligence in you. You ought to sit in the company of learned men," and with that Abu Hanifah was encouraged to embark on his studies.[7]

After completing his education in Kufah, he went on to Makkah and Madinah. There, he enrolled as a student of the famous scholar Ata ibn Abi Rabah. In extolling his virtues, the son of Umar used to say, "Why do people come to me when there is Ata ibn Rabi Rabah for them to go to?"

While in Makkah, Abu Hanifah studied under Ikramah, a discipline of the famous scholar Abdullah ibn Abbas. Ikrimah had the good fortune of learning *hadith* and points of *fiqh* from Ali, Abu Hurairah, Abdullah ibn Umar, Aqrabah ibn Umar, Safwan, Jabir, and Abu Qatadah. It is said of Ikramah that he taught at least seventy of the Successors. Sa'id ibn Zubair was once asked if he knew someone more learned than himself among is contemporaries, and he replied, "Ikramah". Abu Hanifah received a license [*ijazah*] in using ijtihad from Ikramah which was valid even while Ikramah was alive.

Abu Hanifah's first book was *Kitab al-ra'y*, which means the book of reasoning. This book enumerates methods to adopt if a solution is not found to a problem in the *Qur'an* and *Sunnah*. It is not extant, but we possibly have a commentary of it in form of a manuscript of his student Imam Yusuf titled *Kitab al-usul*. Shaibani's *Kitab al-usul* is possibly also a commentary on *Kitab al-ra'y* and is preserved partially in the manuscript of a Mu'tazilah writer named Abu al-Husain al-Basri. Another student, Ibrahim al-Farazi, wrote *Kitab al-siyar* concerning Hanafi *fiqh* on international relations, while Shaibani also wrote a detailed as well as abridged versions of this subject, titled *Kitab al-siyar al-kabir* and *Kitab al-siyar al-saghir* respectively. We should, however, consider a genealogy for Abu Hanifah's book as follows: First his book is absorbed and commented on by Shaibani, whose main pupil Imam Shafi'i then elaborates the concepts and writes his seminal work *al-Risalah*.

His central criteria for making a legal decision are summed up in this statement.

> I accept everything from the Book of Allah; but if I do not find an answer there, I resort to the *Sunnah* of the Messenger of Allah; if I do not find a solution in the Book of Allah and the *Sunnah* of the Messenger of Allah, I accept the statement of whomsoever I chose from the Companions. I will not accept a statement from anyone but a Companion, and if the statement is from Ibrahim Nakhai, Sha'bi, Ibn Sirin, Hasan, Ata, or Sa'id ibn Musayyib, I shall perform *ijtihad*, just as they themselves did *ijtihad*, they are men and we are also men like them [*hum rijal wa nahnu rijal*].[8]

Abu Hanifah was unjustifiably accused of giving preference to reason over revelation. When the news reached his teacher Imam Baqir, he summoned him and asked him saying, "are you the one who has changed the religion of my grandfather by preferring *qiyas* over tradition?" Abu Hanifah responded saying, "I would like to ask you a few questions. Who do you consider to be physically weaker, a male or female?" "A female", Imam Baqir answered. Abu Hanifah followed up with another question to him: "How much is the share of a male and female in the laws of inheritance?" "The male gets double the share of a female" he responded. Abu Hanifah then said, "this is the teaching of your grandfather, if I had changed the laws of your grandfather, reason requires that the lady should get double the share of a man since you agree that she is physically weaker." Abu Hanifah: "Next, which one do you think is the higher duty, the *salah* (daily prayer) or *saum* (fasting in *Ramadan*)?" Imam Baqir: "*salah*". Abu Hanifah: "That being the case, it should be permissible for a woman during her menstruation period to postpone her *salah* but not permissible to postpone her fasting (which is a lesser duty). But I rule that she may postpone her fasting, but she should not postpone her *salah*, and in this I follow the Messenger of Allah." Imam Baqir was so impressed by this dialogue that he arose and kissed Abu Hanifah on the forehead.[9]

Abu Hanifah later studied with Imam Baqir and Imam Ja'afar al-Sadiq. He also attended the *hadith* lectures of Imam Malik, who was thirteen years younger than him, and Imam Malik in return also studied jurisprudence under Abu Hanifah. Abu Hafs counts the teachers of Abu Hanifah to be over 4,000. According to al-Dhahabi, while still a young man, Abu Hanifah was honored by Hammad to replace him at a time when he was on a two-month journey. During that period Abu Hanifah was asked sixty questions which he answered. Upon returning Abu Hanifah presented the same questions to his teacher who agreed with him in forty answers but disregarded the balance twenty answers. Abu Hanifah was so pleased that he vowed never to leave Hammad until death. He also refused to establish his own school while his teacher Hammad was alive.[10]

Abu Hanifah was a very strong opponent of blind following and as we have seen he would rather use his reason than blindly follow anyone. Abu Yusuf, his student was heard saying:

"It is illegal for anyone to blindly accept our views until he or she knows where we are getting our views from."[11]

Imam Malik ibn Anas

Imam Malik ibn Anas also received a very broad education, although he did not have to travel extensively to get it. Instead, the many scholars who came to Madinah sufficed to give Imam Malik a thorough exposure to the progress of *fiqh* in the Islamic world. His work, the well-trodden path [*al-Muwatta*] also is one of the earliest collections of *hadith*. His book was so well appreciated and widely accepted that Caliph Abu Ja'afar asked that *al-Muwatta* be disseminated everywhere, and if anyone acted contrary, he should be persecuted. However, Imam Malik objected to this stand of the Caliph, arguing that each of the widespread communities had learned some particular practice from the Companions, and they were sure to strongly hold on to that practice. If anyone approached them with something different, they were bound to meet with strong opposition from them.[12] So, in this manner, Imam Malik affirmed the acceptance of differences in form, understanding of course that the essence was the same (in this case, the essence was the practice handed down by the Companions.)

The structure of *al-Muwatta* follows a pattern of *hadith* or tradition with its legal ramifications. The collection of *hadith* involved in *al-Muwatta* is one of the earliest works, and his legal opinions are early examples of *ijtihad*. In fact, Ibn Qutaibah (d. 276 A.H.) categorized Imam Malik as one of the *ahl ra'y*, (among those who used reasoning in their legal decisions.)[13]

Imam Malik was also a strong stickler for truth and he suffered greatly for this quality. When he ruled that a divorce proceeding was nullified if it went under duress, Ja'afar ibn Sulaiman, governor of Madinah and a cousin of the Caliph Mansur, forbade him to publicize his decision. Imam Malik, however went ahead and publicized his decision for which he was flogged to such an extent that his shoulder-bones were broken. It is said that from that day onwards he offered *salah* with his hands on his sides as he could no longer fold them.

It is recorded that he would refuse to give legal advice for people in distant and far-off places. In this way he respected the particular practices, all in accordance with Islam, which pertained to different areas. Once a man came to him after travelling for six months seeking his opinion. Imam Malik told him, "Please tell your people that Malik will not give an answer to that question." Ibn Abi Uways recalled that Imam Malik told him that he would get so involved and engrossed in giving legal opinions that he would forsake food and drink. If someone corrected him, he accepted the correction immediately and with due respect.

One of his great contributions was the codification of Madinah *fiqh*. In the absence of a *hadith*, Imam Malik used the unanimous opinion of the people of Madinah [*ahl al-Madinah*]. During his time, there were a number of famous successors still living in Madinah. Sulaiman, the servant of Maimuna, a wife of the Prophet, and Salim, grandson of the Khalifah Umar (who had been taught by his father, Abdullah ibn Umar) were few such people.

Imam Shafi'i

Imam Muhammad Idris al-Shafi'i was born in the same year in which Abu Hanifah died (150 A.H.). He was a disciple of Imam Muhammad al-Shaibani for many years, and he had also studied under Imam Malik. He thus was able to bridge the twin dimensions of *hadith* and *ra'y*.

Imam Shafi'i had trained himself in the area of philosophy as well, and was therefore thoroughly acquainted with the arguments of the *Mu'tazilahs*. His ability to meet the *Mu'tazilah* challenge and to infuse vitality into the *hadith* tradition may very well be a model to which the present scholars of the *ummah* should strive. If we conceive of the pressing contemporary need to be the tension between the traditional legacy and the sophisticated and highly rational onslaught of modern thought, we may see a parallel in al-Shafi'i treatment of the *hadith* and *ra'y* and the Mu'tazilah challenge.

The situation in his times was one where the jurists were moving apart, while one group immersed in the *hadith*, the other studied philosophy, logic, and rational *fiqh*. This conflict of *ahl al-hadith* (represented then by the Hijazi scholars) and *ahl al-ra'y* (represented then by the Iraqi scholars) is perhaps a perennial one, and we certainly see its effect even now. The shortcoming of the *ahl al-ra'y* is that these jurists are often unaware of the tremendous scope of the *hadith*, and they therefore tend to jump to rational tools before exhausting the evidence of *hadith*. The *ahl al-hadith* people tended to narrow the application of *fiqh* and became easy targets for rationalistic sophistication. It took someone completely competent in both dimensions to harmonize between *extreme literalism* of the *hadith* school and the *extreme rationalism* of the *fiqh* school. The fact that there was rigidity in both the schools of jurisprudence did not escape Imam Shafi'i. .

The importance of *Kitab al-risalah*, his *magnum opus*, in the field of *usul al-fiqh* cannot be overestimated. His terminology was as much vibrant and insightful during his time as it is today. As its name implies, the *Risalah* is in the form of a letter instructing a friend in the ways and methodologies of *fiqh*.

Although the Mu'tazilah and Ash'ariyyah positions exaggerated certain truths so much so that they often appeared absurd , the *Mu'tazilah* position has been relegated the loser in the philosophical debate. But lest we give too much weight to the polemic, it must be added that the jurists have always in fact operated or reasoned with a combination of ideas and assumptions which are characteristic of *Mu'tazilah* weltanschauung. This being the case, we find that the Muslims characterized as Mu'tazilah were not at all the villains they have been made out to be. Far from rejecting a *hadith*, the Mu'tazilah rejected only that *hadith* which had just a single transmitter [*ahad*].

154

Now to answer the *Mu'tazilah* stance that single-transmission *hadith* be deemed acceptable, Imam Shafi'i combed the history to find cases of people acting on the authority of a single person (or witness) in the time of the Prophet. He found that on that eventful day when the *qiblah* changed from the direction of the *Bait al-Maqdis* in Jerusalem to the *Ka'bah* in Makkah, a single person was instructed by the Prophet to run through the streets proclaiming this change. In this instance, a single person's authority was enough for the people to change their *qiblah*. Another example concerned Anas and wine. One day when Anas was serving his guests some wine, the revelation descended making wine unlawful. Upon hearing the person running through the streets reciting the verse which prohibited wine, Anas took a hammer and smashed the wine cauldron. He and his guests threw away their drinks that very moment, all on the basis of a single report.

Since Imam Shafi'i studied under Imam Malik, he became very familiar with *ilm al-kalam* and *Mu'tazilah* ideas. It was in his period when a distinction began to be made between ideas, rationality, reason, speculation, and tradition, the *Sunnah* of the Prophet, and the *hadith* literature. It is perhaps best to conceive of this distinction as a spectrum, where a particular scholar would work somewhere toward one end of the spectrum. This spectrum also appears later, in the full-fledged *Mu'tazilah* debate, from which *Ash'ariyyah* doctrine emerged the victor. Much later in South Asia a similar spectrum appeared, opposing the people of *hadith* [*ahl al-hadith*] with rationalists or modernists. Simply put, there need be no contradiction between reason and the tradition.

If we go to either extremes, the results are completely untenable. A scholar who is too caught up in the traditions is unable to appreciate the reasonable and rational background of the tradition. The scholar too caught up in reason and rationality is likely to reject the revelation of Islam itself, contenting himself with a positive and rationalistic religion with no grounding and with great danger. Clearly, some balance is required, and the work of Imam Shafi'i can be seen as a tremendously insightful and developed exposition of a balance, one of the very first systematic works on the *usul al-fiqh*.

After travelling to Iraq, home of the scholars tending toward the rationalistic end of the spectrum, Imam Shafi'i was fully aware of the dangers of unaided reason. With sophistry and rationalistic argumentation, it was possible to create an Islam almost unrecognizable with that practiced by the Prophet. But upon his return he did not take the then practice of the people of Madinah to be normative. He rightly perceived that their proximity to the Prophet was not close enough to justify making their contemporary practices normative. We need not see any conflict in this position with that of his teacher Imam Malik, because already a generation had passed. Neither the new decisions the people of Madinah made were necessarily authoritative nor was Imam Shafi'i confident that the rationalizing of the *ahl al-ra'y* (people of reasoning or opinion) was authoritative.

We can thus see that Imam Shafi'i created and developed a systematic position somewhere between and somehow harmonizing the two teachers, Abu Hanifah and Malik. Again we need not find conflict, because in developing his position, Shafi'i did not have to refute or reject tenets of either school.

If we conceive of Abu Hanifah's school relying on reason in difficult cases of a seemingly silent text, this can be explained by the fact that the Haramain "soil" was not there in Iraq to cultivate a *fiqh* which would have as its basis, practice and tradition. On the other hand, Malik justifiably found great proximity to the Prophet in the practices of the people of Madinah. But, we should also remember that he made sure these practices did not disseminate widely and as exclusive doctrines. Abu Hanifa's school works for particular situations as does Malik's school for particular situations. Shafi'i tried to develop a system which would incorporate both schools in order to cover a broader spectrum of situations. It is fitting that the fourth Imam studied under Shafi'i. The two early schools emerging in the two distinct regions and forms of Islam, Iraq and the Hijaz, developed two distinct aspects of Islam, reason and tradition. Then a scholar studied in both to develop and systematize these two streams and create a systematic *usul al-fiqh* – a fourth scholar then studying under the third scholar.

These are the inter-relationships and resonances coming from the four extant schools of *fiqh* in Islam. Two distinct ideas systematized in one and studied by the fourth. None of these four schools makes sense without the others, none may be removed or rejected without disturbing the inner structures and inter-connections. None can really be understood without reference to the others. When considered together, the tremendous unity in essence and diversity in form of Islam becomes apparent, and the dynamism and vitality of the *fiqh* becomes clearly evident.

Imam Shafi'i also produced students of great eminence. His students in Iraq included founders of new schools of Islamic thought such as the great Imam Ahmad ibn Hanbal whom we shall discuss later, Imam Daud al-Zahiri the literalist and a strong critic of *ra'y* and *qiyas*, in fact Daud al-Zahir became one of the strongest voices against some of Shafi'i's ideas proving that blind following was not the practice of these jurists. Abu Ja'far ibn Jarir al-Tabari the great historian and exegete was also one of his students.[14]

The spread of the Shafi'i may be credited to the efforts of scholars such as Abu Ishaq Shirazi (d. 476 A.H.), author of the famous Shafi'i book of jurisprudence *al-Muhadhdhab*, and Imam Abu Hamid al-Ghazali (d. 505 A.H.), one of Islam's greatest scholar of philosophy, theology, and jurisprudence.

Ahmad ibn Hanbal

Imam Abu Abdullah Ahmad ibn Hanbal (d.241 A.H.) is one of greatest jurists and *hadith* scholars that Islamic scholarship ever produced. He is well known for having been firmly abiding in the truth against the wishes and punishment of oppressive rulers. He was persecuted, beaten, and imprisoned by the Caliph al-Wathiq for not espousing the *Mu'tazilah* doctrine of the "createdness" of the Qur'an.

Imam Ahmad had tremendous knowledge of the *hadith* and became a great scholar in *hadith* literature and *fiqh*. He is reputed to have memorized one million *hadiths*. His aversion to *ra'y* and his strict adherence to the text [*nass*] are well documented. It is for this reason that some writers do not consider him a jurist but a Traditionist [*muhaddith*]. We see that the Muslim bibliographer Ibn al-Nadim classified him along with al-Bukhari, Muslim, and other Traditionist in his *al-Fihrist*.[15] Other biographers of jurists have also not included him in their works suggesting that they do not consider him a jurist. This view, however, is not correct because Ahmad ibn Hanbal is known to have developed a unique methodology of jurisprudence. We should not forget that he was a student of Imam Shafi'i and the two had a close relationship and great respect for each other. Imam Ahmad memorized a million traditions, collected and evaluated thousands of traditions while Shafi'i put together a systematic framework for the *Sunnah*. He also considered reason and analogy as subsidiary sources of law in Islam after the main four sources and *fatawa al-sahabah* (sayings and verdicts of certain Companions of the Prophet).

Although we have discussed four schools of Sunni jurisprudence to which most Muslims belong, historically, Muslims have followed a number of different schools. When we look at a book such as the third century *Hijra* work of Ibn Jarir al-Tabari titled *Ikhtilaf al-fuqaha*, we see that along with the four Imams, we find Laith ibn Sa'ad (d.175 A.H.), the great *faqih* of Egypt, Ibn Shubrumah (d.144 A.H.), Sufian al-Thawri from Kufah (d.161 A.H.), Hammad Zaid from Basrah (d.179 A.H.), Awza'i from Damascus (d.157 A.H.), Tahari (d. 310), Daud ibn Ali (202 – 270 A.H.), Zaid ibn Ali (80 – 128 A.H.), and Ja'afar al-Sadiq (80 – 148 A.H.). These last two represent the *Zaidi* and *Ja'afari* schools of *Shi'i fiqh*.

Imam Awza'i was dominant in Andalus before the Maliki school became prominent there. Muhammad ibn Ali al-Sanusi mentions this in *Iqa al-wasnan*. In *Madinat al-salam* he notes that there were sixteen schools of *fiqh* in Andalus until the seventh century.

Although Muslim thought, including the *usul al-fiqh*, may be characterized by its tremendous diversity, vitality, and openness, we tend to find that the schools of *fiqh* are all very closely knit. This is probably due to the fact that any inherent tensions between the two dimensions of *fiqh* (*ra'y* and *hadith*) was worked out early on by the travels of the Hijazi and Iraqi *fuqaha*. This harmonization is the outcome of the travels of Abu Hanifah, Abu Yusuf, and Muhammad ibn al-Hassan al-Shaibani to Makkah and Madinah and their meetings with Imam Malik and the companions of Ibn Abbas. Also, the Hijazi scholars, such as Hisham ibn Urwah, Muhammad ibn Ishaq, Yahya ibn Sa'id al-Ansari, Rabi'ah ibn Abi Abd al-Rahman, Hamzalah ibn Abi Sufian al-Jumahi, Abd al-Aziz ibn Abi Sulaiman al-Majishun, and others, travelled to Iraq.

The difference centers around the branches [*furu'*] of jurisprudence rather than the fundamental issues of theology. It is important to remember that the great scholars like Shah Wali Allah of Delhi, Ibn Taimiyyah, al-Qadi Shaukani, and Baqir Sadir refused to follow one school blindly, but instead emphasized the coherence and essential unity of the Islamic message as manifested in *fiqh*.

What one discovers from a thorough study of the lives and histories of the founders of the schools of jurisprudence is that they all distanced themselves from contemporary rulers and developed their ideas in an atmosphere of abstraction. Few of them, if any, developed a very meaningful political theory, not because they lacked in political understanding, but because they did not want to have anything to do with the political establishment. For this reason, one can hardly find in their writings any detailed discussion on political science.

These withdrawal stratagems were later reinforced by means of *taqlid*, which we have already discussed above. Meanwhile, the contemporary rulers continued to develop their systems along despotic lines. Consequently, stagnation and despotism, more often than not, represented the position of the Muslim society during its medieval period of decline.

Today's rigid and fundamentalist Islam, with its emphasis on *taqlid*, continue to frown at any call for change in attitude and approach to accommodate social change. What the traditional *alim* fails to understand is that social change is always a feature of human society. It is an unfailing cause of tension when religiously held beliefs fail to accommodate a social change. Islamic revelation affirms that religious beliefs are innate: a divine imprint [*fitrah*] in the nature of man. The inevitability of social change is also confirmed. The Muslims believe (as taught by the Prophet and the *Qur'an*) that all the prophets preached an identical theology and message, what differed and kept on changing as one prophet came after another were the laws to accommodate social changes. Moreover, Islamic social legislation in the *Qur'an* is sparse. Out of the 6000 verses of the *Qur'an*, 245 deals with various aspects of social legislation: 70 verses address personal affairs; 70 deal with financial and civil matters; 30 criminal affairs; 30 on witnessing and adjudication; 10 constitutional matters; 25 international affairs; and 10 address economical issues.

When we call for the revision and *critique* of the *taqlid* regime, we do so knowing that if we break off thoroughly from our roots, if we reject fourteen centuries of Muslim experience of the *Qur'an* and *Sunnah*, we are "sitting ducks" for the sharpshooters of modernity who would relish a world – one billion Muslims – utterly open to capitalism, consumerism, and the new world propagated by advertisement. True, our culture and heritages are heavy and bring with them some *inertia*. But, it is precisely this *inertia* which grounds us in reality, which offers us a firm foundation from which to progress. If we reject the heritage, we condemn ourselves to reinventing the wheel under each generation: and given our "success" in this modern world, we will be condemned to use everyone else's wheel.

Two issues especially arise, *ijtihad* and *ijma'* as an institution. Western scholars are usually completely in favor of *ijtihad*. They reason that if the Muslims use *ijtihad* freely, they will be able to "develop" with the rest of the "civilized" world. This desire on their part must be the strongest warning possible to the Muslims to understand what *ijtihad* entails. We must understand the Islamic legacy before we change it, and any development in Islamic thought must maintain its link with the legacy and not be a radical departure from it.

The modern world is one utterly opposed to Islam in every sense, originating as it did from a world in which the divine was overturned and the human apotheosised. We cannot be true to Islam and exercise an *ijtihad* modifying *fiqh* to the piping of modern western ideas and the modern Muslim elite. If we exercise *ijithad* properly, using our reason grounded in and guided by the direct texts of the *Qur'an* and the *Sunnah*, our *ijtihad* will be a device enabling the *ummah* to regain its confidence and prosperity and position of savior to humankind.

We must also work on making *ijma'* a democratic institution once again. It is the task of Muslims to devise ways to allow themselves to communicate freely in order to reach agreements and make proper decisions. If truly unbiased and well balanced forums can be created for Muslims to decide among themselves how to solve common problems, only then and then alone will the *ummah* be in a state of unity and in a position to give guidance to the entire humankind.

Notes

1. Al-Mahdi, S., *Islam-Society & Change* (Voices of Resurgent Islam. Ed. John L. Esposito.) New York: Oxford University Press, 1983, p. 233.

2. Minister Ishmael Muhammad, the son of Elijah Muhammad and Farrakhan's assistant, confirmed during his visit to London in December 1999 that the Nation of Islam was giving up its doctrines which had kept it away from main stream Islam. 'Remember that 99.9 per cent of our members come from the Christian church so if you are going to introduce a religion to western culture and philosophy and to a people who are right down at

the bottom, you cannot rush...Minister Fard Muhammad is not a prophet. We call him a great teacher, a scholar, a Mahdi is the Arab word for it. He is one of the reformers prophesied by the Prophet Muhammad to come every century to bring the Muslims back to the straight path of God...Prophet Muhammad is respected and recognized by us as the last Prophet.' See *New Nation* (Monday, 13 December, 1999. Issue 158, p. 2).

3. Al-Mahdi, S, op.cit.

4. *Musallam al-Thubut*, vol. 2, p. 350.

5. Ibn Hajib, *Mukhtasar,* 231.

6. Khudrami, Usul al-Fiqh, *457.*

7. *Al-Khairat al-hissan,* p. 37; *Tarikh al-Baghdad,* vol.13, p. 347; & *Siyar a'lam al-nubala,* vol.6, p. 395.

8. See Khatib al-Baghdad, *Tarikh,* 31: 368; *al-Intiqa`* 142; *Siyar a'lam al-nubala,* vol.6, p.399.

9. Ibn Bazar al-Kurdi, *Manaqib al-imam al-a'zam,* Beirut: Dar al-Hikmah, 1342 A.H., p. 99.

10. *Al-Khairat al-hisan,* p. 39.

11. Al-Zuhaili, Wahbah, op.cit., p. 1130.

12. Ibn Abi hatim 'Abd al-Rahman al-Razi, *al-Jarh wa al-ta'dil,* Hyderabad, 1337 A.H., p. 29.

13. See also Ibn Qutaibah's *kitab al-ma'arif.*

14. See Ibn Nadim's, *al-Fihrist;* Ibn Khalikan, *Wafayat al-a'yan*; & Husayni, *Tabaqat.*

15. Ibn Nadim, *al-Fihrist,* pp. 314-320.

Chapter Six

Toward a New Methodology
in the Study of *Fiqh*

uslims, as they come in contact with the acute problems that exist in the world today, they experience the need to take part in solving them. This means they have to participate with people from other religious and cultural traditions since the nature of some of the problems is such that they do not discriminate on the basis of religion, gender, or cultural background. Deciding to participate will mean that, as Muslims, we would like to do so "Islamically", by recourse to the *usul al-fiqh al-islami*. But then again this *usul al-fiqh* is one that was developed to deal with problems that may be described as "local problems" in the Muslim lands. The universality of the *usul al-fiqh* discourse, which we claim, requires that we broaden the science of *usul,* or even revise it so that it can cope with the contemporary global situation. Thus, there is an element of contingency here, which means that there can be no final approach and methodology to *usul al-fiqh.* We are certainly not dealing with a closed system, but rather, a very open and dynamic one. Indeed, a closed system of *usul* would be impossible from an Islamic point of view as that would limit Allah to our own particular systems and Allah cannot be limited. He speaks today through the *Qur'an* to the villagers in Transkei as he spoke to the Bedouins in Arabia some fourteen hundred years ago.

When we say that the inherited *usul al-fiqh* is "local", we acknowledge the socio-phenomenal dimension present in this discourse; the influence exerted by *usul* on social process, and the conditioning imposed by the dynamics of society on the interpretation and understanding of *usul.* The new methodology in *usul*, therefore, should predominantly be concerned with ways to re-construct the *usul* discourse independent from the medieval Arab socio-cultural influences. It is an attempt to bring our existential experiences to the discourse, what is typical of our social locations and searching for an intellectual self-definition. We have seen how Abu Hanifa's methodology in Iraq developed in a very distinct way from that of Malik in Madinah. Socio-political as well as cultural factors affected the development of these two *usul al-fiqh* genres. Therefore, to propose that there is still a possibility for another development and methodology of *usul al-fiqh* whether it may be African, European, or Chinese is not implausible or a *bid'ah*.

A contemporary *usul al-fiqh* discourse will have to be critical toward economic and socio-cultural factors which condition the life and reflection of the society. To disregard these factors is to deceive both oneself and others. It will then necessarily be a *critique* of both society and theology insofar as they are convoked and addressed by the *Qur'an*; it will be a critical discourse, worked out in the light of the *Qur'an* and *Sunnah* and inspired by a practical purpose and therefore indissolubly linked to historical praxis.

Classical books of *fiqh* do not always provide the answers to contemporary social realities. Not because the writers of these books did not possess enough knowledge of the *Shari'ah* and society, but because we cannot expect them to exercise some unearthly power and speak to us from their graves. We should not force the Imams to deal with issues that did not concern them in their societies, nor to ask them questions that they never asked themselves. Social analysis are matters of scientific rationality. Their selections, while they must conform to the spirit of the *Shari'ah*, must be justified rationally. An *usul al-fiqh* engaged in the struggle for social justice and liberation therefore, needs to use the tools and procedures provided by the social sciences. They enable us to move beyond the level of sentimentalism and mere moralism which was described by the Prophet as *az'af al-iman* (weakest faith) in his *hadith*: "whoever among you sees an injustice being done, then he should stop it with his hands, and if he is unable to do so, then with his mouth (he should speak out), and if again he is unable to do so, then he should at least distaste it with his heart, and that is the weakest form of faith."[1]

The social sciences will enable the *mujtahid* to do his work more thoroughly. They can make the *ummah* aware of how its beliefs and practices help either to support or change the social order, and they offer a sense of how the society's beliefs and practices either encourage or suppress the struggle for freedom, justice, and equality. Thus, they make the Muslim realize the *maqasid al-shari'ah* and *Shari'ah*'s duty in the liberation of humanity.

When we call for the introduction of the social sciences in *usul al-*

fiqh, we do so realizing that these disciplines are not apodictic and beyond criticism. In fact, the contrary is true. When we agree that they are "sciences" we also have to agree that they cannot evade critical examination but rather submit to it. Scientific knowledge, as we know it, advances by means of hypotheses that provide diverse explanations of one and the same reality. Therefore, to say that a thing is scientific is to say that it is particularly true with regard to the ever-new and changing field of social sciences. Nonetheless, these sciences do help us understand our social realities.

The *Qur'an* and Islam sanction no representative or representatives of Allah [*khalifat allah*] who should establish religious authority. It entitles no one to be the exclusive interpreter of the texts. On the contrary it recognizes and cites all the known means of knowledge: revelation, intuition, reason, and experience. It encourages interest in the achievements of other peoples. Thus, the *Qur'an* takes an open attitude to the adoption of useful ideas and institutions of foreign origin. The Caliph Umar adopted several such ideas and institutions, for example, the *kharaj* (land tax) and the *diwan* (bureaucratic system).

Empirical and rational knowledge must not be discredited since a Muslim believes that Allah is the source of all knowledge. The underlying essence of knowledge in Islam is *tawhid*, and this essence must be the generator of our research, work, and our efforts. This was the attitude of Islam's great scholars during the golden age of Islamic civilization.

We see that Al-Farabi accepts knowledge acquired by sense-perception as true knowledge. To him, man's first knowledge is perception. Perception comes after sensation. It is an individual knowledge and it does not require mental activity. In his work, *al Madinat al-fadilah,* he argues that because of the inherent weakness of our mental powers we cannot comprehend God completely. According to him, every idea comes from sense-experience:

> There is nothing in the intellect that has not first been in the senses. The mind is like a smooth tablet on which nothing is written and it is the senses that do all the writing on it. The senses are five: sight, hearing, smell, taste and touch. Each of these has a proper sensible thing for its object. In every sensation the senses receive the form or species of sensible things without the matter, just as wax receives the form of a seal without any of the matter of it. [2]

165

The sensations we have once experienced, he maintains, are not utterly dead. They can reappear in the form of images. The power by which we revive a past sensible experience without the aid of any physical stimulus is called imagination [al-mutakhayyilah] while the power by which we combine and divide images is called the cogitative [al-muffakkarah]. If we were limited merely to the experience of our actual sensations, we would have only the present, and with it there would be no intellectual life at all. But fortunately we are endowed with the power of calling back a former experience, and this is called memory [al-hafidah or al-zakirah].[3]

We see how Thomas Aquinas as a representative of religious realism and living in the 13th century, developed a theory of knowledge parallel with his metaphysical conceptions. We can explain his theory of knowledge by showing that he was influenced by Aristotle and al-Farabi. God is "Pure Reason", thus the universe is also "Pure reason". It follows that we can understand the truth of objects by using reason, as suggested by Aristotle and al-Farabi. To obtain information about the external world, however, we have to use our senses. Even though the truth has been conveyed to humans by revelation from God, He has also provided men with the intellect to seek the truth. Aquinas gives second place to intellect after revelation.[4] He further maintains that sense is a power and is naturally changed by the exterior senses. Wherefore the exterior cause of such change is what is directly perceived by the senses. Now, change is of two kinds, one is natural, the other is spiritual.

Like Thomas Aquinas, John Locke, another western scholar, also follows the path of Muslim scholars in his interpretation of knowledge:

Let us then suppose the mind to be, as we say, white paper, void of all characters, without any ideas; how comes it to be furnished? Whence comes it by that vast store, which the busy and boundless fancy of man has painted with an almost endless variety? Whence has it all the materials of reason and knowledge? To this I answer, in one word, from experience; on that all our knowledge is founded, and from that it ultimately derives itself. Our observation, employed either about external sensible objects, or about the internal operations of our minds, perceived and reflected on by ourselves, is that which supplies our understandings with all the materials of thinking.

These two are the foundations of knowledge, whence all the ideas we have, or can naturally have, do spring.[5]

Al-Ghazali also explains how the five sensory organs function and which characteristics of objects they perceive:

In the creation man was formed empty of knowledge and simple, knowing nothing of Allah's worlds. His worlds are many...Man only comes to know about them through the use of his senses. Each of those senses is created so that man perceives himself and one of those worlds of the universe. By worlds, we mean the different variety of beings.[6]

Foreshadowing Bacon, he claims that knowledge can only be through induction, and uses Qur'anic verses to support his case. Knowledge, he says, cannot be obtained by deduction, only induction. Thus, discarding the Aristotelian method of deduction, he laid the foundation of modern science that the Western world would notice in the 17th century.

According to al-Ghazali, "there can be no thought of Allah's person, but the power and grandeur of the Creator can only be conceived by thinking about the created."[7] Inductive knowledge, he claims, comes from the *Qur'an*:

Verse 190 of al-Imran, which commands us to study "*the creation of the earth and skies, and night and day as they follow one another.*"

These are particulars, and through a study of them the generalization can be made that Allah is the Creator of all. Al-Ghazali notes in his book, *Ihya'*, that each of the senses alone is insufficient; only with the combination of all five organs can a complete sense form in the mind. This complete sense [*al-hiss*] forms in the fore of the mind and cannot reach conclusions. Here Al-Ghazali introduces the intellect. The complete sense uses each of the five as "spies", collects the information brought by them and turns it over to the intellect. In the final analysis, knowledge issues from the intellect, and at this point, just as Al-Ghazali's thinking differs from Locke with the notion of complete sense, it also diverges from other Muslim thinkers.

Al-Ghazali does not stop at placing sensory information at the basis of knowledge, but accepts as well experience as one of the sources of knowledge. In other words, there is the natural intellect and there is the later, accumulated intellect. The accumulated intellect is gained through experience, it is born of experience.[8] We may conclude that Al-Ghazali, like other realists, sees the role of the mind in the acquisition of knowledge about an object to be equal. On the other hand, Al-Ghazali, though not as much as Locke, tries to prove with Qur'anic verses that observation is another source of knowledge:

His heart did not deny what he saw.[9]

As this, we show the secrets of the earth and the skies.[10]

Eyes cannot be blind, but hearts in the chests are.[11]

Using the above verses, he argues that observation is necessary to understand the divine-order of the universe; but also says that there are two kinds of eyes; the eye as the organ of vision, and the eye as the eye of the heart. Thus the sense provided by observation is rooted in two separate sources: the eye in the head, and the eye of the heart. The eye in the head achieves the observation of objects, and then the eye of the heart confirms it. However, all metaphysical issues can be observed and understood only through the eye of the heart.[12]

We can understand from the above analysis of early Muslim scholars' concept of science and knowledge that all objective knowledge of the world is knowledge of Allah's will, His arrangement, His wisdom. All human willing and striving is by His leave and permission. It ought to fulfill His command, the divine pattern He has revealed in the *Qur'an*, if it is to earn for its subject happiness and felicity. This means that the process of referring to Allah and His Messenger must inform and generate our efforts, and as a consequence our *usul al-fiqh* must certainly be unified and directed by the concept of *tawhid*.

If science is understood in its larger definition concerned by methodology, then certainly our sciences in Islam will span domains from the physical world to the social world, from the level of the individual to the level of the imagination. This perspective acknowledges that "science" must be described distinguishing domain and method. As Ken Wilber notes in an extremely insightful work, "when these scales are confused or equated, then science comes to mean "lower and genuine". The battle, thus stated, can never be resolved, because both parties are half-right and half-wrong."[13]

The mystical statements of the 20th Century physicists is a result of recognizing that the real important questions cannot be answered, or even addressed, by "science" if science is to mean the study of merely physical reality. Instead, using Lovejoy's concept of levels of Being, Ken Wilber explains that physicists came to understand that "Physics deals with shadows; to go beyond shadows is to go beyond physics; to go beyond physics is to head toward the meta-physical or mystical – and that is why so many of our pioneering physicists were mystics. The new physics contributed nothing positive to this mystical venture, except a spectacular failure, from whose smoking ruins the spirit of mysticism gently arose."[14]

This spectacular failure was seen when the old and new physics were compared. The two were both dealing with shadow-symbols, "but the new physics was forced to be aware of the fact that it was dealing with shadows and illusions, not reality."[15] With this, we understand that methodology may be "scientific" in its criteria of public demonstration (non-dogmatic), experiment, verification, and system, whether the domain studied is imaginational, spiritual, physical or social. But along with the concept of methodology, we recognize that study has its values and subjective objectives, and so the Islamic scientific effort must also have motivations generated from Islam.

One other problem that *usul al-fiqh* needs to address is antinomianism and legalism in contemporary Islam. On one hand you have some Muslims believing that their religious allegiance frees them from obedience to any secular law; that secular laws are evil and ought to be deliberately broken as a sign of one's Islamic stature. This certainly is against the *maqasid al-shari'ah* which recognize, any just legal system as Islamic. On the other hand legalism has led other Muslims to believe that because they have followed a set of Islamic laws, they are guaranteed salvation, and because there is no prescribed *hadd* (punishment) in the Islamic legal system for prejudice or exploitation, therefore it is not that serious to be prejudiced and to exploit others. We need to be ever aware that it is never the purpose [*maqasid*] of *Shari'ah* to establish a society where the penal laws are applied, but rather it aims at establishing a society where the penal laws may not even be applied because of Allah, one's consciousness prevents one from crime.

Legalism tends to create in an individual a false feeling of pride that crime is committed against the state or the authorities and as long as the state or authorities do not find out, there is nothing wrong in committing a crime. On the contrary, the *Shari'ah* makes an individual aware that any kind of crime is bad and it is also a sin committed against Allah who is forever seeing, and even though no specific penal laws may have been stipulated by the Almighty Allah, displeasing Him is serious. Laws therefore become secondary to keep the society in order.

There is a need to move from legalism and antinomianism, and a departure from the letter of the law to the spirit of the law [*ruh al-shari'ah*]. *Shari'ah*, as we pointed out in this book, does not primarily demand us to follow a set of defined rules and laws, but rather requires us to love Allah and His Prophets; to be able to stay away from stealing not because your hand will be cut off but because of your love for your Creator whom you know does not like you stealing and who is ever watching all actions we perform. That is why a Muslim judge is not only the person who will have you stoned to death for adultery, but also the person who is trained to bring you nearer to Allah.

Social Change and Innovation

As far as the fundamental principles of Islamic legal theory are concerned, they have been revealed in their entirety in the Holy *Qur'an*. The *ayat al-ahkam* or the legal injunctions of the *Qur'an* have been divided by some scholars into three categories. The first being the injunctions declaring what is *halal* (lawful things); second is the declarations of what is *haram*, that is the prohibition and the third category is *afw* which actually refers to those situations that are not covered by *Shari'ah*. Such situations can be decided by legal reasoning, based on the guidelines provided in the other two categories.

In those situations which are not covered by *Shari'ah*, the jurists would decide by applying established rules or through extension of these rules. However, no extension can ever take place in the case of *ibadat*, obligatory ritual practices, like s*alat, zakat, siyam* and *hajj*, but only in *adat*. The reason is that *ibadat* are only for the sake of Allah who can decide what is good for mankind. Since Prophet Muhammad happens to be the last Prophet of Allah, the Holy *Qur'an* is the last complete revelation and it contains all that man needs for his welfare, both worldly as well as spiritual. The *ibadat* are fully explained and demonstrated in the *hadith* and the *Sunnah*. Hence, there is no need of extension of *ibadat* beyond what the *Qur'an* and the *Sunnah* prescribe. If one tries to extend anything in *ibadat,* such an extension would be termed as *bid'ah* (innovation) which must be whole-heartedly condemned.

It should also be understood that the *ibadat* are not rationally intelligible, while the *adat* are. Besides, often in the *Qur'an* and the *Sunnah,* an *illah* (*ratio legis* of law) is mentioned in case of *adat* which means that *Shari'ah* not only considers them intelligible, but also extendible.

Since the Muslim believes that there will be no more revelation and no more *hadiths* to guide humanity after the death of the Prophet, the situation demands that some system be developed to respond to the changes and to extend and apply the rules which are derived through legal reasoning but still within the framework of the *Qur'an* and *Sunnah.*

This process of legal reasoning responds to social change in the framework of the legal system termed *ijtihad. Ijtihad* as we have seen before, is not simply a process of adaptation of legal theory to social changes but it also aims at a rational attempt to accommodate the change and still maintains the continuity of the Islamic legal system, the *Shari'ah.*

The Muslim society today is confronted with formidable problems on all fronts. The problems are economic, social and political in nature and are overpowering by any standard and this happens to be only the tip of the iceberg. The whole "iceberg", or complex of causes, manifestations, dialectic with other phenomena and consequences of the society's problems, requires empirical survey and critical analysis. The wisdom of the discipline should be brought to bear upon the society's problems, i.e., to enable the Muslims to understand them correctly, to assess with precision their effect upon the life of the society, and to chart out exactly their influence upon the cause of Islam in the world.[16]

It is an intrinsic part of the Islamic vision to bear responsibility not only for the welfare of the Muslim society but for that of the whole human race with whom Muslims live and for whom Muslims are "witnesses" [*shuhada'*]. Therefore, any legal reasoning on *usul al-fiqh* which demands us to adjust ourselves to various social changes taking place in the world must not be considered as *bid'ah* (mere evil innovation). The need to distinguish between *masalih al-mursalah* and *bid'ah* is therefore very important.

Shatibi, the famous Maliki scholar has discussed the implication of *bid'ah* as a legal change and the problem of its legitimacy. First of all,

Shatibi condemns *bid'ah* on more than nine grounds. His reasons for condemnation can be summed up by saying that since *Shari'ah* is complete and final, anyone who innovates, commits, among other sins, two very grave errors. One is the implication of equality or rather superiority to Allah, the original Law Giver, because the promulgation of *bid'ah* implies that the innovator knows more than Allah about *Shari'ah*. Secondly, he relies more on human reason and vain desires than on the "intentions of the Law Giver."[17]

Shatibi explains that etymologically *bid'ah* comes from *bada'a* which means to invent something new, the like of which has not existed before. In a technical sense, however, this "new-ness" and "invention" is only in reference to *Shari'ah*. Human acts can be of three kinds: required, prohibited, or voluntary. The category of prohibited actions is governed by two considerations. Firstly, that it is prohibited by law, and secondly, it literally opposes the rules of *Shari'ah*. It is the latter consideration to which the technical sense of *bid'ah* pertains.[18] Therefore, if innovation belongs to *dunya* (mundane matters) exclusively, it would not be a *bid'ah*.

There can be many examples cited like innovations in crafts, in plans of cities, and all the technological innovations, the quick means of transport, the modern amenities available to us to make our lives easy. The qualification of innovation excludes those matters which have their bases in *Shari'ah*.

Shatibi further elaborates the relationship of intention of an act to the purpose of *Shari'ah* by describing four situations. First, if the intention of an act and the act itself conforms with the purpose of *Shari'ah*, the act certainly is valid. Second, the act is not valid if the act and the intention for it are not in keeping with *Shari'ah*. Third and fourth are the cases where one of them (the intention or the act) conforms and the other does not. Shatibi makes a distinction if the intention conforms and the act does not, it is to be called *bid'ah*. If the act conforms but the intention does not, the act belongs to the category of *riya'* and hypocrisy.[19]

The mechanism of *masalih al-mursalah, istihsan, istidlal* or *istishab al-hal* illustrate the type of new things where the intention and the act both conform to the purpose of *Shari'ah*. An example of this type is the levying of new taxes in addition to those prescribed in the texts. The conformity of the act with the purpose of *Shari'ah* and the intention in this case show the right understanding of *Shari'ah* and further, the intention does not conflict with the objectives of *Shari'ah*.

In fact, it is this conformity of *masalih al-mursalah* with the *maqasid al-shari'ah* that disassociates them from *bid'ah*. Even some jurists have also wrongly identified *masalih al-mursalah* as *bid'ah hasan*. But these two terms are completely opposed to each other. To refute such views Shatibi has argued that first of all the jurists have not agreed upon an exact definition of *al-masalih al-mursalah*. Even Ghazali expressed two different views on this point. Secondly, Shatibi explains, *al-munasib al-mursal* (synonymous with *al-masalih al-mursala* in Ghazali's terminology) which is neither specifically supported by the legal text nor is it outrightly rejected, and hence it cannot be called a *bid'ah*. On the contrary it is supported by the existence of the genus which is common between *Shari'ah* and *al-masalih al-mursalah*.

Imam Shatibi has provided ten best examples of *masalih al-mursalah* like the collection of the *Qur'an*; determining the penalty for using intoxicants; allegiance to a less qualified person for an office in the presence of a better qualified one.[20] He finds three elements common in all the ten examples. First is the element of suitability with the objectives [*maqasid*] of *Shari'ah*.[21] In other words, *masalih al-mursalah* does not conflict with the fundamentals or with the evidence of *Shari'ah*. *Masalih* are rationally intelligible since they do not belong to *ta'abbudiyyat* (acts of worship), which are not rationally intelligible.[22] *Masalih al-mursalah* mainly refers to the protection of (human) necessities, removal of impediments, which are harmful to religion, and protection of an indispensable means to the end of law.[23]

This is the reason why the acceptable *masalih* cannot be equated with any *bid'ah*. They are not limited to the category of *darurah* (necessity) alone as some jurists have maintained; they cover other categories as well.

If every new thing in *adat* is regarded as *bid'ah*, then every modification (modifications) in matters such as eating, clothing speaking, etc., would stand condemned. As Imam Shatibi has put it: "There are *awaid* which change with time, place and persons. If every change is condemned then everyone who differs in this respect with those Arabs who were in contact with the companions of the Prophet will be considered as not following them and hence deviating from the right path. This is quite difficult to accept."[24]

Lack of distinctions in various types of new things in will make the concept of *bid'ah* both confusing and controversial. Those who would not accept anything new in Islamic law would reject *bid'ah* absolutely. Some jurists maintain a broad distinction between good and bad *bid'ah*. Scholars such as Ibn Abd al-Salam and Qarafi have even divided *bid'ah* into five categories of corresponding legal valuation: obligatory, recommended, indifferent, reprehensible and forbidden.

Shatibi regards such a division as meaningless and irrelevant. With the exception of those *bid'ah* mentioned by these scholars in the categories of "reprehensible" and "forbidden" the others are not *bid'ah hasanah* (good *bid'ah*) at all but fall under *masalih al-mursalah*.

Muslim scholars have categorized *bid'ah* in two kinds: *bid'ah haqiqiyyah* (absolute innovation) and *bid'ah idafiyyah* (relative) innovation. *Bid'ah haqiqiyyah* is that which is not proven by any evidence such as the *Qur'an*, *Sunnah*, *ijma*, or a reliable basis of reasoning, neither in general nor in particular. *Al-bid'ah al-idafiyyah* is the one which touches upon both the aspects. In one aspect, it is connected with evidence, in the other, it is not. It is only in the latter aspect that it is really *bid'ah*.[25] The common point in the two definitions of *bid'ah* is the intention of the innovator to equal the Law Giver.

It is not sufficient to declare a new methodology in the study of jurisprudence a *bid'ah*, unlawful [*haram*] or disliked [*makruh*] simply by saying that it did not exist during the time of the Messenger of Allah, or his Companions. By giving the revealed sources like the *Qur'an* and *Sunnah*, Allah never willed to bring an end to the human capacity of new discovery. Nor did Allah wish to declare lawful [*halal*] the human efforts to discover new things or new methods for a specific period only. Obviously, Allah did not wish to declare unlawful these human efforts though, He wanted us to look at various scientific phenomena, ponder over them, and continue conducting researches within the limits of *Qur'an* and *Sunnah*. We see how by man's stepping on the moon, it created problems for those who believed that the moon was the boat in which their duties sailed or those who had other such obnoxious ideas about various natural phenomena. But for the true Muslim, who believed that Allah is the Lord of the Worlds and the constellation of stars and planets both known and unknown, it was nothing but man's subjugation [*tashkir*] over nature and it gave him another opportunity to prostrate before Allah the Creator of the known and unknown.

We should not forget that our Muslim forefathers established *Bait al-tarjumah* (House of Translation) and studied different languages in order to understand the various scientific disciplines. Furthermore, they established the *Bait al-hikmah* (House of Wisdom) perpetuating modern philosophy and providing the tools to the Western World for conducting research, in the Middle Ages.

By giving the revealed sources of i.e., the *Qur'an* and *Sunnah*, Allah taught the human being to harness the principles of the forces of nature for his benefit. The practical life style of the Holy Prophet has provided us with sufficient examples to show how the early Muslims made proper use of the natural resources. This is how the Companions and the great Imams of the first century understood the *usul of fiqh*. They actually provided solutions to the problems by following the spirit   of the *Qur'an* and *Sunnah* and by deriving various principles from these sources. They demonstrated how Islam could be practiced in different geographical locations where various cultural patterns existed and where various new things were employed for their use.

If we understand these *usul* correctly, whatever new things will be discovered from the creations of Allah both in the firmament and in land, water and mountains and whatever new energies we will be able to discover and overpower, we will not have any problem to make proper use of them nor will we be confused when new situations would arise in various parts of the world. If we understand the *usul* of *Shari'ah* properly, we will be undaunted and will neither be the slaves of new discoveries nor will we commit excesses, while using them. When new situations arise or new discoveries are made, we shall accept the challenge and delve into the *usul* of *Shari'ah* and will come to realize whether we should make use of them or not. It also states whether using them meets the approval of Allah and His Messenger or not. By getting shocked at the sight of new discoveries, and letting our so-called *ulama'* make confused pronouncements about them, we in fact misguide ourselves by following the minor and inconsequential details which have no actual value in the work plan of *Shari'ah*.

What we have actually learnt from the *Qur'an* and *Sunnah* is that unless something is definitely proved to be unlawful in the text of the *Qur'an* and *Sunnah*, we have to presume that it is lawful. The Holy

Qur'an says: "*Everything that is created in the earth, it is created for you by Him.*"[26] Likewise, it further says: "*He made everything subservient for you that exists in the Heaven and the earth.*"[27]

It is quite evident from the above verses that everything that exists in the heaven and earth are meant for human beings to derive benefit from. There is absolutely no need to catalogue each thing that exists in the universe and declare by name whether it is lawful or unlawful. If something or its use is forbidden categorically, in the *Qur'an* and *Sunnah*, then certainly it is unlawful, else there is no need to debate about its lawfulness or otherwise. The Creator has not left us in complete darkness about what is profitable or what is injurious or what is good or bad for mankind, so that in our utter helplessness, we may declare something beneficial or harmful. Thanks to Allah, we have been given definite guidelines in respect of these matters.

Whatever is going to restrict us in carrying out our religious obligations will be considered as harmful and therefore we will have to abstain from it. Whatever, on the other hand, will help us in carrying out our obligations will be declared as lawful. For example, loud speakers will help people sitting outside the mosque to listen to the sermon or other religious discourses. It should, therefore, be deemed lawful. Likewise, the use of telescopes to see the moon for the timing of our months will be recommended rather than seeing it with the naked eyes; the use of easy and quick means of transport to go for *hajj* are few examples of deeming the actions lawful. To say that these inventions were not used during the time of the Prophet or the Companions will amount to putting the clock back and will be taken as gross misunderstanding of the *Shari'ah* and its real intent.

The greatest blunder that some traditional *ulama'* commit is to argue that the study of the *Qur'an* and *Sunnah* are complete and to attempt any further interpretation will amount to *bid'ah*. In actual fact, the quest for knowledge in the religion of Islam is eternal. The object of this quest is transcendent and therefore inexhaustible. The technique developed by our learned forefathers of *ilm al-rijal* or the science of *jarh wal ta'dil* used in the study of *hadith* actually proved this point and they were used to establish an oral tradition, in the study of *hadith*. The application of scientific and religious knowledge to the life of the *ummah* must be considered as eternal and infinite. Just as the door of *ijtihad* is open, the

176

door of internal criticism and quest is also open. The vertical unity of the Muslim society in time and horizontal unity in space actually has come from Muslim commitment and attachment to their firm belief in the *Qur'an* and *Sunnah*. Therefore, critical study in the interpretation of the *Qur'an* and *Sunnah* must not be considered as lack of love and faith in these two primary *usul* of *fiqh*.

Usul al-fiqh, if properly used by Muslim scholars today, will help us bind together and unite in our purpose to understand the *nass*, with clearly defined principles of grammar and syntax which are very well established in the *fiqh*. There are also principles of linguistics and semantics, *tafsir* and contemporary hermeneutics which will help us to solve our present day problems. For the deduction of laws from the *nass*, *fiqh* has also further established rules of *qiyas* and *ijtihad* which we have already discussed in the earlier chapters in this book. In order to keep us steadfast in our faith, and in order to present Islam as a solution to problems rather than being the problem, and to discover the new laws needed, *fiqh* has defined the *maqasid al-shari'ah*, i.e., the goals of the law as well as the precise mechanisms of their discovery, of their establishment and actualization in the life of the people, known as *masalih al-mursalah, istihaan, istidlal*, etc. They provide legitimate re-interpretation which is needed in addressing social changes in the ever evolving contemporary society.

All the great scholars and reformers starting with Ibn Taimiyah and more recently Shaikh Muhammad ibn Abdul Wahab, Shah Wali-Allah al-Dehlavi, Muhammad Ali bin Sanusi, Muhammad al-Mahdi of Sudan, Shaikh Uthman Dan Fodio of West Africa, Shaikh Hassan al-Banna, Syed Abul Ala al-Maududi, Shahid Ismail Raji al-Faruqi, Syed Baqir Sadr, have all emphasized that the greatest necessity of our time is to do *ijtihad* on the basis of the *usul* provided in the *fiqh* of Islam.

It is a pity that many Muslims have started thinking that it is only in Muslim lands that *Shari'ah* can work and are not fully convinced that *Shari'ah* is workable anywhere in the modern world and times. This is mainly because Muslims and Western scholars have come to perceive *Shari'ah* only as criminal and penal laws. It must be borne in mind that *Shari'ah*, afterall, is the establishment of peace, social justice, and equality for the entire human race. If this is archived by suspending the criminal and penal laws of Islam, then this is acceptable and true *Shari'ah*.

Muslims who are facing modernity have to resort to the mechanism of *Shari'ah* to bring about the necessary revival in the modern times. In the words of Ismail Faruqi, "those who stand immobile before the challenge are of no consequence and will be swept aside by both history and the forces of dynamic, creative Islam. With its built-in suppleness and readiness to conform with the demands of the time, the *Shari'ah* will continue to be as it was ordained right at the beginning, fit for all and at all times and for all places."[28]

In fact, the vision of Islam is its social ideal since it is not merely a piece of utopian thinking. These ideas were not left to the personal effort of the noble-minded Emirs, Kings, Emperors to be actualized when they so desired, and to suffer neglect or violation when they were not happy. Indeed, what humans compose can only be tentative, and what they resolve can only be temporary. With partial knowledge and passing interests, humans can continuously contend with each other either in agreement or disagreement. The values of Islam embodied in its vision cannot be subject to such vicissitudes. That is why vision and its axiological content had to be translated into the *Shari'ah*, i.e., into a system of laws which cover human life 'from the cradle to the grave'. The values of Islam, therefore, did not remain ethical desiderata that could not be invoked in legal processes. As *Shari'ah* or law, the ideal values enjoyed the full force of established law. As laws, the values or ideals of Islam, became known to the literate and illiterate almost a whole millennium before the advent of printing. They were understood, if not pursued, by everyone. Kings and cobblers appreciated and invoked their provisions on a daily basis, whether to feed their hope, to justify their actuality, or bemoan their plight. The social ideal became so much a part of life that no spirituality was conceivable to them which did not begin with the fulfillment of the law. This realism has protected Muslim piety against the speculative flight of the mystic, and worked for the reawakening of Muslims in the modern times.

Islam is not merely a creed or a set of rituals, but it is life to be lived in the present, here and now, a religion of right-doing, right-thinking and right-speaking. The practice of the social ideal of Islam does not lie enshrined in the limbo of false sentimentalism. It forms the active principle of life for all Muslims in all ages. Therefore, the *usul* of *fiqh* inspires Muslims even in the most difficult circumstances to live honorably and meet up with whatever challenges they may have to face. There is no situation in which Islam as a dynamic way of life does not offer a solution. All the precepts in the *Qur'an* and the *Sunnah*, with the help of active *ijtihad* are practicable. However, in Islam of today, unfortunately the precepts which inculcated duties have been so utterly devoid of practicability, so completely wanting in a knowledge of human nature, and partaking so much of the dreamy vagueness of enthusiasts, that they have rendered the real battles and struggles of life simply useless.

Eclecticism in Islamic Jurisprudence

Moreover, our approach towards *fiqh* should enable us to choose "the preferred verdicts" from the various verdicts we already have before us. Islam is an easy way of life, so says the Messenger of Allah, "*al-din yusrun*". Aishah reports that whenever the Prophet was presented with two or more options, he would always opt for the easier one. We see among some of the new *ulama'* that eclecticism in the *madhahib* (schools of jurisprudence) is condemned while this attitude is supposedly required to be greatly encouraged. Eclecticism was, in fact, the method of the greatest *fuqaha*, as we see in various writing of scholars such as Shah Wali allah al-Dehlavi and Abu Hanifah, and while we do not suggest that local preferences be overthrown, we do point out that for the Muslim who has contacts in other parts of the world with other Muslims, there must be respect for different styles [*madhahid*] and interpretation of Islam. Muslims must stop parceling themselves in their respective boxes and acknowledge that there is some good in every school of thought just as there is some good in every religion. When Muslims were confident and full of vitality, they welcomed new Musiims and made contacts with new ideas and new people. When eclecticism in the schools of jurisprudence was widespread, the inner and outer dimensions of Islam got equally developed. If we are to emerge from our insecurity, we as the *ulama'* must have the bed laid for eclecticism and future co-operation among Muslims as well as people of other Abrahamic faiths.

Unity is the goal and integral content of the Islamic vision. The majority of the Muslims believe that all the great Imams in *fiqh* were respected servants of the same cause of Islam. But in the present times, it is heartbreaking to see that the proper functioning of the society is disrupted from certain quarters. We continue to see followers of Imam

Shafi'i, Ja'far Sadiq, Malik, Ahmad, and Imam Abu Hanifah offering prayers separately in a mosque rather than praying together. One is reminded of the painful situation of the four *musallah* in our most sacred area, the *haram al-sharif*, praying separately behind their own Imams. Some of the *ulama'* have even given obnoxious remarks against the followers of other schools of *fiqh*. We even see that some would gladly adopt all kind of innovations in religion in the form of secular law, laws utterly harmful to Islam, rather than co-operate with Imams of other schools of *fiqh*.

Eclecticism, in Arabic: *takhayyur* and *talfiq*, is an ideal way to keep *fiqh* relevant and applicable. In the language of *fiqh*, *takhayyur* is the opposite of *taqlid*. Because of the increased interaction between Muslims in various parts of the world, the instilling of the concept of *takhayyur* is doubly important. If we can re-install this concept, which truly is the norm for the Prophetic period and those of the Companions and the Successors, we stand to make *Shari'ah* more easily acceptable and practical all over the world. *Takhayyur* may then enhance *talfiq*, the piecing together or patching up through combination and fusion of the various legal decisions of diverse sources. *Talfiq* is the mosaic of local decisions which constitutes and expresses the essence of Islam. By eclecticism and fervent application of the *Shari'ah* to all our needs, the society demonstrates the unity of purpose and that is the way it should be.

Utham Dan Fodio applied the principle of *takhayyur* and *talfiq* in the Sokoto State. In his *Tafsir al-millah*, he set out his program to liberate the application of *Shari'ah* from the narrow confines of a single school [*madhab*] by emphasizing that the concept of "ease in religion" certainly meant making the *Shari'ah* understandable and accessible to the Muslim who made an effort to learn. He asked the judges to rule according to the most well known and authentic opinions [*al-mashhur wa al-rajih*] of the scholars of any school. He wrote:

> Neither Allah in His book nor the Prophet in his *Sunnah* made it obligatory that one particular *madhab* be allowed, nor did we hear any of the early scholars enjoin a person to follow one *madhab*. If they had, they would have committed a sin by not allowing people to act in accordance with any *hadith* that particular *madhab* had not considered.[30]

As a way of illustration, let us employ the method of eclecticism to examine the case of divorce in Islam. Each of the four Sunni scholars has an opinion about the dissolution of a marriage by a judge. We start with the premise that the best decision will be the one which is beneficial to both parties. We also start with the position that divorce should be considered within the two extremes as follows: the discouragement of divorce comes from the *hadith qudsi* "divorce is the worst of all permissible things" while the other extreme is that making divorce too difficult benefits neither the wife nor the husband. This of course means that the other supports of Islamic Law must be in place, because where alien values have permeated Muslim communities, the situation exists (e.g., in South Asia) where divorce must be almost disallowed in order to give a modicum of support to the wife.

According to the jurists, there are five conditions which may dissolve a marriage. They are:

1. The husband fails to provide for the wife.
2. The husband has a fundamental defect.
3. The husband has molested the wife.
4. The husband is absent for a prolonged period.
5. The husband is incarcerated.

Now, the Hanafi school does not recognize non-maintenance of the wife as a ground for divorce, whether the non-maintenance is occasioned by inability or mere maliciousness. The Maliki, Hanbali, and Shafi'i schools, however, do recognize non-maintenance as grounds. Allah has warned against using marriage as a means of inflicting injustice or hardship on the wife. They base this view on the following evidence: "*Do not retain them (your wives) with the object of causing them injury*" (2: 231). Similarly, for the second divorce, the *Qur'an* stipulates that the wife may be retained with amenity or released with amenity. The weight of this evidence suggests that the judge should dissolve a marriage where maintenance is absent.

The Prophet said that married life must not have either injury or molestation, and so the judge must forbid any injustice to the wife arising from the lack of maintenance.

If the husband has a defect, and cannot provide a necessary kind of companionship, the wife may suffer hardship. It follows by analogy that lack of maintenance could similarly result in the need for judicial dissolution of the marriage.

The Hanafis base their decision not to make non-maintenance a grounds for divorce on this Qur'anic evidence: "*Let him who is possessed of resources maintain (his wife) out of his resources; and let him whose means are limited maintain (her) out of what Allah has given him; Allah shall not impose on a person an obligation beyond his capacity; Allah provides relief in difficulty*" (65: 7). They reason that a husband who is unable to maintain his wife due to poverty, is not thereby required to have the marriage dissolved.

When the Prophet's wives would make economic demands which he could not fulfill on account of his limited means, he stayed away from them for a month to chastise them, thereby indicating that excessive demands beyond the husband's means need not be met.

The Hanafis also reason that while there must have been quite a few Companions without much wealth, there never was a time when the Prophet dissolved a marriage on account of non-maintenance.

The Hanafi position applies solely to husbands whose means are limited. It does not apply to the miserly husband. The example of the Prophet only applies to excessive demands. The Prophet was often so poor that he did not "eat two dates together"[31] (did not live a luxurious life). Furthermore, the *Sunnah* of the Prophet with regard to his wives is not always applicable to everyone, as the *Qur'an* says "*O you wives of the Prophet, you are not like any of the other women*" (33: 32).

According to the Malikis, maintenance must either be proved or the wife must testify that she is provided for. But the Shafi'is and Hanbalis hold that the admission by the husband of insolvency is sufficient to dissolve the marriage. The Shafi'i judge will give the husband three days to provide for his wife. The Maliki judge also gives time. The Hanbali judge offers no time period, but gives the wife the discretion in waiting for maintenance or dissolving the marriage. Our view is that giving the judge flexibility and giving the wife discretion are important aspects of this case. After all, the judge should be a member of the community and most involved in these matters; he should be best informed about the circumstances. Similarly, the wife may want to persevere too, and these desires and conditions must be respected.

The three schools agree that if there is any indication of maliciousness (and again, the wife and the judge will know better about this), the judge should order immediate dispensing of funds from the husband's property for maintenance. The Shafi'i judge will look for hidden assets if no visible property is found, while the Hanbali and Maliki judge will stop at the tangible and declared assets. Again, the question of search is sensitive, and leaving the discretion to the involved and informed judge is the approach most likely to render justice for all parties.

Therefore, if we understand the *usul al-fiqh* correctly, we will be able to respond to this changing world in ways that make our lives worthwhile and devoted to Allah. The changes and "innovations" we make must not continue the process of alienation and desanctification, and they need not. Our changes must originate from the desire to follow the path of divine guidance, a path that goes here and there without fear or trepidation, always right and always straight.

The current dilemma that Muslim society faces is two-fold. Those who want to innovate Islam so that it becomes uprooted and a path for modern secularism, and those who are so rigid in their understanding of Islam that Islam becomes, likewise, a relic unsuited and unsuitable for contemporary times. Neither path is true to Islam. Instead, we must, while maintaining and supporting the essence of Islam also apply Islam to our changing challenges and problems.

A dynamic *usul al-fiqh* will entail preserving the essence of Islam while creating new forms and diverse patterns of solutions and adaptations. Perhaps one of the problems is that at the time of the vibrant and dynamic interpretation of divine guidance which took place in the first century *hijrah,* no one imagined that a time would come when Muslim empires would decline and some of the areas once ruled by Muslims would be ruled by non-Muslims and that Muslims would have to live as minorities under non-Muslim jurisdiction. This is why we must develop *ijtihad* to reflect the divine guidance for the contemporary problems of Muslims minorities.

If we continue to use the classical terminology of *dar al-Islam* and *dar al-harb* (land of Islam and land of war, respectively), we should consider that the government is not the sole criterion of the ability of the Muslim society to survive. Thus, countries where Muslims can "call towards good and reject evil", where they can freely perform their religious duties and build mosques, should not be considered *dar al-harb,* even though non-Muslims rule them. In fact, today we can say that many Muslim countries could be classified as enemy countries [*dar al-harb*] while some non-Muslims have become friendly countries since it is becoming increasingly difficulty to exercise free thinking as well as practice Islam in some Muslim countries while non-Muslim countries have become truly pluralistic. Our *usul al-fiqh,* therefore, should provide the tools that will enable us to participate with people from other religious and cultural backgrounds in working for the betterment of our peaceful and pluralistic societies.

The need for fresh and timely applications of *fiqh* is especially apparent now as the Muslims in "independent" Muslim countries and countries where they are in the minority try to improve their lives. A new methodology of doing *fiqh* will enable them to find new solutions to the various problems that they face.

Usul al-Fiqh and Socio-Economic Change

If we consider the concept of need [*hajah*] and necessity [*darurah*] as it applies to issues in economics, we see that contemporary issues concerning economics revolve around two requirements. The first is one of survival and necessity [*darurah*] and is necessarily temporary. The second is the perennial requirement of economic justice and distributive prosperity.

We must conceive of these two requirements or themes to be parallel. As we saw with the concept of necessity in *fiqh,* the emergency suspension of an Islamic injunction must only be temporary and local, without question of bad intent. These stop-gap measures never pass into legality. Further, the ideal of Islamic economic justice may be almost unattainable, but the duty to work toward this goal is perennial and may not be frustrated.

Since recasting the *usul al-fiqh* entails making Islamic guidance more relevant to contemporary challenges and problems, we must engage *fiqh* with economic activities as well. But, as decisions in *fiqh* may be temporal or local, or subject to debate or disagreement, no final rulings are attempted. Instead, the theme of parallel tracks of the *usul al-fiqh,* that of the ideal and the practical, will be developed in reference to the following issues.

One question frequently asked of Islamic economics is if interest and its prohibition apply to both consumption and production loans? Some people argue that it is interest on consumption loans which is prohibited in Islam, but not interest on production loans. They argue that a production loan will lead to the generation of profits, and the lender, therefore, should charge interest on the loan. The *ulama* in the 1930s and 1960s generally accepted this argument, possibly because there were no viable alternatives.

But now, alternatives are there, and the general consensus seems to be that the prohibition of interest is comprehensive and makes no distinction between consumption and production loan. Instead, Islam provides an outlet for that lender of money to share some of the benefits derived from the loan by the borrower, through the principle of profit-and-loss sharing. As for borrowing from conventional banks, Muslims should avoid this if there are alternatives (Islamic bank, private savings, friends, and family) at no interest cost. However, if there are no alternatives, a Muslim may find it necessary to borrow from a conventional bank in order to buy basic necessities. This of course, entails payment of interest, but may fall under the rule of necessity.

While the concept of necessity may make temporarily acceptable the taking of an interest loan, the devastating power of interest is sometimes sufficiently visible to make the costs truly frightening. Let us take the example of eating food that is usually *haram* (unlawful) during an emergency. There is unlikely to be much effect on the body if the food (for instance, pork) is reasonably clean from a purely medical perspective. But "eating" a loan with interest may put the Muslim in perpetual slavery to a bank. The tremendous burden of debt servicing which is becoming visible in the United States, for instance, with people using one credit card to pay off another, is just one illustration of the terrible costs of interest. While the concept of necessity may make "eating" a loan with interest temporarily legal, the high costs must be compared to the degree of emergency. It will be an extreme emergency indeed which would make an interest loan palatable.

One serious problem we find, as the capitalistic values make deep inroads in the Muslim communities of South Asia, is the high degree of consumption required of a family with daughters. This family must, according to the new rules of consumption, live high above its means in order to attract offers of marriage. The problem of dowry being paid to the husband's family is very much entrenched in the Muslim communities in South Asia, and its eradication will take a multiple level, multifaceted reformation of the economic and social structures of these communities. But, this example brings out the tremendous tension between the requirements of an alien value system and the *fiqh*.

The *fiqh* concerning these issues is clear. First, we have the utterly clear precept of money or wealth going to the woman, who then keeps and invest this money as she pleases. If Islam weights the divorce process by giving the husband one notch of advantage, in the *mahr* (dowry to the bride) Islam gives the woman the advantage. Clearly, taking both the advantage of the divorce process and the dowry is a double burden on the woman, and it is no accident that many "Islamization" of the law programs tend to punish women without giving them their due, where the "gradual" process of installing the *hudud* punishments becomes nothing more than yet another way to wage war against women. Islam quite clearly makes punishment directly associated with responsibility (no responsibility, no punishment) as in the case of Umar who would not punish theft of food if he himself had not ensured that everyone had enough to eat. Thus, any true implementation of *Shari'ah* must come holistically, all of the *fiqh* must apply, not just some of the parts.

In the case of the father who is led to believe that he must borrow constantly and consume conspicuously, what are we to say from the point of view of *fiqh*? First, we must ourselves be involved in the local communities. Only then is our knowledge put to good use. Secondly, we must approach the problem holistically and be sensitive to the many factors involved. We may find that the prerequisite to an interest-free society is the instillation of Islamic values such as *mahr* to the bride, *taqwa* over money, honesty over appearances. The father forced by local circumstances to act against the precepts of Islam is the victim, and changing those circumstances assumes greater importance than making this person's life even more difficult.

Let us now consider what wholesalers and retailers in a majority Muslim country should do about credit and interest. If Muslim retailers in a majority Muslim country have to go to non-Muslim wholesalers to buy goods on credit, and pay interest, should they engage in such a transaction? The preferable course is to go to Muslims who do not charge interest on credit sales. If this is not possible, then they may be able to go to the non-Muslim wholesalers and pay the interest. Otherwise, it could be shown, those sectors would be left to non-Muslims to dominate and

Muslims will become economically weak in their own country. But, since this example is drawn from a Muslim majority country, the Muslims should be able to implement *Shari'ah* and create the relevant mechanisms of trade. All other measures are stop-gap measures not addressing the real issue. The case of a wholesaler or retailer taking goods on credit with interest is to be different from the individual Muslim who takes a loan and has serious trouble repaying it. The businessman may understand the true costs of the loan, while the other Muslim may not. Especially when we see the way credit is advertised as "easy", we should realize that a gullible person could fall too easily into a debt trap. In the United States, for instance, credit cards are advertised and sent to people complete with checks. One company even suggested you pay your other credit card off with the check and then they would give a "rebate" of some amount. Quite clearly the winners of any such transaction are those offering the money, and the losers may lose everything under the lure of the seductive advertising.

We must also accept that advertisement, and especially that found on commercial Television, is nothing but the pernicious penetration of ideas into the minds of the audience. We are shown, subtly, continually, skillfully, what the "good life" is. The fact that only a small percentage of people live such a life, even in countries like the United States and United Kingdom, is important to note and remember. But, perhaps even more important is to realize that such a level of consuming rests on the labor and oppression of the vast majority of the people. It also rests on ecologically harmful and destructive technologies, and furthermore, offers nothing but sickness – physical and mental – for the participants as well as those "supporting" the rich in their lifestyles. These ads are such that the viewer has an instant and complete touchstone to judge the good from the bad, the cool from the not-so-cool. Whether it is a cigarette or a soft drink, alcohol or another drug to pop, ads convey entire world-views directly into the conscious and subconscious of the viewer. The total destruction of this system will be a necessary prerequisite of justice, whether it is justice to the bride with her *mehr* or justice to the worker who must now borrow to live.

Muslim wholesalers and retailers living as minorities in a non-Muslim country may also choose to go into interest-charging sectors if they have to. But they should also form political and economic associations to pressure governments to establish economic and social justice. Muslims should also form their own co-operatives. One of the many values conveyed by the modern West is that of government as the provider *par excellence*. Now, such a position was sounded in the conservative years of Reagan and of Bush, where the government expenditures went drastically away from welfare to defense and interest-payment.

But Muslims must realize that the *Shari'ah* has traditionally been the government of the people, imposed not from above but self-imposed by the community. In this sense, Muslims who form co-operatives are doing their best to make Islam work for them, and this is entirely opposite.

Secondly, concerning interest earned by state-owned banks and financial institutions, it goes to the state exchequer and is therefore not appropriated by an individual, some people claim that such interest is like a form of tax, which is permissible in Islam. This kind of reasoning does not hold up. Firstly, the harmful effects of interest on an economy far outweigh any benefits it may have, the levying of interest has an adverse effect on production in the economy and in the distribution of wealth. Interest charged by state-owned banks should not be allowed. Secondly, the concept of a corporation is of dubious legality. Can there be in Islam a corporate body, not a person? The weight of the *fiqh* is on the concept that transactions take place with entities that may be regulated or characterized by trust and honesty.

This "entity" can only be a person, not a corporate body. Can the fiction of corporate identity fit in the *Shari'ah*? Can personal liabilities be dodged with corporate identities?

Furthermore, we saw that punishment is always directed to the person in proportion to his responsibility, never to the victim or the incompetent, never vicarious and never against a group.

Thirdly, there is the issue concerning an interest rate which is equivalent to inflation rate. Inflation erodes the value of money and an interest-rate which is equivalent to the inflation rate will simply keep the value of the money intact. It must be remembered that indexing will never be a solution to the problem of inflation. Both inflation and interest are evil forces in the society and hence need to be eliminated.

The concept of *zakah* is based on indexing, where *zakah* is not money value but weight value or commodity basket. Thus, it does not matter how much the commodity basket costs from year to year: what matters is that *zakah* consists of such and such a weight of grain and food.

The general consensus, however, is that indexing is not allowed in Islam because there can be no exchange which entails a decrease or increase in value. But an economy based on the partnership [*mudarabah*] would almost eliminate the problem of inflation. Now in a *mudarabah* based economy, the value of one's investment would correspond to the wider economy. If someone has 100 units of money and invests it with some partners, if the cost of living increases, so, too, will the investment in question. And since Islam discourages hoarding, the more active money there is, less will be the cost associated with fluctuating prices.

However, one group of people at least will be affected – those who took a consumption loan and it is they who will have trouble paying back money which is becoming to be of increasingly less value. In such a circumstance, the institution of *zakah* should be able to help the parties affected. This again, however, emphasizes the importance of a *zakah* institution which is fully responsive to the needs of the community.

Money, not only commodities, depreciate. As Mahmoud Abu Saud mentions, Islam does not recognize money as an inherent good, and so it too, should depreciate. He mentions that "If money were subjected to depreciation, nobody would be interested in holding it back." This would have the effect of "boosting production to increase supply, leading to more employment and higher wages."[32]

Fourthly, should Muslims accept interest from interest-based banks? If an Islamic bank is available, then a Muslim should bank with it. If there are none, the Muslim may be able to deposit in a savings or deposit account. He should collect the interest on these accounts and use it for welfare and charity purposes, but not for personal use. If a Muslim were to refuse to collect the interest, the cause of the interest-based bank would be unwittingly furthered. However, some people believe that the *haram* aspect of the interest makes the entire money *haram*. It should be remembered, however, that money that was ill-gotten by non-Muslims could still go into the *baitu al-mal* of the Muslims and become *zakah*.

Fifthly, is interest and banking in itself an institution prohibited in Islam? The function of a bank is to mobilize savings and make them available for productive use. Islam forbids hoarding and encourages investment. Further, the practice of Muhammad when he put Ali in charge of the Muslims' money in Makkah suggests that depositing money is not a bad thing. Moreover, the lesson to be learned is that the emphasis placed on Ali's trustworthiness suggests that the prime characteristic of the bank should be trustworthiness. However, when some Islamic banks are found out to be speculating with depositors' money, the question of trust arises. When investments are made without consent or adequate overseeing, then the bank is no longer worthy of the full trust required to be Islamic.

Further, the rigid division of labor and concentration of money is surely something working against human values. There are even a number of scholars noticing that "theorizing" is a top-heavy approach that tends to demean the value of "fieldwork". And the theory level is certainly operating with cumulated fieldwork. If we look at wealth, the same situation applies. The production of value through labor is increasingly looked down upon, while the investment bankers and lawyers who "earn" millions in take-over bids make a mockery of the worker's efforts.

The bank is an ideal place for money to accumulate and become unattached from its true producers. Accumulated money also becomes "faceless" so much so that investments of a dubious nature are easily effected. The corporate bank cannot be controlled by the contributors, and at some point becomes an institution divorced from the realities of everyday labor, whether those realities are characterized as profit-loss or *zakah* or *sadaqah*. As a force of food in the community, the bank is at best a mixed bag. Some scholars feel that Muslims should be gathering their wealth together in the form of co-operatives so as to set their own priorities and help themselves. This kind of local, community-oriented banking is a system with great potential for good, empowering people, giving them resources for their own directions and priorities, and allowing communities to act without waiting for their governments to implement the *Shari'ah* laws.

Sixthly, we have the question of interest being replaced by a service charge. When service is provided, such as a money transfer, there should be a payment for it. But if the service charge becomes an interest charge – where a 10,000 unit loan gets a 100 unit service charge and a 50,000 loan gets a 500 unit service charge– then such a case is not allowed in Islam, because the service involved in the two loans should be the same amount and at the same cost. Furthermore, if the bank has already accounted for the employees' service as a cost of production, there can be no justification for charging the customer once again for the work done by an employee.

Seventhly, is the situation where the cash price is lower than the future price deferred sale, [*murabahah*] legal? One argument runs that the cash price may be lower because the seller will have the opportunity to use the cash for investments and earn a profit. But, if the customer cannot pay the deferred sale price on the due date, the seller cannot increase the price. The original price is still in-effect. Moreover, the difference between the cash price and deferred sale price should be reasonable.

Another argument suggests that there is no problem with traders buying something and selling it again at a different price, and this form of *murabahah* is perfectly legitimate. But this concerns commodities. The bank which lends out money and then adds a 10 % mark-up is doing nothing but dealing in interest. The argument that the banks are simply acting as traders is doubtable and debatable.

What emerges from these issues is that while many scholars of Islamic economics call for the predominance of *mudarabah* (partnerships), the vast proportion of banking activity is *murabahah*. Thus, the ratio of approximately 95% *murabahah* and 5% *mudarahah*, those Muslims who have been actually setting up commercial banks are implementing about 95 % *mudarahah*.

Two conclusions emerge from the above discussion: Firstly, the discipline of Islamic economics must break out of the cage imposed by the entrance after "independence" of various Muslim countries into the entirely hostile international political economy dominated by the United States and now perhaps by an equally hostile structure, which is probably characterized by interdependence. Very easily the structure was installed which paralleled colonial systems of dominance, creating an indigenous elite to take the place of outside agents of repression. Islamic economics will never be more than rationalization of continually perpetrated evils unless it gives more than lip-service to the concepts of justice emanating from the *fiqh* and Islamic systems of business transactions [*mu'amalat*]. Secondly, Islamic economics must be part of the larger effort of *usul al-fiqh* to address all matters to Allah and His Messenger. This means in effect that economics must be once again part of politics and sociology and cultural sciences. The problem of dowry in South Asia, as we saw, was one entirely subsumed in complex factors, some of them religious (syncretism with Hinduism, for example), some of them political, and some arising from social structures. Until all of these forces are under-stood and addressed, no "economic" solution will be in sight. When we tie in the television advertisements or the Western penetration (often at the behest of the government and its elite) to the problems bedeviling the society of today, we not only begin to see that the problem is not easily solvable, but also that we can take courage from the recognition that our intellects are not deficient, because the problem is not going to be resolved by an equation or a formula.

Also, while the commercial impetus of banking on the debt-financing model may be superficially Islamic, many issues such as large consumer debts, the incorporation of a bank (without personal responsibility), and so on are not adequately addressed by commercial Islamic banks.

It is often the case that we have situation where even in Muslim majority countries, the Muslim has no real choice but to participate in an economic system, which is detrimental to the society's economy and a continual frustration of justice and distribution of prosperity. Its not easy for one to decide for the Muslims whether they are sufficiently in an emergency to warrant participating in these destructive economic activities. The battle against the elite firmly tied into international economic systems, the devastation wrought by multinational corpora-tions, the destructiveness of capitalism and state controlled economies, and the cut-throat tactics of groups controlling economic sectors, will not be that easily won.

The combination of seduction and repression, which characterize contemporary economic powers, is truly formidable. If the Muslim is not seduced by the market to join the capitalist system and take huge loans and become so dependent so as to never criticize the *status quo*, he is repressed visibly and forcibly by the police and government to participate in the rampant rape of modern economies. In this situation, Muslim communities must decide for themselves how best to confront these issues, how best to maintain enough prosperity to make their worship of the divine possible and facilitated. There can be no condemnation of a community working to improve their condition, because indeed we are in an emergency situation. If this evil can be changed without hands, we must make it our concern to do so. If we can speak out against it, we must surely do so.

This means primarily that we should never legitimize what we know to be evil. We must never accept for all time the tremendous inequalities and widespread economic injustices. Muslim communities may find it necessary to engage in activities of dubious legality, but these activities must be judged not by the dispassionate outsider, but by the *faqih* involved and cognizant of the complexities and problems facing the community.

Practical and ideal, the Islamic perspective allows for necessity but perennially calls for justice. One evil is to strangle the community and make economic activities unattainable so as to make not a purified Islam but an irrelevant Islam. Muslim communities will survive; the task of the *ulama'* is to consult within the communities to survive in a manner most in keeping with the divine guidance. A second evil, perhaps even worse than making Islam irrelevant, is making the *haram* or doubtful *halal* or permissible.

All that has been said above only means that the contemporary *alim* must not be constrained either by the subject-content or approach of the Western disciplines, but should and must examine, instead, issues from the background of *usul al-fiqh*. This implies that we discover, above all, how to make Allah and His Messenger, in the form of the *Shari'ah* our everyday and ultimate criterion of our political, cultural, social, and economic life, here on earth, the temporal residence of all.

Notes

1. *Muslim,* kitab al-iman.

2. Hammond, R., *The Philosophy of al-Farabi and its Influence on Medieval Thought*, New York, 1947, p. 149; Al-Farabi, *Political Regime*, pp. 47-51.

3. Hammond, R, Al-Farabi`s *The Gems of Wisdom*, p.39.

4. smon-Craver, *Philosophical Foundations of Education*, New York, 1971, p.46.

5. Calkins, M. W, *Locke's Essays Concerning Human Understanding,* New York, pp. 25-26.

6. Al-Ghazali, M, *Al-Munqid,* Beirut: al-Maktabah al-Sha'abiyyah, n.d, pp. 78-79.

7. Al-Ghazali, *Ihya',* Makkah: al-Maktabah al-Faisaliyyah, n.d, vol. 4, pp. 435-447.

8. Idem, *ibid,* vol.1, pp.75-76.

9. *Al-Najm,* verse 11.

10. *Al-An'am,* verse 75.

11. *Al-Hajj,* verse 46.

12. Al-Ghazali, M, *Ihya',* Makkah: al-Maktabah al-Faisaliyyah, vol.1, p. 104.

13. Ken Wilber, editor (1984) *Quantum Questions: Mystical Writings of the World's Great Physicists* (Boston: Shambhala) 21.

14. Wilber (1984) 11.

15. Wilber (1984) 9.

16. Faruqi, Ismail Ragi, *Islamisation of Knowledge: A Work Plan,* Herandon, Virginia, 1987.

17. Shabiti, *Al-Hisam,* vol. 1, p. 82.

18. Ibid, p. 18.

19. Shatibi, *Al-Muwafaqat,* vol. 2, p. 337.

20. Shatibi, *Al-I'tisam,* pp. 99 - 110.

21. Ibid, p. 111.

22. Ibid, p. 111.

23. Ibid, pp. 113 - 115.

24. Shatibi, *Al-Hisam,* p. 67.

25. Ibid, P. 232.

26. *Qur'an,* chapter 2: 29.

27. *Qur'an,* chapter 45: 13.

28. *Arabia: the Islamic World Review,* No. 26, October , 1983, p. 47.

29. *Sunan Abu Dawud,* Bab fi tajawuz fi al-amr.

30. F. H. al-Masri, editor, *Bayan Wujub al-Hijrah* of Shaikh 'Uthman Dan Fodio, pp. 90-91.

31. This is how 'Aishah described the Prophet's living conditions. See *Sahih al-Muslm* and *Shamail al-tirmidhi.*

32. Mahmoud Abu Saud (1989) Toward Islamization of Disciplines (III T).

Bibliography

Primary Sources

Abd al-Aziz, Sultan Turkey,
  Al-Majallah (the Civil Code of Turkey, Constantinople, 1880.

Abd al-Raman; al-Jaziri,
  Kitab al-Fiqh ala al-Madhahib al-Arb'a, Cairo, n.d.

Abu Daud, al-Siristani, Sulaiman ibn al-Asha, *Sunan*, Cairo, 1863.

Ahmad Baba, *Nayl al-ibtihaj* (on the margin of Ibn Farhun's
  al-Dibaj al-Mudhahhab). Cairo: 'Abbas b. 'Abd al-Salam, 1351 A.H.

Al-Albani, Nasir al-Din, *Silsilat al-Ahadith al-Da'ifah wal Maudu'ah,*
  Beirut 1384 A.H.

Al-Alwani, Taha Jabir, *Usul al-Fiqh al-Islami-* Manhaj Bahthin wa
  Ma'rafah, Herndon, Virginia, U.S.A., 1988.

Al-Amidi, Sayf al-Din. *Al-Ihkam fi usul al-ahkam*, Cairo: Matba'a
  Ma'arif, 1914.

Al-Ayni, Budr al-Din, *Umdat al-Qari Sharh Sahih al-Bukhari,*
  Cairo, 1348, a.h.

Al-Baihaqi, Abu Bakr Ahmad ibn Al-Husain, *Sunan al-Kubra*, 10 vols.
  Hyderabad 1344, A.H.

Al-Basri, Abu al-Husayn. *Al-Mu'tamad fi usul al-fiqh.* Dimashq: Al-
  Ma'had al-'ilmi al-firansi, 1964.

Al-Bukhari, *Jami' Sahih*. Beirut, n.d.

Al-Ghazali, Abu Hamid Muhammad, *Al-Mustasfa min Ilam al-Usul;*
  Baghdad: Muthanna, 1970.

Al-Ghazali, Abu Hamid Muhammad, *Al-Mustasfa min Ilam al-Usul;*
  Cairo, 1937.

Al-Hakim, Abu al-Hasan 'Ali ibn Yusuf. *Al-Dawhat al-Mushtabika fi
  dawabit dar al-sikka.* Edited by Husayn Mu'nis. Madrid: ma'had
  al-Dirasat al-Islamiyya, 1960.

Al-Hakim, Muhammad bin Abdullah, *Al-Mustadrak,* 4 vols.,
  Hyderabad, n.d.

Al-Kasani, *'Ala al-Din, Badai' al-Sanai' fi Tartib al-Shari'ah*, Cairo, 1327-28 A.H.

Al-Kazimi, Muhammad mahdi, *'Anawin al-Usul*, Baghdad, 1432 A.H.

Al-Khallaf, Abd Al-Wahhab, *Khulasat Tarikh Al-Tashri al-Islami*, 9th ed. Cairo, 1971.

Al-Khassaf, Ahmed ibn Umar, *Kitab al-Hiyal*, Cairo 1314 A.H.

Al-Khatib, Abu Bakr Ahmad bin Ali al-Baghdadi, *Tarikh Baghdad*, Sa'ada Press, Cairo, 1931.

Al-Khazin, 'Alauddin Ali ibn Muhammad, Al-Tawil fl Ma'ani, al-Tawzil, Cairo, n.d.

Al-Khazraji, Ahmad bin Abdullah, *Khulasat Tahdib*, 12 vols., Hyderabad, 1325 - 1327 A.H.

Al-Marghinani, Burhan al-Din, *Al-Hidaya*, Cairo 1326 - 27 A.H.

Al-Mawardi, Abu al-Hasan Ali, *Al-Ahkam al-Sultaniyah*, Cairo n.d.

Al-Munawi, abd al-Rauf Muhammad, *Kunz al-Daqaiq*, Cairo, 1305A.H.

Al-Muzani, Ismail, *Al-Mukhtasar,* Cairo, n.d.

Al-Qasimi, Jamal al-Din, *Qawaid al-Tahdith*, Cairo, 1961.

Al-Qarafi, Shihab al-Din, *Al-Dhakhira,* Cairo 1961.

Al-Qurtubi, Abu Abd Allah Muhammad, *Al-Jami' li-Ahkam al-Quran,* Cairo, 1937.

Al-Razi, Fakhruddin, *Tafsir Kabir*, Cairo, n.d.

Al-Sarakhsi, Shams al-Din, *Al-Mabsut,* Cairo, 1906-13.

Al-Shafii, Muhammad ibn Idris, *Al-Umm,* Bulaq, 1320-25 A.H.

Al-Shara'ni, Abd al-Wahhab, *Al-Mizan al-Kubra*, Cairo, 1932.

Al-Shatibi, Abu Ishaq Ibrahim, *Al-Muwafaqat,* 4 vols, 4th print, E. M. M. 'Abd al-Hamid, Cairo: Muhammad 'Ali, 1969.

Al-Shatibi, *Al-I'tisam,* Rashid Rida. (Ed.) Cairo: Mustafa Muhammad, 1915.

Al-Subki, Taj al-Din, *Jami al-Jawami*, Cairo, 1354 A.H.

Al-Suyuti, Abd Al-Rahman, *Al-Ashbah wa al-Nazair*, Cairo, 1936.

Al-Suyuti, Jalal al-Din Abd Al-Rahman, *Tadrib al-Rawi*, Medina, 1959.

Al-Suyuti, Jalal al-Din Abdur Rahman, *Tahdhir al-Khawass min Ahadith al-Qusas,* Beirut, 1972.

Al-Tabari, Muhammad ibn Jarir, *Tafsir al-Tabari,* Cairo 1955.

Al-Tirmidhi, Muhammad ibn Isa, *Al-Jami',* Cairo, n.d.

Al-Zailai, Uthman ibn Ali, *Tabyin al-Haqaiq,* Cairo, 1313-1335.

Dahlawi, Wali Allah, *Hujjat Allah al-Balighah,* vol. 1,
   Cairo, Dar al Kutub al-Haditha.

Dan Fodio, Shaikh Uthman, *Hidayatut tullab,* Zaria, n.d.

Dan Fodio, Shaikh Uthman, *Irshad al-Ummah ila Taysir al-Millah,*
   MS in A.B.U. Zaria.

Abu Dawud, *Sunan Abu Dawod,* Karachi, n.d

Fullani, Saleh B. Muhammad, *Iqaz Himam Uli al-Absar,* Pakistan 1394,
   A.H. 1974.

Hattab, Abu Abdullah Muhammad b. Muhammad, *Mawahib al-Jalil,*
   (*Bab al-Aqdiya*), vol. 6, Libya.

Husain Hamid Hassan, *Nazria al-Maslaha fi al-Fiqh al-Islami,*
   Cairo, 1971.

Ibn 'Abbad, *Al-Rasa'il al-sughra.* Edited by Paul Nwiya. Beirut:
   Imprimerie Catholique, 1958.

Ibn Abd al Barr, Abu Umar, *Jami Bayan al Ilm,* 1 & 2 Cairo 1388 A.H.
   1968 A.C.

Ibn Abidin, Muhammad Amin, *Radd al-Muhtar,* Cairo 1324 A.H.

Ibn Adi, Abu Ahmad Abdullah al-Jurjani, *Muqaddimah al-kamil,*
   Hyderabad, n.d.

Ibn Al-Jauzi, Abdur Rahman bin Ali, *Al-Maudu'at al-Kubra,* Maktabah
   Salafiyyah, Medina 1386.

Ibn Amir al-Hajj, Muhammad ibn Mahmud, *Al-Taqrir wa al-Tahbir,*
   Cairo 1316 - 18 A.H.

Ibn Farhun, Ibrahim ibn Muhammad, *Tabsirat al-Hukkam,*
   Cairo 1302 A.H.

Ibn Fudi, Shaikh Uthman, *Hidayah al-Tullab,* Zaria, Nigeria.

Ibn Hajar, Ahmad bin Ali, *Tadhhib al-Tahdith,* 12 vols.
Hyderabad, 1325-1327 A.H.

Ibn Hajar, Ahmad bin Ali, *Lisan al-Mizan*, 6 vols.
Hyderabad, 1329 A.H.

Ibn Hajib, Usman ibn Umar, *al-Mukhtasar*, Bulaq, n.d.

Ibn Hanbal, Ahmad bin Muhammad, *Kitab al-Ashribah*,
ed. by Sughi Jasim, Baghdad, 1396 A.H.

Ibn Hazm, Ali, *Al-Ihkam fi Usul al-Ahkam.* Al Bab as Sadis wa
al-Thalathun Ed. By Ahmad Shakir, Cairo.

Ibn Hazm, Ali ibn Ahmed, *Al-Ihkam li Usul al-Ahkam,*
Cairo, 1345 - 48 A.H.

Ibn Kathir, Imaduddin Abu al-Fida, *Tafsir*, Beirut, 1969.

Ibn Kathir, Ismail bin Umar, *Al-Bidaya wal Nihayah*, 14 vols.
Cairo 1932.

Ibn Khaldun, *al-Muqaddimah.* Beirut: Dar al-Fikr, 1988, vol.1.

Ibn Nujaym, Zayn al-Abidin, *Al-Ashbah Wa al-Nazair,* Cairo 1322 A.H.

Ibn Qayyim, al-Jawziyah, *I'lam al-mawaqqi'in 'an Rabb al-'Alamin*,
Cairo, n.d.; Al-Turuq al-Hukmiyah', Cairo 1317 A.H.

Ibn Qayyim, Shams Al-Din, *I'lam al-Muwaqqi'in,* vol. 2,
New Edition, Cairo, 1968.

Ibn Rushd, Abu al-Walid Muhammad, *Bidayat al-Mujtahid,* Cairo, n.d.

Ibn Taymiyyah Ahmad b. Abd al-Halim, *Raf'u al-Malam 'An al-A'imati
al-A'alam,* Makkah, n.d.

Ibn Taymiyyah, *Al-Siyasat al-Shariah,* Cairo, 1969;
Al-Hisba fi al-Islam, Madina, n.d.; *Majmuat al-Rasail al-Kubra,*
Cairo 1323 A.H.

Kudari, Muhammad, *Tarikh al-Tashri al-Islami,* 8th ed. Cairo, 1967.
Al-Mu'allaqat al-sab'ah, Cairo, 1315 H.

Muhammad Abduh, *Tafsir*, Cairo, 1330 A.H.

Muhammad Sa'id Ramadan, al-Buti, *Dawabit al-Maslaha fi Shariat
al-Islamia* Demascus, 1966-67.

Muslim ibn al-Hajjaj, *Jami' Sahih* (Nawawi's commentary). Beirut, n.d.

Mustafa Zaid, *Al-Maslaha fi al-Tashri al-Islami,* Cairo, 1954.

Al-Raghib al-Isfahani, *al-Mufradat.* Beirut: Dar al-fikr, n.d.

Sabuni, Abd al-Rahman, *Muhadarat fi al-Sharia al Islamiyyah,* Damascuss, (1392 A.H.) 1972.

Sanusi, Muhammad b. Ali, Al-Majmuah al-Mukhtarah. *Eqaz al-Wasnan,* Libya 1388 A.H. 1968.

Shaikh Ibrahim ibn Abdullah, *al-Adhba al-Faid Sharh Umdat al-Farid,* Cairo 1372 A.H.

Syed Qutb, *Fi Zilal al-Quran,* Beirut, 1971.

Suyuti, Jalal al-Din, *Mukhtasar al-ittiqan fi ulum al-Qur'an.* Beirut: Dar al-Nafais, 1987.

Yusuf al-Qardawi, *Shariat al-Islamia,* Doha 1973.

Al-Zarkashi, Badr al-Din, *Al-burhan fi ulum al-Qur'an.* Beirut: Dar al-fikr, 1980.

Al-Zubaydi, Muhib al-din, *Taj al-arus min jawahir al-qamus.* Beirut: Dar al-fikr, 1994.

Secondary Sources

Ali Engineer, Asghar, *Islam and Liberation: Essays on Liberative Elements in Islam.* New Delhi, 1990.

Amina Wadud Muhsin, *The Qur'an and Women.* Kuala Lumpur, 1992.

Calkins, M. W, *Locke's Essays Concerning Human Understanding.* New York.

Doi, Abdur Rahman, I. *Non-Muslim under Shariah.* London 1979.

Edward W. Said, *Covering Islam: How the Media and the Experts Determine How We See the Rest of the World.* New York, 1981.

Gai Eton, *Islam and the Destiny of Man.* Cambridge: Islamic Texts Society, 1985.

García, Ismael, *Justice in Latin American Theology of Liberation.* Atlanta, 1987.

Hammond, R, *The Philosophy of al-Farabi and its Influence on Medieval Thought.* New York, 1947

Bibliography

Kiogora, Timothy. G, *Black Theology* (Initiation into Theology: The Rich Variety of Theology and Hermeneutics) ed. Maimela, Simon and König, Adrio. Pretoria, 1998.

Gutiérrez, Gustavo, *Essential Writings.* New York, 1996.

Noam Chomsky, *Language and Responsibility.* Harvester Press, 1977

Parker, Stuart, Reflective *Teaching in the Postmodern World.* Philadelphia, 1997.

Ricoeur, Paul, *Hermeneutics and the Human Sciences.* trans. Ed. Thomson, T.B., Cambridge, 1995.

Simon-Craver, *Philosophical Foundations of Education.* New York, 1971.

Windelband, W, *A History of Philosophy: The Formation and Development of its Problems and Concepts.* London, 1914.

Index